Ann,

THANKS —

Mike Marra

Lancy Ruff

DEFENDING GOD'S
GIFT OF FREEDOM

From 1776 to the 21ˢᵗ Century

MIKE MORRA

authorHOUSE®

AuthorHouse™
1663 Liberty Drive
Bloomington, IN 47403
www.authorhouse.com
Phone: 1 (800) 839-8640

Published by AuthorHouse   03/15/2016

ISBN: 978-1-5049-7617-6 (sc)
ISBN: 978-1-5049-7615-2 (hc)
ISBN: 978-1-5049-7616-9 (e)

Library of Congress Control Number: 2016901522

Print information available on the last page.

Any people depicted in stock imagery provided by Thinkstock are models, and such images are being used for illustrative purposes only. Certain stock imagery © Thinkstock.

This book is printed on acid-free paper.

KJV
Scripture quotations marked KJV are from the Holy Bible, King James Version (Authorized Version). First published in 1611. Quoted from the KJV Classic Reference Bible, Copyright © 1983 by The Zondervan Corporation.

NIV
Scripture quotations marked NIV are taken from the Holy Bible, New International Version®. *NIV*®. *Copyright © 1973, 1978, 1984 by International Bible Society. Used by permission of Zondervan. All rights reserved. [Biblica]*

Dedicated to the American veteran who loves God

CONTENTS

PROLOGUE

Since the 18th century, 1000's of scholarly books have been written about America's wars. Some of these manuscripts featured economic dynamics, others military tactics or long term strategies, still others accredited victory to the brilliance and character of generalship, or to the individual heroics in the heat of combat. Or, to a particular battle unexpectedly won. Many of these victories must be attributed to the wisdom of the socio/politics of freely elected leaders. Most all of these writings alluded the human cravings for freedom. Other than conventional history, this one of its kind book, ***Defending God's Gift of Freedom***, will bring to light the religious/spiritual determination of free people who have been energized to fight America's crusades in defense of God's gift of liberty.

Specifically, this book is about one of the paramount attributes of God, ***freedom***. Failing to fully understand the spiritual/theological implications of ***Liberty*** surely will detract from one's knowledge of God. As we know it today the character and personality of Deity includes Divine freedom that joins justice, love, truth, and righteousness. God is all-knowing, all-present, all-mighty, and being intimate with each of us. To grasp these precepts will put evil, Hell, and sin in a clearer theological perspective. Simply stated, God did not create evil, sin, or hell. Mankind did, through his free-will that comes about from the frontal lobes of the brain mass. Evil, the cosmic darkness that tempts and afflicts each of us daily is a negative forcefield that acquires its strength from the world-wide human free-choices to sin. So too, hell is a place or state of human alternative to either accept Jesus as Lord and Savior and His compassionate Will for each of us, or to live marooned forever in the Outer Darkness surrounded by weeping and gnashing of teeth. Surely, the freedom-to-choose has eternal consequences for each of us. If truth be told. Divine freedom is a gift offered to each soul to decide our timeless fate with either Jesus or to live within the cosmic darkness and its alienation away from the Kingdom of God.

Mostly via Sacred Scripture, over the millennia of cultural progress, Mankind's theological consciousness has been able to discern a number of qualities of the Creator, Redeemer, and Majestic Nature of God. In an abridged capsule: (a) redemptive freedom for the individual soul; (b) the creation of the physical and organic realms; and (c) as the Divine Manager of the majestic course of history. These three attributes allow us to be able to better define and spiritually appreciate the free nature of the Deity. In the Judeo/Christian Bible freedom is cited from the Torah, the OT Prophets, the Gospels, and throughout Paul's writings. Believers of Divine freedom understand, or should have been aware of, that God is all-knowing, is everywhere all-powerful, and who fashioned the Multiverse out of a dark nothingness. While His Nature transformed cosmic darkness into spiritual light, God also offered love, justice, goodness, truth, freedom, compassion, forgiveness, the sharing of His Divine life, and His incarnation to help humanity understand and experience the Organic stages of human development, the spiritual perceptions offered by the five senses, and the power of the role of free-will generated by the frontal, brain capacity, all needed to fathom an invisible God by way of a visible Messiah, Jesus.

Throughout human history, freedom vs bondage has been the underlying, socio/political factor in almost all of the armed and unarmed, national and societal conflicts. Well organized, powerful affairs of State dictated by emperors, despots, and autocrats have sought the domination and enslavement of those seeking freedom and independence, only to find that these tyrannies became challenged by the intervention of God's might. In many ways, history can be typified as the struggle between the transgressions of predator nations and the freedom yearnings of "preyed-upon" minorities. Often, while these "predator empires" seek to carry forth the ideational advances of Mankind's progress, ultimately their absolute power corrupts their leaders who eventually turn into barbaric tyrants by rationalizing away more and more of their oppression, moral decadence, ebbing ideational relevance, and the cruelty of innocence. For example, in the ***Modern Age of Human Carnage (1940-1945 AD),*** over a 100-million innocent men, women, and children were slaughtered by godless, predator dictators in Europe and

Asia. Out of a deluded self-importance, ebbing, socio/political power, and receding, spiritual credence, tyrannical justice never has been a valid option offered to the freedom-loving soul. Always with the passing of despotic political influence, absolute rulers perceive the less powerful as the enemy and national security threats to be crushed into submission. Time and again, in order to prevent their bondage vs their freedom, the preyed-upon minorities that simply seek more of God's freedom "to be," "to worship," and "to express the new ideas" are forced to go underground, dispute publically, confront, and defy the excesses of powerful, quasi-kingdoms. These factors underlie the nature of war. With civil and/or military resistance and with the God of Freedom on their side the might of a vulnerable people seeking liberty eventually win-out. As God's chosen people, as set-apart nations, this has been the history of the Israeli and American wars. Why so? Freedom exudes a Divine energy that can't be compromised, surrendered, or defeated. Accordingly, the pursuit of freedom has been delegated to God's set-apart people. Throughout the Eras we see socio/predator power first arising to prominence, then citizen acceptance of prideful socio/greatness, followed by the national sinking into obscurity from their outdated ideas, gone-by. All the while, victimizing their "prey" which only seeks greater and greater freedom "to be," "to think," "to express," and "to worship."

America's major wars from 1776 to the present day only can be understood as the struggle between "totalitarian predators" and "democratic-seeking prey." None-stop, from the 18th to the 21st centuries, those who hoped for America's demise have sought socio/political enslavement, economic exploitation, along with the destruction and eradication of democratic institutions. If so, it must be concluded that America the Beautiful has been the carry-over of God's Ancient Israel to be set-apart, protected, upheld, and sealed with: (a) free market and job opportunities; (b) free citizenship and a judiciary committed to just laws, regulations, and rules for all; (c) free travel across State to State; (d) free speech; (e) free political assembly; (f) free equal educational availabilities; (g) free political elections; along with, (h) the freedom to worship. For this to have come about over 240-years in democratic America, it took God's direct and indirect intervention between the righteous forces of freedom and those seeking bondage. As well, individual, spiritual freedom must have become part of these societal struggles. God, who shared His perfect, righteous Nature with each human soul, insists upon the free choosing of: (1) good over evil; (2) Jesus as Lord and Savior over being eternally marooned in the Outer Darkness; (3) the surrender of one's path of life to God's Way of trust and obedience; (4) the spiritual mode that transforms one's abrupt, impulsive, sinful inclinations to the enduring, virtuous commands of God; (5) the selection of the treasures of eternity over the fleeting offerings of Planet Earth; (6) the renouncing of independent decision-making to a full dependency on God's guidance and certainty; and (7) the rejection of the continual imposition of one's will over Divine reality.

In parallel by way of the inerrancy of Sacred Scripture, the shared, spiritual histories of both Ancient Israel and modern-day America include a number of Biblical events and campaigns in support of the view of despotic, predator oppression seeking bondage over those "upright prey," who simply yearn for greater and greater righteousness, socio/ spiritual freedom, and civil/economic liberties. Both in the OT and the history of the American wars, we find that with obedience to God the powerless ultimately shall inherit the Earth. For example, Moses led the Exodus, Gideon prayed with only 300 warriors who then conquered a large number of Midian troops and their allies. So too, Joshua and Caleb liberated Canaan under God's protection when fully surrounded by the powerful armies occupying the Holy Land. In the year 1948 AD, Israel had no army and surrounded by overwhelming Muslim forces. Yet, Israel survived, prospered and became democratic. David, not yet King, prayed for God's safety from a deranged King Saul and his pursuing military forces. Not unlike Moses and Joseph who also prayed for freedom from the mighty Pharaohs. Daniel, who predicted 400-years of sequential empires, (from Assyria to Babylon to Persia to Greece on to Rome) prayed for religious freedom in opposition to the mighty Assyrian king. Paul prayed against the horde of unbelievers, false prophets, and Jewish tyrants, who renounced Jesus' Incarnation; this after observing three years of healings, miracles, parables, and teachings. After Jesus' Resurrection and Ascension, two hundred fifty years of Christian martyrdom took place from a fading Roman Empire led by brutal, wicked Caesars, all who sought universal bondage. Highlighted by predator, Roman oppression against the freedom of a budding Christianity was the overriding theme of that socio/political day. That is, until Jesus appeared to Emperor Constantine in the 4th century AD asking him why he was persecuting the Lord and Savior. In a nutshell with God as the all-mighty the prayers for freedom to worship by the subjugated Christians never has gone Divinely unanswered. It was faith, trust, conviction, and obedience to God's promise to protect the freedom to pursue goodness by the vulnerable against the powerful that was one of the principal thesis cited in the OT, NT and America's wars. For three hundred years, (18th-21st centuries AD), the compassion and lovingkindness of an Almighty God, who created the Multiverse with His laws of science and mathematics, from a dark nothingness to multi-billions of stars, took time to protect America, Israe, l and a miniscule Planet Earth from Galactic catastrophe by looking-after our evolving, defenseless humanity from predator bondage. Indeed, *freedom* is incredibly important to God.

Over the millennia of cultural progress, Mankind's theological consciousness has been able to discern a number of qualities of the Creator, Redeemer, and Majestic Nature of God. In toto, (a) freedom for the individual soul; (b) the creation of the physical realm; and (c) as the Divine Manager of the majestic course of history. These three theological features have been able to better define and spiritually appreciate the amazing nature of Deity. Believers understand, or should have been aware of, that God is all-knowing, all-powerful, is everywhere, and who fashioned the Multiverse out of a dark nothingness. While His Nature transformed cosmic darkness into spiritual light, God offered love, justice, freedom, goodness, truth, compassion, forgiveness, the sharing of His

Divine life, and His incarnation to help humanity understand and experience the Organic stages of human development, the spiritual perceptions offered by the five senses, and the power of the role of free-will generated by the frontal, brain capacity needed to fathom an invisible God by way of a visible Messiah, Jesus. After Salvation, spiritual maturity comes about as grace offered by the Holy Spirit, greater and greater faith. increased Christlike righteousness, justification, sanctification, redemption, our resurrection, and finally the bodily glorification of our unique identity.

After our brief stay on Planet Earth, all human souls, being stranded in the vast Multiverse without the care, security, freedom, intellectual truth, protection, providence, guidance, unconditional love, and cosmic meaning of each individual life, would certainly prove to be existentially catastrophic. Within this theological context, this book, ***Defending God's Gift of Freedom,*** will attempt to historically explore the set-apart Israeli/American encounters, i.e. wars, fought against unbelieving nations and their evil, all within the framework of the vindication of God's gift of freedom.

By way of American warfare and the shedding of blood by millions of military lives, this book is about God the Creator and His indirect role in the theological and historical pursuit of freedoms for Planet Earth.

Still in progress, Mankind's imperfect, intellectual progress ought to be telling us that God is the God of the Multiverse, the Lord of history, and the indwelling, personal

Counselor of every human life. Ranging from the Outer Reaches of Space to the individual, human heart qualifies God as breathtakingly awesome. His cosmic character has created a remarkable, intellectual design of a planetary enormity that is embroidered with an overload of splendor and majesty that saturates the entire Multiverse. Appended to this majestic Creation is the Divine resolve that insists upon zero-tolerance for unholiness for human acts, thoughts, language, injustice, and hatefulness that occur daily within the context of human freedom. If truth be told, no more and no less, Divine ***Creation, Redemption, and Beauty*** are what describe the cosmic dynamics of Planet Earth.

Today is the 21st century, the potential onset of a new Era of budding, ideational illumination. At the start of this 3rd millennium AD, what is ushered-in is an inspiring Epoch that must incorporate unequivocally the theological wonders of God in all its ideational proceedings. By first renouncing the godless arrogance propagated and proliferated by the influence of the 18th century's literati of the Enlightenment Era, by the cynical skepticism of its Age of Reason, or by the oppressive Age of Authoritative, Religious Rule, these three periods of 18th century's 'history, which featured "it's all about reason" as the definitive truth of philosophical thought, along with, later in the early 20th century, that fashioned an outbreak of neo/Marxism that gave birth to the grisly ***Modern Age of Human Carnage***, when the evil pride of Mankind morally lacked the full-bodied, spiritual appreciation of the existence and role of the Divine in all human affairs. From 1940 to 1945 AD, if they happened to be lame, last, least, or lost, 100-million innocent men, women, and children were tortured, slaughtered, and annihilated by godless, neo/Marxists. It seems logical that for Mankind to progress in its ongoing history of ideas, God's attributes set within His intentions must become incorporated and highlighted with the current-day Philosophy of Man, the aspirations of Science, and a truthful theology of God.

Simply stated, who would deny that both the origin and maintenance of the Multiverse have been presided over by the fundamental laws of science and mathematics? If so, then who would deny with simple logic that you cannot have Cosmic Laws without a remarkable Cosmic Lawgiver? Or, who could dare deny that each of us within our species is but a speck orbiting the Multiverse that could never survive the fiery cauldron of the Space environment that would result in the finality of human extinction? Or, who could deny that the tenure of individual human life is brief? Without Divine freedom, presence, protection, providence, guidance, and intervention, only the spiritually arrogant among us would deny that the uplifting, ever-evolving forces of Divinity steers and funnels the course of the physical, organic, socio/political, historical, military, spiritual, and economic conditions affecting Planet Earth. Mankind must be ever-reflecting upon the free and transcendent attribute of the Godhead. Undeniably in the 21st century, to grasp the wonders and mysteries of *Creation, Beauty, and Redemption*, God first must be allowed through faith to become the principal focus of Man's, philosophical and spiritual attention. In order to be able to fill-in the full picture of "cosmic comprehension," the understanding of this basic wisdom will take **Faith**, i.e. the gift of spiritual logic, as affixed to our album of reasoning capacities. Perhaps, the godlessness of scientists, academicians, journalists, misguided, Old World clerics, and other self-anointed literati ought to give up their transparent spiritual ignorance, self-serving pride, blind arrogance, and Divine alienation in their intellectual pursuits. Within the enlightenment of the 21st century, 18th century's 200-year infatuation with the **Epoch of Reason,** with all its errant, philosophical fallacies, has stalled human progress, placing us at the trailing edge of the backside of our ideational evolution.

With reasoning alone, devoid of faith, we can expect that a "truth drag" of socio/intellectual non-sequiturs to continue to burden Humankind with a plague of "ideational nothingness," Otherwise with God as the focal point and with spiritual inspiration, an *Age of Intellectual Belief* could emerge, poised to position Mankind again at the cutting edge of His ideational/spiritual wisdom.

This book is about God and His unswerving role in the "freedom creation" of the Multiverse, along with His dynamic involvement in the ideational evolution of the history of human liberty, all set within the deliverance of the individual spirit.

Yet within the righteousness of the freedom theme, the neuro/spiritual evolution of the human brain also raised the issues of sin and death. These matters require resolution by a new, self-reflective species that became capable of perceiving "right from wrong," along with the realities of infinity and the finality of organic life. Surely, this human voyage was Divinely launched, whereby Man and his adventurous ideas ever-evolved to be understood as a difference between human discovery vs Divine revelation. To claim **discovery** through human reasoning alone by self-anointed philosophers, scientists, scholars, and theologians is disingenuous and most-offensive to a Deity who is an "all knowing," all-powerful, all-loving, all-righteous, and all-just. When in fact the essentials of the transcendent accomplishments of Mankind have been acclaimed as *revealed* by God, not *discovere*d by scientists, academicians, scholars, philosophers, and/or theologians. Only by accepting the difference between discovery and revelation will Mankind continue to intellectually progress.

For instance, George Washington, who prayed and read the Bible set on a Ottoman for two hours daily on his knees, did not *discover* political freedom by refusing to become an American king. In his prayer life, it was revealed to him that *freedom* was a fundamental attribute of the Divine. Political freedom was *revealed* to George Washington, in tandem with the Founding Fathers of the USA. The US Constitution was directly scripted by God. No doubt, America the Beautiful was Divinely revealed, a "socio/political" miracle intended for a more righteous, communal life&love style. So too *revealed* **by God** might be said of: (1) the amazing findings by modern physicists; (2) the intricacies of the Organic Realm by a corps of bio/scientists; (3) the Adam Smiths of the free marketplace; (4) the astro/engineers of the Space Age; (5) the oceanic explorers of the Renaissance; and (6) those who searched the healing wonders of modern medicine. All this and much more have been selectively *revealed* through the timeline of Divine wisdom. Surely, within the context of the 21st century, to claim a *rational* d*iscovery,* in lieu of a *Divine disclosure,* is an egregious, idolatrous sin and a fundamental violation of the 1st and 2nd, Mosaic Commandments worthy of spiritual consequences. Bar none, the evolution of the sciences, the musings of philosophers, and the speculations of theologians all were advanced by the *revealed truths* of God, not *discovered* by the rational brain-mass of quasi-enlightened humans.

Day by day, the bio/spiritual, bio/political, and socio/economic marvels of Divine Creation are being revealed through the mechanics of *freedom,* along with, the components and dynamics of the Physical Realm, the engineering of Space travel, medical micro/technology, the scope of the Internet, global communications, and the greater truths of the Moral Evolution of Western Man. Add to these amazing, freedom-generated, awesome "ideational innovations" lies the genetic dominion of the DNA that administers our individual physical and spiritual lives. Freely, the workings of both these tangible and metaphysical attributes surrounding human life are being transmitted by the mysteries embedded within the free-acting genes. Body&soul, not unlike the protons, electrons, and neutrons of atoms, function as one cohesive unit. To date, this is what we suspect about the human Genome as being *revealed* to the scholars of Divine intelligence.

Genes are the Carriers of Bio/Spiritual Attributes

Think 21ˢᵗ Century: Not unlike the Homo Sapien, all higher mammals are capable of expressing: (a) the spiritual dynamics of *love,* in lieu of pointless violence; (b) *intelligence,* as in adaptation; (c) the *beauty* of their own existence; (d) the *freedom* to be; (e) *goodness,* as expressed as parental responsibility; (f) the dynamics of *transcendent* evolution; and (g) *socio/fairness.* In different ways, these metaphysical traits are carried and transmitted by species-specific Genomes.

Genetic science is in the process of edifying and confirming the writings of the Biblical account of the origin of Man. Thusfar, these studies found that the Garden of Eden was not located in the Tigris/Euphrates Valley. With indisputable DNA/evidence, well-known to the scientific community, it has been determined that with a free-roving, male genetic/marker the Adam&Eve narrative originally occurred in the South-Central region of Africa. At this locale, the evolution of the frontal lobes, as neuro/developed optimally, allowed Adam&Eve, i.e. Homo Sapien, to perceive with his/hers newly acquired competence of free-choice, the implications of "right from wrong," as well as to gain them the capacity to grasp the meaning of infinity, i.e. eternity. This account, consistent with the Divine predisposition, gave Mankind a frontal neuro/center and the brain-faculty to passionately desire freedom. Furthermore in order to wisely utilize the intellectual ramifications of deduction, induction, sequential logic, generalization, differentiation, a wide range of languages, and aesthetic expressions, Man must grow intimately with a loving God. Assuredly, from the instincts of the single-cell organism to the frontal lobes of the human brain has been an amazing feat of phylogenetic transcendence. Genetically, armed with these intellectual attributes SubSaharan Man was now ready to freely journey out of the African Garden of Eden and explore and partake in the offerings of Planet Earth, all the while mutating geo/environmentally across a number of racial categories (Black, Brown, Yellow, and Hybrid forms). This process was consistent with the "freedom character" of God and His transcendent dynamic, called evolution.

Seeking the unknown implications of a bio/spiritual journey trekked by Early Man across Planet Earth, which had been estimated to occur over a period of thousands of years, field scientists launched a 2-year, well-controlled study of human migration, surprisingly to discover that a male gene/marker could reliably be identified and tracked "out-of-Africa." These specific genes then fanned-out across the Globe by way of a handful of trailblazing, freedom-seeking Sub-Saharan, Negroid adventurers, traveling eastward toward the African coastline, then northward into the Middle Eastern region, called the "Cradle of Civilization," a region that caused Ancient, quasi-civilized Humankind to blossom and further evolve within the confines of this lush area, i.e. the legendary Tigris/Euphrates, a geo/site that was as favorable to the basic needs of organic life as was SubSaharan Africa. Accordingly, for over a millennia of time tribal life became sustained by ample water supplies, ideal climate conditions, and ample foodstuffs; such as, olive oil, figs, vineyards, livestock, and grains, all of which resulted in an ever-expanding, tribal demography.

Eventually, this unique bio/spiritual, male/marker pointed outward from this agri/lush Mideastern platform. A restless, impatient Homo Sapien became anxious to freely tryout its newly evolved brain/soul capacities by further venturing into the geo/unknown. While exploring northward, this higher species began mutating into a variety of ecologically adaptive bio/breeds; and became color-coded as Black, Brown, Yellow, White, and Hybrid races. Scattered across the confines of Planet Earth., some drifted north-westward into the European terrain, while others ventured southward toward India, Southern Asia, and across a number of islands into Australia and Micronesia. The Eastern leg of this bio/spiritual voyage took Early Man into China-Proper, and across the Bering Straits into the Americas, both North and South. The freedom drive to seek greater and greater fulfillment filled Planet Earth with human life.

Allegorically, this journey ought to be considered part of a "genetic narrative" of the Garden of Eden, including Adam&Eve, Cain&Abel, Tower of Babel, and Noah's Ark. Structurally and operationally, we know that God's "love to be shared" with us intended that the transcendent evolution of the Human Genome becomes freely expressed neuro/morphologically, overtly physically, fine-tuned physiologically, socio/politically, and bio/spiritually. All three attributes, intelligently designed in due course, was meant to deal with Man's future, including his sins and the evils spawned by human acts, thoughts, and words.. By way of the DNA, this bio/metaphysical mystery, via the dynamic transmission of Divine forces, resulted in the joint development of both body and soul.

Suitably for the 21ˢᵗ century, it is futile to attempt to fully understand the mathematical, scientific, socio/political, emotional, and spiritual dynamics of the Divine "intelligent design" accounting for both the Multiverse and the complex nature of living organisms. If scholars and theologians examine closer and deeper into the "black box" of the bio/spiritual Genome, they will find that *freedom* has been one of the universal drive of life on Planet Earth. The "good and evil" forces that both enable and plague Mother Earth pose a paradoxical mystique to the DNA/properties of the physical, psycho/social, physiological, and spiritual domains. To date, the workings of the DNA encompassing the fundamental attributes of life&love seem to be intriguingly complicated, yet-minimal, often simple, always consistent, and enduring. All the while, it had to be God who is reflected in this intelligent design as unadorned, reliable, and intact. Surely, when existential principles become considered, both structurally and operationally, who else might have created the compelling, shifting energies of the astrophysical and chemical compositions of the Universe, along with that of the Organic Realm? This basic truth alone ought to negate the godless socio/politics and dehumanizing technologies of the 18ᵗʰ thru the 20ᵗʰ centuries, which ultimately resulted in the immoral and amoral slaughter of countless innocence. In the 21ˢᵗ century, Neo/Marxism, Islam, and the insidious corruption of the Papacy pose analogous threats to the continuation of human life.

Philosophically plain to see, the spiritual genius of the organic DNA, when set within the Redemption Plan, was intended for the eternal life of the human soul. As Divinely networked and intimately woven within the realities of Planet Earth, for sure the nature and intentions of a holy, just God, who also is all-knowing, in all-places, all-loving, and all-powerful, yet dotingly attentive to each constituent of his Creation, are mystifying. Ranging from the science and mathematics of the Multiverse to the daily needs of an individual soul are consistent with a miraculous, Divine character and fully consistent with the continuing, revealed, ideational enlightenment of the Post-Modern Era. It is now becoming apparent that both the organic genes floating about in an inorganic, micro/atomic realm must be the operational carriers of, and conduit for, the seven, metaphysical building-blocks of existential life on Planet Earth. Henceforth, the grisly, socio/political encounters of the early 20ᵗʰ century will be harshly judged by the moral standards emitted by these seven, universal attributes of God. Surely, the bio/spiritual model that explains our socio/political motivations and decisions to seek freedom, in lieu of misguided, conventional, academic paradigms, account for the cosmic evils, sin, and hell that have inflicted the soul of humanity being victimized as recurrent, reiterating phenomena.

Divinely conceived, the seven, bio/spiritual factors that define our existential ambiance include: (1) the upward thrust of *transcendence,* not chaos or mindless randomness; (2) *intelligence*, not the irrational or insane; (3) *freedom*, not bondage; (4) *love*, not hate; (5) *goodness*, not evil; (6) **justice,** not inequality; and (7) *beauty*, not the grotesque. All, bar none, whether subatomic, micro/genetic, macro/cultural, or religious expressions are subject and accountable to these seven rudimentary, preestablished principles of the Divine Creation Plan. In the early 20th century, the **Age of Human Carnage, t**he amorality of Secular Socialism, the immorality of dehumanizing technologies, and the theology of religious bondage have become the survival plagues and challenges facing the 21st century.

The spiritual workings of both the genetic and subatomic, inorganic realm are part of a Divine device driven by the ascendant thrust of the physical world, the phylogenetic evolution, the military history of socio/politics, and an individual's free-will seeking a greater and greater intimacy with God. These enfolding, upward progressions can be readily observed in a variety of settings. As an example, the biological evolution from the single-cell to the Homo Sapien, which has been well-documented by contemporary bio/research, should signify that a Divine plan of intelligent design has been set into motion. Individual, spiritual growth, which comes about from an intimate relationship with a personal God, also should qualify as a transcendent phenomenon of the conscious soul. To understand the latter, one's thinking processes must not be restricted by the constraints of time, energy, mass, and/or space. Furthermore, to grasp this cosmic, spiritual truth, one can't hope to understand with "primordial certainty" when a mindset is burdened solely with the godless limitations of economic, political, historical, technological, and cultural models. Without doubt, only the bio/spiritual paradigm best separates the real from the irreal. Only by acknowledging the noticeable manifestations of the transcendent, Divine attribute of organic and inorganic evolution can we ever begin to appreciate the development of philosophical, cultural, technological, military, economic, socio/political, or bio/spiritual ideas, theories, and their truths. This Divine factor has been operating as a dynamic transformation influencing a variety of circumstances ranging from the physical to the spiritual.

Throughout history, the upward transformation from lower to higher has been guiding a host of human endeavors. To be sure, this ideational evolution of Planet Earth has been neither random nor haphazard, but instead anchored to the "transcendent energy" of Divine intercession. In time, driven by this surge, the models and their forcefields of economics, politics, theology, technology, transportation, the sciences, socio/psychology, numerics, the full scale of the arts, finance, and medicine, all have aperiodically and freely tracked upward by *revealed*, Godly ideas. This existential drive of human institutions is deeply embedded within the Natural Order. Hence with certainty, not by way of the lateral slippage and sliding, such as the conservative vs. liberal politics or neither by Marxism vs democracy, nor by the Yin&Yang revered in ancient, Chinese philosophy, has life and all its components accelerated continually to escalate toward greater and greater maturity and perfection. The vigor derived from this robust, transcendent feature is hardcore evidence of an ever-present, Divine freedom.

As events that resolved forever the issues of death and personal wickedness, the Crucifixion and Resurrection of the Messiah became the "ultimate transcendence." Any leader or nation without an intimate relationship with the personal God, i.e. Jesus, is destined to cause socio/political havoc on Planet Earth. Both in Europe and Asia, the dreadful events of the early 20th century became irreal and horrific, confirming the desperate need for God's deliberation and continuous guidance. Assuredly, the Divine principles of intelligent design, as opposed to the irrational, chaotic, or insane, have been guiding the proceedings of the bursting cosmos. All elements of the Multiverse are governed metaphysically by valid premises, logical conclusions, sound judgments, and Divine wisdom. As a glaring example, at the higher levels of the phylogenetic scale, zoologists have been researching and reporting a broad range of creative, animal adaptations to their specific, but merciless geo/environments. These creative acclimations to various, planetary conditions are logical manifestations, not illogical, Darwinian happenstances. If so, survival adjustments to the volatile, geo/idiosyncrasies of Planet Earth have been, and will continue to take on the organic forms and outcomes of both a vertical evolution (i.e. lower to higher species) and a horizontal evolution, (i.e. speciation). As a case in point, biologists have noted that within a particular, evolved species, e.g. the bear, there are polar types, black bears, brown bears, along with a dozen or so other bear-types. Simultaneously, in the bear world, that's vertical and horizontal evolution in play. Hence, these simultaneous adaptations in both directions are tantamount to intelligent survival. These distinct subspecies of bear life have been finely honed to their particular habitat and can't otherwise live elsewhere. Indeed, that's tailored, intelligent, Divine design by any standard of rational analyses. Or, consider parental behaviors across the full spectrum of higher, organic life by which the precarious survival of offspring is at stake. At any echelon of scholarly scrutiny, what becomes visibly evident is the importance of "intelligent parenting" that lovingly fosters and manages offspring care and adaptation. Surely full of twists and turns, whether cosmic or organic, science and theology must continue its "systematic peek" into the mechanisms within the "black box" of survival. As revealed, they will discover that the Divine handprint of "intelligent design," and not the Darwinian premise of "haphazard selections," is what is happening out there in the Multiverse.

Add to these bi-directional dynamics of evolving creation, God includes the *freedom factor* to the Natural Order; "freedom" is a Divine attribute. Whether individual, social, organic, or related to the physical dynamics of the Multiverse as ordained by God, *freedom* ought to be assumed a basic reality for all expressions of the Creation Plan. In their socio/politics, Secular Socialism, Evil Empires, autocratic societies, fundamental Islam or the Papal theology of bondage, fail to recognize freedom as a basic Divine dimension of life itself.

If "God is Love" then the freedom-to-love must have been a specification of the Divine blueprint for Planet Earth. God extended the endowment of "existential liberty" to all facets of his handiwork. Muslims do not acknowledge the right of socio/political freedom for women or "infidel societies." So too, Marxism, the root of Secular Socialism and modern-day Liberalism, lacks "political trust" for the self-reliant decisions of the individual. The 6000-year history of China Proper is another example of this lack of trust in the free insights of the individual citizen. Ranking in common with these socio/spiritual plagues is the full range of the theology of Roman Catholicism. "Spiritual bondage" has been uncompromisingly promoted by the Papacy and its global clerics for over a millennium. This bondage theme of Catholicism has been cynically imposed on believers to service the Global ambitions and finances of the Vatican. Even within the vast physical and chemical array of the Multiiverse, as maintained by its predictable scientific and mathematical orbits, have been set-free to function and evolve from its hydrogen base to an oxygen envelope that encompasses and sustains life on Planet Earth. Indeed *freedom* is a basic ingredient in the survival performance of Planet Earth.

As intended by God, socio/political freedom, which came about from the neuro/evolution of the brain's, frontal lobes, becomes a decisive element to a nation's life. Only the free-will mechanism of each society enables each of us to choose daily "righteousness and social justice" vs. "evil and socio/immorality." Likewise, the freedom-to-choose an intimate relationship with our personal God, Jesus, also impacts our destiny. Despots throughout history, who are intellectually anchored to the reasoning of Earth-bound realities, reject the notion that God in his wisdom has given us a free consciousness, a choosing soul with the power to select the good vs. evil. Indeed, we are forgivable for our "bad choices," although socio/cosmic evil can never be sanctioned by Divinity. Why! Simply because the Divine Nature is good, holy, just, loving, and righteous and we have been created to His image and likeness. On the other hand, world-generated evil, which inflicts each generation culturally and socio/politically, either by a particular society or by an evil Era, is a Malthusian forcefield that acquires its energy and density out of the accrual of Global, human sin. Evil is the reverse replica of goodness. God didn't create evil. Out of His "love Nature," He allows wickedness so as to afford the human soul the opportunity to freely choose and share in his majesty. To intimately partake in His Nature or to warrant His protection, guidance, love, grace, and providence, every soul has been given the strength to seek and freely choose salvation, justification, and sanctification, rather than being marooned in the Outer Darkness, surrounded by weeping and gnashing of teeth, forever. Truly, the search for individual salvation is a "freedom option" that ought not to be denied or repressed by the illegitimate authorities of any form of despotism. Plainly in support of the perils of freedom, God's Creation Plan appended *seven* basic, metaphysical attributes of life itself that are preset to our daily, spiritual expressions.

In addition to the three above mentioned building-blocks of Divine Creation, *(transcendence, intelligence, and freedom)*, *love* becomes the fourth, basic DNA/module needed for the initiation and continuance of life on Planet Earth. Undeniably, expressions of love can readily be observed in all parental behaviors across the full, phylogenetic scale. Scientists may call it instinct. Yet wrongly depicted, as if the gentleness and care afforded by parental, animal behaviors instinctively are emotionless, robotic, and perfunctory. Actually, many expressions of laws energize, stabilize, and normalize the Organic Order.

Love is always good. Evil, socially or individually, is always opposed to life. De facto, the presence of love within the socio/ confines of each subspecies exudes a strong, positive valence needed to preserve the adaptive cohesiveness and integrity of each species and their communities. As seen across the Epochs, this principle is especially true for the socio/bonding needs of the Homo Sapien. Surprisingly, as tailored at each level within the phylogenetic scale, there seems to be more, natural love expressed within the subhuman sector than among humans, where the power-of-choice often detracts and deflects away from the display of selfless caring. Thus, in human societies the reoccurrence of socio/political evils occurring from century to century ought to be anticipated. Since God is love, all aspects of His Creation reflect a concerned ambiance, especially designed to impact the human, spiritual level. Yet, it matters not if it's a lion, whale, horse, bird, deer— or human, freely, love is patient, kind, not proud, enduring, relinquishes to others, serves desires, is protective, provides for the needs of others, teaches willingly, and generates a warm, inviting, approachable, pleasurable aura—to the soul of Man—or bear, elephant, dog et.al. Who would deny the unconditional love of the domesticated dog? Indeed, love is what binds, nurtures, and makes meaningful the proceedings of organic life on Planet Earth. Bio/spiritually, it is carried from generation to generation by the genes across species. Out of love comes **goodness**, the fifth of seven primal DNA/ attributes of all existence, whether displayed in the physical cosmos or organic sphere. As proof positive, in Sacred Scripture God said of his creation: "...the waters ...sky ...land ...seed-bearing plants ...trees ...the day and night ...the sun and moon ...every kind of fish and wild or tamed animal—it was good." Yes, good, holy, righteous, and noble.

For human life and its ability to f choose freely, a capacity newly acquired by virtue of the evolved frontal lobes of the brains of Adam&Eve, and by way of Abraham&Sarah over four millennia ago, God commissioned Moses to dispatch the *Moral Evolution of Western Man* to draw attention to the worth of holiness. As never seen before in the Ancient World, the formalization of the Mosaic Code defined, directed, and enhanced the density of the Moral Order. Why so? Simply because with the introduction of "evil," a cosmic forcefield created, embolded, and augmented by human sin, the chances of the Homo Sapien surviving as a species always would remain precarious. God would never directly interfere with the freedoms He endowed to His individual and social creation, as He preestablished at all echelons of His handiwork. Yet "goodness," as an unwavering truth of existence, oughtn't to be compromised by the accrual of wrongful, socio/political choices as happened prior to the Revolutionary Epoch of

American history. Now in the 21ˢᵗ century, Secular Socialism, the Papacy, and Islam have become the socio/evil expressions to be challenged and contested. God, the God of History, who is holy, loving, and just, would never tolerate a lasting departure from His hallowed Nature as set in Divine freedom.

So, dating back to about three millennia BC, a "set-apart people," who were fully devoted to a monotheistic, holy Godhead, was introduced to the morally corrupt, Ancient World. So too in the year 1776. Over 800 of the last of these 3000 years BC, Israeli prophets guided and predicted the proceedings of "goodness and justice," along with the arrival in Bethlehem of a new covenant with the coming of Jesus. By Divine fiat, the tribe of Judah was selected to set the stage for the advent of the Messiah and his message of salvation, justification, and sanctification for each human soul. Since, many modes of Malthusian evil were expected to appear from subsequent Era to Era that threatened the very survival of Humankind by compromising the choices of freedom, justice, holiness, and goodness. At that point in history, importance arose in theology for Man to pursue liberty, the wholesome, the spiritually spotless, the pious, the pure, and socio/ congruity. Operationally, at the very onset of this "moral evolution," the Israelis and later, the American Founding Fathers were expected to: (1) praise One God; (2) honor the Sabbath; (3) adhere to the disciplinary laws; (4) show generosity to strangers and foreigners; (5) expect males and females alike to be ceremoniously cleansed or circumcised: (6) reject idolatry,; and (7) denounce the socio/heinous practices of both the Ancient World and the 18ᵗʰ Century AD, e.g. child sacrifice, Temple prostitution, and the violent tribalism accepted by family life. As a new covenant, which best defined "goodness," the messages of Jesus, who was an Orthodox Jew and a Rabbi, upgraded and guided the spiritual density of the Homo Sapien. Later in history, by the 15th century, the Reform Movement of Judeo/Christianity further added clarity to the meaning of "goodness" by redefining the theological message of Jesus. What's important to grasp is that God operates beyond the constraints of time, energy, mass, and space, thus, the 3500 year voyage of Judeo/Christianity simply connoted that to God: a day is like a thousand years and a thousand years is but a day.

Sixth ranked in the assortment of the existential components of God's prelude to His Creation Plan is **justice**. Unsurprisingly, freedom, fairness + goodness + love are the four overriding macro/themes found throughout the Bible. While goodness and love pertain to our relationship to a personal God, freedom and justice relates to our relationship with our neighbor, society, and the environment. As an answer to the soul-piercing, Biblical question: *"what must I do to enter the Kingdom of Heaven,"* the unambiguous answer given by the Christian Way is unmistakable. Man must love thy God with all thy might, followed by, to love thy neighbor as thyself; that implies freedom. These thematic dictates, beautifully scripted within the 1200+ pages of the Judeo/Christian Bible, have been encapsulated as "freedom +holiness + love + justice." Indeed, these spiritual directives ought not to be socio/politically appeased. If so, then this command of God plus neighbor must be included in our democratic institutions. For every nation, a "fairness doctrine" must be legally established to embrace: (1) the Global principle of universal, human rights; (2) civil liberties for all; (3) social justice, bar none; (4) economic parity, for those who dare apply; (5) the humane treatment of animals, birds, and fishlike, whether domestic or wild; along with (6) the care of the physical environment, whether oceanic, atmospheric, planetary, or beyond the cosmos. Certainly, "fairness," i.e. justice within the context of the free-will of individual self-reliance, not societal liberation via pan-victimization, ought to be viewed as a compelling, fully accountable, existential fundamental to our eternal future.

Lastly, but not least, is **cosmic beauty**, the seventh genetically driven, building block of existence. All beautiful expressions reflect a majestic glimpse of the Divine Nature. No doubt, God is beautiful. Bio/spiritually, this all-encompassing quality of existential life is both DNA/driven in humans and atomically guided in the physical Multiverse. All natural elements of the cosmos are capable of exuding an intrinsic aura of splendor. Whether it's the brilliance of the stars, fiery volcanic eruptions, the endless variations of fauna and flowers, or within the dynamic, ever-evolving, Organic Order, in truth, the majesty of all existence joins equally to the other six inscriptions of God's, created reality. Moreover, at the human level, every person has locked into its psycho/spirit an individualized beauty, which in potential is capable of expression in someway, somehow, and somewhere.

Freely across the broad extent of available art media offered by the cultures of yore, endless, open-ended modes and methods of beauty include the visual, auditory, kinesthetic, gustatory, olfactory, motor, spiritual, and/or as communication. Add to these senual/language conduits, art can be freely expressed as: (a) social comment; (b) abstraction; (c) impression; (d) expression; (e) bionic; (f) realism; (g) gestural; (h) social outrage; or (i) art for art sake. Interestingly as a compelling art-factoid: *"it is no accident that there are no colors in the Natural Order which clash, or are dissonant, or inharmonious."* Ugliness was never included to God's creative specifications. Only human intervention is capable of producing the grotesque. Hence it can be concluded that these standards and expressions of beauty represent an affirmation implying that an underlying aesthetic principle is operating that connotes that there exists an inbuilt majesty to all of the elements of the Divine Creation Blueprint. Indeed, God is beautiful and so are all the aspects of His intelligent Handiwork.

If truth be told by scholars, theologians, and academicians the cosmic role of these seven ABCs of Divine Creation has been undervalued, underestimated, and ignored by the spiritual ignorance by godless, Secular Progressives of all Ages. Simply stated, the socio/politics of godless bondage are guided by a worldly, non-Divine, perspective. Dangerously limited, today's philosophers, journalists, authors, Popes, academicians, and Imans are wearing "philosophical blinders" that have been fashioned, aided, and abetted by an extremist, ever-decaying, intolerant, Liberal and/or defective ideology. Beyond doubt, God both created and predestined paradoxical "complex/simplicity" of the DNA ribbon, along with its micro/atoms, so as to act as carriers of His seven, metaphysical principles of existence. In the 21st century, we are beginning to see the infinite, cosmic implications of the Divine working within the Genome, the engineering of the astro/sciences, and in the expanding abstractions of theoretical physics, and academic chemistry.

Moreover, at the onset of this Neo/Renaissance Age that seeks to include God's freedom in all its splendor, theories, and ideas, honest and mature scholarship untainted by the ideological bias of self-aggrandizement, will be asking more poignant questions concerning the role of the socio/spiritual and socio/political liberty. If so, this neo/scholarship will expand and dilate with the encouragement of the astounding technologies of the day. If so, the unresolved Q&As, pertaining to the basics of "being," will drift to the forefront of human imagination and investigation. A new erudition will emerge that will spin-off and make available more plausible replies to the freedom questions of; who, what, where, when, how, and why. In return, the philosophies of Man, Science, Politics, and God will become forward-looking, transformed, illuminating, and spiritually humbling. In many ways, whether viewed on or beyond Planet Earth, the seven, building-blocks that define existence on Planet Earth, will produce a greater, enlightened marketplace and more compassionate, democratic societies, as legislated within a bio/socio/spiritual context. In view of this, both Secular Socialism will be thrown-out into the "junk yard" of Malthusian ideas gone by.

Within this context, the prophetic urgings of Thomas Jefferson will be confirmed. His inspired insights alluded that in a democracy each generation must expose and resist the Malthusian tyrannies of the given day to launch the next, ideational revolution based on *freedom*. To be sure, this "genetic vision" and its bio/spiritual implications will comprise the next level of fundamental thought. Within the constraints of the Moral Evolution of Western Man, i.e. the Judeo/Christian belief, the arrogance of the "reason alone" crowd will be renounced giving rise to: (a) the sagacious DNA/management of *Criminal Justice*; (b) the scripting of history as *Bio/Spiritual*; (c) the revealing of the neo/scientific/theological principles of *Bio/Anthropology*; (d) the featuring of the fair implications of *Bio/Social Diversity* and its *Sociobiology* of speciated humans; (e) the religious methodology appended to *Pedagogical Genetics*; (f) the responsible morality of *Industrial Eugenics* and its *Free Marketplace*; along with (g) the politics of an upgraded democracy, which will include *Bills of Genetic, Victim, and Patient Rights*. Indeed, the exploration of the workings of the "bio/spiritual gene" and its just socio/politics will entail the teamwork of the Space technologies of the day. The Internet, world-wide TV, in conjunction with affordable, commercial air travel will lead the way for this neo/enlightenment. Followed by, Space travel, Global Satellite Positioning, micro-communications, and personal handsets. Hopefully, these humanizing technologies will act to abate the current-day, bondage plagues of Humankind. Pandemic disease, famine, ignorance, tribal warfare, Divine estrangement, Islamic terrorism, and the theology of bondage, will be fading away by way of neo/modern medicine, affordable energies, global ecology, and neo/psychology. All these high-tech trends and their allied events ought to confirm the unitary nature of our bio/spirit as well as verify the Intelligent Design of our Creator.

CHAPTER 1

God's Gift of Socio/Political Freedom
The American Revolutionary War

America is first and foremost known for pursuing socio/political and religious freedoms. Israel is first and foremost known for its approachable relationship with God and the initial defense of the Moral Order. Over the many centuries of yore, with the protection, providence, guidance, love, freedom, truth, and Divine grace readily made available by God to Man, both these nations, America and Israel, have had to fight many wars of liberty to fulfill the Divine Will.

The search for liberty dates back eight centuries with the scripting of the Magna Charta. It was the most important document scripted of all times as it set the common citizen at odds with the arbitrary rule of despots. King John, who placed his royal seal on the parchment in the county of Surrey, assured its continuity as etched on a monument placed there much later in the year 1957 AD by the American Bar

Association. However, almost three millennia before God made the decision that He wanted a set-apart nation, Israel, to carry-forth and defend His moral message to the souls of Planet Earth. Later in history America too became Divinely selected to implement, expand, and endorse God's gift of freedom for all human life and their societies. In the 18th century's USA, a colonial rebellion erupted in the New World just before the defeat of the powerful British Empire in the Revolutionary War. Freedom became an idea that began to germinate in the mindset of pioneers prior to the year 1776 AD. While many academic factors have been proposed by scholars as the decisive causes of this American socio/experiment, it was the spiritual/religious determinate of a confederation of States with Viking DNA from Scandia, Northern Germany, Northern France, and across the British Isles that conquered the mighty armada of King George's England. Inspired with colonial leadership, sea-roaming privateers, ragtail State militia, and an insufficiently financed, Continental Army, the Revolutionary War became the righteous conflict of religious resistance between a ruling class and those seeking God's liberty. In this regard, Thomas Jefferson led the way with his stirring script that gripped the imagination o fhe common pioneer to seek the Great Cause of freedom. Biblically, again we see that the upright and the weaker of us shall inherit the Earth. No doubt, this American War of Divine freedom only can be explained as a sacred, religious victory for Mankind. God's intervention expressed through an enlightened, Christian leadership, known as the Founding Fathers, set this imaginative, historic stage intended for a political paradigm needed for future, socio/legal freedom. The Declaration of

Independence, the Articles of Confederation, and ultimately the US Constitution became the incentive for this momentous happening. Actually, it was the Saxons in the 10th century that gave rise to the English Common Law. They valued the rule of law over the might of kings. Surely the Magna Charter of England written a hundred years or so later became the socio/political archetype for the democratic ideal, although its principles were not adhered to by the English monarchy and King George III in their attempts to silence, defeat, and exploit the American colonies. The Revolutionary War proved that the cause of liberty will never tolerate or submit helplessly to regal hypocrisy.

In the main, the Founding Fathers, bar none, were deeply religious men who sought out the Christian Lord for guidance and reassurance. Away from home and family, they suffered untreated maladies and loneliness for a stretch of time since they sensed and knew that their political destinies had far-reaching implications and existential meaning. At the very least John Adams, his son, John Quincy, George Washington, Benjamin Franklin, Thomas Jefferson, and James Madison, all avid, devoted readers of Sacred Scripture, knew that God was promoting "freedom" through them as set-apart leaders. No doubt, the Revolutionary victory was a God-sent miracle of spiritual courage; unlike the French Revolution, whereby freedom was based upon human reasoning-alone devoid of the guidance of God. This conceptual difference between these two 18th century Revolutions proved to be vital to the course of history. As a matter of historic fact, throughout

America's tenure, the Good Book, the Bible, could be found at the near-reach of any Presidential desk.

At the onset, it was Thomas Jefferson who became the forerunner and champion for the cause of religious freedom. He knew that our understanding of God's Nature, His Will, and His Word must deeply relish the freedom to believe. Jefferson's entire life was devoted to his opposition to all clerically managed, established Churches, especially the entrenched Anglican Church of Virginia. He was an Evangelical who fervently believed that individuals should be allowed to seek God's intimacy in their own time, ways, and means. Both the freedom of religion and political liberty should have no commanding injunction by the tyranny and one-party outlook of a State or religious denomination. In this regard, Jefferson drafted both the Declaration of Independence and the Virginian Statue for Religious Freedom that summarized the rights of Man as coming from God not "political or clerical Man." As never seen before, these two "freedom documents" had the potential to advance the political, intellectual, and spiritual growth of America, the Western World, and universally, Global Mankind. In the 21st century, the cry for freedom can be heard ringing throughout the Globe. However it took the personal sacrifices, national treasure, and much bloodshed of the American Revolution to create the intellectual and spiritual demeanor needed for political rights to emerge out of God's gift of freedom for the common citizen. The Christian principle of both private and public sacrificial service can be readily observed troughout Jefferson's political career when at twenty-five years of age he was elected to the House of Burgesses in the State of Virginia; followed by its Governorship and Presidency of the USA. During his lifetime, Jefferson was a servant via his political offices, who believed that "active goodness" should be at the core of all democratic life. For his country, not unlike Jesus who came to serve Mankind, Jefferson also served his neighbor and country throughout the tenure of his adulthood. Within a political context, Jefferson advocated the natural rights of Man as God's gift, which were premised upon freedom, self-government, a war of independence against Mother England, and the disestablishment from the ruling classes of both Church and State. Jefferson's view of spiritual deliverance included the modernizing of advance education. Based at West Point, NY, he set up a Corps of Engineers so as to better educate the officer corps by teaching engineering, technology, languages, and the mathematics of artillery. As President, Jefferson's prophetic achievements also included the acquisition of the Louisiana Purchase from Napoleon, which expanded the geo/politics of America well past west of the Mississippi River. It took years of bloodshed and untimely deaths by many thousands of colonials and frontiersmen to implement and actualize the basic freedom ideas and ideals of Thomas Jefferson. What had to be endured during this 8-year war, a bloodbath, were starvation, disease, nakedness, years of mistreatment in British prisons, cold weather, sickness, and hunger. In anticipation of this suffering ought to have been expected side-by-side with the spiritual purity of a Christian character and fortitude of a George Washington, his Generals, and Congressional allies. Out of the blue, this sorrow became comforted by the direct intervention of God who interceded during notable battles won-over at Bunker Hill, Valley Forge, Lexington, Dorchester Heights, and Salem. At these sites were the inspiring heroics of the American "freedom crusade." By taking the high ground, the victory at Bunker Hill so devastated the confidence of the British generals that it gave General Washington a year and a half breathing space so as to assemble a formidable Continental Army. At these victorious battle sites, when understood at the spiritual level, the loss of blood that represents life itself, first shed by Jesus for the forgiveness of human sin, justifies warfare as needed to further God's Will. Carried on for over eight years, the Revolutionary War of socio/political freedom finally ended at Yorktown when the British General Cornwallis had to unconditionally surrender after the French blockaded the American ports. Along with, when a much smaller British brigade faced a much larger Continental Army and Navy. Just prior to this British defeat, thousands of British and Hessian soldiers walked unsteadily to surrender to George Washington. As a counter tactical reaction, toward the end of the War the British desperately tried to make use of the Tories, i.e. American Loyalists, along with a vast array of Indian tribes to reinforce its now-evaporating troop strength. During this War there were over 20,000 Tories either under British command or serving as a Tory militia. As a military counterpoint, the American West had 10's of thousands of sturdy settlers, who were harden as frontiersmen and accustomed to adversity as a given circumstance of life itself. These settlers stood ready to defend their freedoms, to explore new lands, to seek greater prosperity, and to face Indian threats while under the protection of the newly forming Federal government.

Indeed, the hopes of the democratic ideal, where all citizens are deemed equal by law, paved the way of future socio/political thinking for the expanding Frontier experience. Now, most of America's territory that had no royalty and no State Church, but only Divine freedoms as outlined and mandated in the US Constitution. Although once in jeopardy by the social bondage by powerful ruling classes, slowly the destiny of Americans was becoming historically realized and set in stone at a point of no return.

Unquestionably, George Washington was the spiritual personification of the American War for independence. As a member of the gentry class, a social standing just below nobility, he radiated Christian dignity, integrity, and sincere humility. God's handprint selected him to lead the cause of socio/political freedom for human life and their nations. Washington displayed the Christian virtues as scripted in the Bible by Paul. Washington was humble, courageous, compassionate, patient, stalwart, stately, dependable, disciplined, loved God, and his country. Today, any tourist visiting his estate and gravesite on the Potomac River at Mount Vernon will leave honor-struck with Washington's profound, religious character. When at home, Washington would read the Bible two hours a day on his knees in front of a wooden Ottoman. Out of deep respect for his military temperament and unwavering integrity, both officers and troops alike would follow him along, unconditionally inspired by his Cause for national independence from England, along with socio/political liberty for all. His tactical commands and military strategies during the harshest of environmental conditions or during the physical exertion of long marches into battles or with the looming certainty of being wounded or killed was proof-positive of his Divine destiny. Granted as historians have revealed, Washington was not a great military tactician like the British generals. He made a number of critical battle choices that proved to be decisively incorrect and costly. But wisely as a diplomat dealing with Congressional politics and funding for his Continental Army, Washington proved to be cunning and unmatched. His leadership was highly successful mainly due to his Christian moral fiber, his just political outlook, his stately appeal, and his diplomatic tenacity.

George Washington died in his late 60's from a throat infection as America's first President, who refused to be anointed as King and to serve no more than two presidential terms. Then, like many generals and military commanders, he was a tobacco farmer whose English immigrant roots dated back to the year 1657. As a pre-adult his father died unexpectedly.

George was sent to Western Pennsylvania by the Governor of Virginia to survey the wilderness. Washington, who was tall and strong, acquired some of his combat skills during the French and Indian War. Later in his career, unanimously and wisely, Congress selected him to take command of the Continental Army to deal with a number of major encounters against the powerful British Army and Navy in Boston, New York, Trenton, Philadelphia, Princeton, and Saratoga. Within the military context of 8-years of war, Washington had to deal with Hessians, Indians, ministers, Courts, Tories, traitors, deserters, corrupt politicians, troop gloominess, wounded soldiers, death, paymasters, drunkenness, prostitution, kings, Parliament, slaves, single and married women, foul language, dysentery, typhus/typhoid fevers, and the betrayal of undercover agents. Yet he survived Loyalist plots to have him assassinated. Surely, all these intrigues was Divinely thwarted.

When possible, Washington regularly attended Sunday services to beseech the American Cause with prayer for God's protection, guidance, and providence. Most of his army that he had to train did not consist of professional soldiers. They were common Americans seeking freedom. Blacksmiths. Tailors. Shoemakers. Saddlers. Fishermen. Noblemen. Farmers. They all fought together, shoulder to shoulder, with 18th century's lowlife as the New England States eagerly supplied Washington's citizen soldiers with new regiments and ample foodstuffs consisting of ducks, geese, fish, pigs, beans, lamb, citrus fruit to prevent scurvy, and hay, along with monthly rations of rum and brandy. Truly, these provisions fortified the colonial spirit that wrestled with the cause of freedom, truth, justice. God's inspiration as scripted by Thomas Jefferson in his ***Declaration of Independence*** and later ***Common Cause*** and ***The Crisis*** by Thomas Paine ***were the times that tried men's souls***. The appeal to a "Gracious God of Providence" was widely implored by American commanders during ruggedness of battle circumstances. By appealing for retribution for their fallen comrades during combat campaigns, Washington's commanding voice could be openly heard by his troops engaged in battle. When George rode a white stallion and became visible to is troops, spirits soared. From his headquarter, Washington wrote to John Adams: *We have nothing to depend on but the protection of a kind Providence.*

To overpower and eventually conquer overwhelming military and economic odds, the American War for God's gift of freedom had to have had three persuading, prominent components. *One*, the "scripted word" to inspire combatants to fight for freedom as written by Thomas Jefferson's, ***Declaration of Independence*** and/or Thomas Paine's ***The Crises*** or ***Common Cause***. *Two*, although yet untried, but potentially exceptional, a military leadership, as per a George Washington, who relied Biblically on God's guidance, protection, and provisions. Throughout 8-yesrs of war, Washington knew thatGod's grace was to be spiritually petitioned and not to be taken for granted. *And three*, the knack and cleverness of national and international socio/politicians, as crafted by a John Adams, Benjamin Franklin, and most of the other Founding Fathers. Historically, it has become apparent that God's individual selection of the special attributes of the Founding Fathers and generals as set-apart people to promote the cause of freedom was astonishing.

As the third component to the spiritual/military triumph of the Revolutionary War for socio/political liberty for all, John Adams became God's selection to intellectually, spiritually, and politically lead the way to execute the philosophical clarity of Thomas Jefferson's writings, along with the military gallantly of George Washington. Without a John Adams and his diplomatic and Puritan, political genius America's crusade for freedom surely would have faltered and faded away. One (Jefferson), two, (Washington)) and three (Adams) became the tri/factor core, a prescription accounting for the British defeat in the 18th century.

A great deal has been written by scholars about the political relationship of John Adams and Thomas Jefferson. As proof-positive of the handprint of the Divine gracing their spiritual and intellectual affiliation in their defense and promotion of the noble idea of government by law, not rulers, they both died on Independence Day, July 4th, in the year 1826. God was pleased with their destined lives and obedient souls. Both men were opposites in many ways, yet alike, they intensely loved their country and the cause of socio/political liberty.

John Adams was born in Braintree, MA, a hundred years prior when in the year 1638 his family migrated from England with 20,000 other Puritan families, which simply sought separation from the repressive Church of England. They were among the first Evangelical Christians who came to America to renounce the false doctrine, heresies, idolatries, and clerical corruption of the Old World "religious Kings" i.e. the Pope, the Archbishop of Canterbury, and the Patriarch of Eastern Christianity. Today, not unlike Puritans and Quakers, Billy Graham's simple message: "it's all about Jesus" exemplifies the theological evolution of the modern Christian Church. Persecuted Christians of the 17th-18th centuries, i.e. Baptists, Quakers, Pilgrims, Congregationalists, and Lutherans, only sought the guidance, protection, providence, unconditional love, and grace for one's individual destiny as individually supplied by the Holy Sprit, their indwelling King.

Consistent with Quaker beliefs, John Adams, a Massachusetts farmer was the only Founding Father who never owned slaves. Otherwise, Jefferson and Washington from the Gentry class were slave owners who believed in the gradual emancipation of the Black race. Due to his spiritually mature, religious faith, Adams brought into play the unconditional search for truth, love, courage, strength, virtue, and friends into his professional and personal lifestyle. Instead, Jefferson was reclusive, suffered a lifetime of grief with the unexpected death of his two children and demise of his 33-year old wife to child birth fever. Left with raising three other children as a widower caused Jefferson to experience a chronic, emotional depression and in turn, the over-compensatory motivation to write about great, new ideas, while seeking sexual comfort and love from a beautiful slave, Sally.

Enthused by George Mason's ***Virginia's Declaration of Rights*** as scripted in his ***Thoughts on Government***, John Adams brilliant intellect fortified with Christian maturity led him to formalize what a democratic nation might look like, as ruled by the laws of citizens, not the arbitrary autocratic fiats of rulers. Adams insisted that this new style of governing must be premised and summarized by "all men are born equal" and ought to be set free to self-govern. He insisted that any hierarchal passing-on of socio/political power, whether regal or by social standing is aberrant. Socio/political rights coming directly from the God of Freedom and Justice are innate and absolute. Some of these rights include: (a) freedom of speech; (b) a free press; (c) against unreasonable search and seizure; (d) trial by jury; and (e) the assurance of all religions and their denominations to freely worship a Supreme Being. Most importantly, no citizen or his property ought to be arbitrarily detained In addition; structurally, Adams proposed that this new democratic concept assures that government by the people ought to have three independent branches: the executive, legislative, and judicial. To assure a sovereign balance among States, Adams designed a bicameral legislative assembly with two senators for each State and a House of Representatives based on population size. For John Adams, to preserve the natural rights and liberty for all will always require spiritual virtue, critical thinking, and valid, educated information.

In order to understand the unique, American ideal of socio/ political freedom as the Will of God based upon law and morality, it might be said that John Adams' moral fiber directly came out of a Puritan/Quaker, Biblical conviction. Both these Christian denominations and others were made up of New World persecuted Separatists, who after the Reformation renounced the corrupted Christianity of Old World "religious kings" and instead became committed fully to the spiritual leadership of the Holy Spirit. In Sabbatical, liturgical, and theological practice, both Puritans and Quakers lived out Jesus' mandate of loving the lame, the last, the least of us, and the lost. This also was the socio/political standard of living of John and Abigail Adams

As family custom, John Adams grew up as a Puritan. Like the Protestant theologian, John Calvin, a Swiss Reformer, Adams believed in a simplified religion with plain vestments, simple liturgy, and Biblically-based Lutheran theology, all to be free of an absolute, centralized Church and its preestablished religious politics. Puritans became separatists when persecuted by the Church of England. In tandem, during the War for independence Americans also were persecuted by the British. Originally, some of John Adams' family had to migrate to Holland, then a religiously tolerant nation. Not unlike the American colonies Puritans and Quakers came to the New World, some of them as Pilgrims, traveling on the Mayflower ship to Plymouth a harbor in New England. A short while later, the Adams' descendants with thousands of other Puritans crossed the Great Ocean and settled in Massachusetts. These historic events must have shaped the mind, character, and destiny of John Adams. Throughout the next two centuries Puritanism became the overriding belief in New England. In America, the Puritan interpretation of the message of Jesus had a long-lasting impact, with independent churches and denominations appearing throughout the land. The Founding Fathers and in particular, John Adams, initialized and put into a socio/political context the rationale for the American Revolution.

Collectively, the Quakers along with the Puritans also were prominent, vibrant, influential, and well-known to the American/Christian democracy. In actual practice, not in theological theory, Quakers believed in the basic message of Jesus that tells us: He loves the lame, the last, the least, and the spiritually lost, among us. John Adams spiritual maturity emulated the Quakers who were the leading advocates for the immediate emancipation and justice of slaves. In the 17th century there were over 40,000 Quakers in America. In many ways, they were pretextually persecuted, murdered, jailed, fined, and ostracized. Why? They wanted to hold their own Sabbath services, refused to bear arms, or pay Church tithes. For Quakers, the plight of the Black slave, the Indian, the unfairly convicted criminal, the poor, the mentally ill, and the uneducated, all were forms of human suffering that translated into the pure Christian spirit and became eligible for Quaker participation. Not unlike the Puritan/Quaker moral fiber of those pre-Revolutionary days, ii was Jesus who inspired the American religious separatists to love the cripple and sick, the last in social standing, the least important of us, and those nowhere to be spiritually found. No doubt America was brought into being by Judeo/Christian principles and brave separatists as put into operation through the Divinely selected, Founding Fathers and brave generals. In addition to the Quaker/Puritan soul, it was the full range of evangelical denominations that led and sustained the cause of religious freedom. In addition to the nucleus contributions of Jefferson, Washington, and Adams, the other Founding Fathers of America also were Divinely selected to perform some unique role in the Freedom Crusade. Add, Benjamin Franklin, James Madison, Alexander Hamilton, and others to fill the fuller picture of the miracle of the American democracy.

Without a doubt, above all America originated out of religious intentions that explain why God set-apart the

Founding Fathers to conduct the Revolutionary War and why the Pilgrims, landing in Plymouth on December 11th in the year 1620, chose to sail across a perilous Atlantic Ocean to establish a new society based on Christian values and the Kingdom of Heaven. England, despite its commitment to universal freedoms via its Common Law and Magna Charter was in fact an ungodly and amoral Empire in the 18th century. Instead as a Great Awakening, the colonists were regular church attendees and ardent Bible-readers. One might easily deduce that the Declaration of Independence was a theological manuscript and the US Constitution arose out of the Torah, i.e. the Mosaic Law. The socio/political dynamics of the 1st Amendment alone, which rejects a national Church and the Congressional establishment of a collective denomination, should confirm the Christian view of freedom as a Divine mandate.

While much as been voluminously written about Benjamin Franklin, Alexander Hamilton, John Marshall, and John Jay, as noteworthy contributors to the evolution of the American democracy, it was James Madison who ranked highest when compared to the intellectual brilliance of his lifelong political friends, Thomas Jefferson and John Adams. Madison's first year in higher education was spent in a seminary where he became instructed and intellectually challenged with theological matters. For this reason, during the rest of his political career, Madison he took the position that religion played a considerable role in the "freedom politics" of democratic science. His subsequent formal education was acquired at the College of New Jersey, i.e. Princeton. What followed became

Madison's sizeable writings that intermittently included notes and quotes from the Bible to embellish a point or an argument. Seeking spiritual maturity during the years 1772-1775, Madison embarked on a far-reaching study of Sacred Scripture. These religious years proved to be indispensable to his intellectual pursuit of a new "freedom conception" for government by law, not rulers. Soon thereafter, the major role he performed was in the transition from the Articles of Confederation, whereby power rested with the sovereign States on to the US Constitution, which shared power between Central/State governments. In this regard, Madison chose to pray often at his home, Montpelier, during his remarkable career that included the 4th Presidency of the now-USA. The same religious dedication might be said for most of the signers of the Declaration of Independence, the attendees of the Constitutional Convention, and those who framed the celebrated First Amendment that guaranteed freedom of worship. These men were faithful, involved Christians, who fashioned a Judeo/Christian America that acknowledged the providence and protection of God, obeyed His Will, and were thankful for His salvation. For a good society, most all of the Founding Fathers believed in religion, moral education for children, and the acquisition of knowledge. Even after 2 ½ centuries, the Revolutionary remnants of Judeo/Christianity include a Congressional Day of Prayer and a public holiday, Thanksgiving Day.

James Madison was born in Virginia in 1751 of English heritage. His family was wealthy rich landowners passing on to young James a sizeable fortune. He was physically frail and fragile in health so could not militarily serve in the Revolutionary War. Nevertheless, Madison was busy recruiting troops for the Continental Army and scripting wartime leaflets to inspire the troops and other colonists. Under the new Virginia government Madison became elected to its Assembly and later represented his State in the Continental Congress. It might be said that Madison's debates during the Constitutional Convention were some of his greatest accomplishments. Eventually, taking the written form of the ***Federalist Papers,*** these formal documents became the argumentative contentions between the Anti-Federalist, e.g. Alexander Hamilton, and those that were hoping foe a strong national government. Straddling the years of the War for Independence to the Post War period was marked by Madison's political brilliance that facilitated the taking of a new nation from a number of relatively powerless and decentralized Sovereign States to the political potency of Federalism and the US Constitution. Now renowned and fortified with the Declaration of Independence and the US Constitution Madison, who composed 29 out of the 85 now-revered Federalist Papers became a political clairvoyant whose vision pointed Westward by proposing greater freedom on the seas in the form of free navigation on the Mississippi River.

Indeed, America was and is a set-apart, exceptional nation that was fashioned as a Divine happening. Within the context of freedom and the bloodbath of war, not unlike the forgiving bloodshed of Jesus' Crucifixion, became spiritually indispensable. This first major American war for freedom and independence came to pass as a Divine episode. It reflected God's Nature, His Word, and His Will to directly intercede socio/politically during the tenure of human existence. Evangelical religion played a major role in the rise of the American people. The first pioneers that had the DNA to make this happen were the descendants of the Neatherthal, who begot the Vikings, then the Nordics, Northern Germans, Northern French, and those inhabiting the British Isles. Indeed the energy of Old World genetics played a decisive role in the socio/political expressions of freedom. Up to the Modern Era, all other non-Euro societies continue to struggle with the notion of government by "we the people." Neither the youth revolution of the 1960's nor the Vietnam protests were able to topple the American aspiration and fortitude. In truth, the US Constitution has been an everlasting, Divine document of liberty for all. Now in the 21ˢᵗ century, moral corruption challenges to our democracy include residual racism, the rise of female power, abortion, same-sex marriage, the Islamic terror, plunging educational standards, mindless litigations, a subjective journalism, the secular progressives who spew cultural correctness, atheism, and the gridlock of Congress. Will God allow America to continue to survive at the cutting edge of spiritual evolution? Will America continue to be the only and last hope for a dying world?

Mosaic Law and 21ˢᵗ Century Democracy

American Christianity and American Democracy run parallel. They both emanated in substance out of the Mosaic

Law. At the near onset of human civilization, this covenant addressed the universal, socio/political concerns of Mankind, which were then slighted by the tribal outlook and debauchery of those Ancient times. While the 10-Commandants set the stage as the core of moral living, the expanded Mosaic dictates dealt with false accusations, rights of the family and women, individual dignity, just economics, equal law, and rest on the Sabbath. From the Israelis to the message of Jesus to the development of the democratic order, this Mosaic covenant accounted for the Moral Evolution.

By existential theme, there are three overriding, spiritual building-blocks featured within the 1200-plus pages of the Judeo/Christian Code, i.e. the Bible. *One*, is the command of *righteousness* that is a Divine, nonnegotiable condition of which both the organic and inorganic Realms within the Multiverse has been preestablished. Creation in itself is good, neither neutral, nor evil, nor in bondage to scientific law, nor chaotic, and not devoid of inherent beauty. Indeed, goodness is beautiful. This righteousness or goodness or holiness is a primordial, metaphysical, dynamic attribute of all organic and inorganic creation. Why? Simply because, the Nature of God is indubitably holy, good, and righteous, and His creation must become this likeness of Divinity. *Secondly*, for living-and-loving on Planet Earth, *social justice* is another spiritually nonnegotiable reality, fundamental to all of human proceedings, e.g. socio/politics. Indeed, when a young man asked Jesus: what will it take to enter the Kingdom of Heaven, the answer was "…love your God (who is good) with your whole might" and "love thy neighbor as thyself." *Thirdly*, the aura of *love* is paramount in the understanding of creation. Love cherishes. Love serves. Love considers all creation as precious. In sum, although God's nature supersedes all of our human capacities to fathom the totality of the Divine, these four existential, conditions, i.e. love, freedom, justice, and righteousness, reflect the reason and justification of both our species and individual creation. In the 21st century, these four attributes became the forewarnings by Jesus, along with serving as socio/political beacons for Global, democratic living. Straddling time from Abraham to the 21st century, personal holiness, love, freedom, and social fairness have been the four religious presuppositions, which have been avowed and affirmed throughout the 3500-year history of the Moral Evolution of Western Man. The Mosaic Law, written over 3000-years ago, initiated and formalized these three themes for Western Mankind to abide by.

Throughout the chapters of this book the role of the "freedom aura" of personal holiness and love has been dealt with from a 21st century perspective, the matter of socio/political manifestations of justice, as the second building-block of the Creation Plan, hasn't yet been fully elucidated and fulfilled. Surely as spiritual dynamics, while personal holiness, love, and social justice, can be understood as partially overlapping; two factors (love and goodness) address individual relationships with Man and God, while one (social justice) tackles the spiritual mechanisms of community affairs. Freedom covers them all. Accordingly, in order to understand what "justice," as a spiritual entity entails, a socio/political discourse on the transcendent evolution of governments should cause us to see the glaring differences among despotic dictatorships, autocratic oligarchies, benevolent monarchies--and the compassionate, Mosaic-based democracies. As it stands today, historic logic should ordain that 21st century America ought to be considered the ideal consequence of Biblical expression. Unequivocally, both the Torah and the USA stand for universal human rights, civil liberties for all, social justice, and economic parity for those who dare apply. Biblical scholarship has revealed that these commitments have been originally implied and codified by Mosaic Law. Likewise both structurally and operationally, the socio/political "justice devices" of America are the outcrop of Israel's tradition that has been spiritually crafted over 3000-years ago. While throughout Western history, Mankind has been victimized by "spiritually inept" political models, which summarily have failed to connect and recognize the evolutionary significance of "righteousness, love, freedom, and justice" to the survival and fulfillment of the Homo Sapien. The American democracy, as a gift of God, has been telling it otherwise. If so, by virtue of its flourishing, 230-year tenure, adaptively and spiritually, America, as the concluding socio/political paradigm, ought to be regarded as the last and only hope for a dying world.

Via God's Creation and Redemption Plans, both of which unequivocally respected freedom-of-choice for each soul, the Mosaic Decree became launched by way of a Divinely chosen people, the Hebrews. In a theological context, this religious code formalized the rules, regulations, and spiritual laws for both individuals and their ruling bodies of government.

Henceforth both in their leaderships and daily proceedings so as to survive and succeed as human, social institutions, all regimes of nations, tribes, and communities must reorganize their socio/political ways&means to echo the preconditions of holiness, love, freedom, and social justice. So, what did the Mosaic Law allude about the spiritual attributes of democratic socio/politics?

<u>On Personal Worth</u>: the right afforded every person to be respected; highlighting the non-exploitation of the powerless (rights of the poor, disabled, orphan, the sick, widows, and foreigners). Moses told us….

…do not murder (Exodus 20:13)

…kidnappers must be killed…an assailant must pay…because of injury…if a slave is beaten and dies, the owner must be punished (Exodus 21:16-21)

…show your fear of God by treating the deaf with respect and by not taking advantage of the blind (Leviticus 19:14)

…cursed is anyone who steals another's property…or who leads a blind person astray…or who is unjust to foreigners, orphans and widows… or who kills in secret for pay…or has sexual relations with animals, or other family members (Deuteronomy 27:17-26).

<u>On Untrue Allegations:</u>(the right against perjury, slander, and libel.

...do not testify falsely against your neighbor (Exodus 20:16).

...do not pass along false reports...or tell lies on the witness stand...do not be swayed in your testimony by the opinion of the majority and against the poor (Exodus 23: 1-3).

...do not spread slanderous gossip among your people (Leviticus 19:16).

...never convict anyone of a crime on the testimony of just one witness (Deuteronomy 19: 15).

<u>Rights of Women:</u> the right of females to be protected from exploitation.

...if a slave owner's son marries a slave girl she becomes free and must be treated as a daughter (Exodus 21:9)

...on the Sabbath no one must work, including your daughters and female slaves (Exodus 20:10).

...if a man seduces a virgin, he must pay the customary dowry and accept her as his wife (Exodus 22:16)

...if you see a captive, foreign, beautiful women you may marry her, but not humiliate her or sell her or treat her as a slave (Deuteronomy 21: 10-14)

...do not accuse a virgin falsely or have intercourse with his father's wife (Deuteronomy 22: 13-30).

…a newly married man must not be drafted in the army but must be free to be at home to bring happiness to his new wife (Deuteronomy 24: 5).

…if a man dies and has no sons, give his inheritance to his daughters (Numbers 27:8)

<u>Punishment</u>: the right not to be punished cruelly and inhumanely.

…if a person is sentenced to be flogged, no more than 40 lashes may ever be given so as to avoid the public humiliation of the accused (Deuteronomy 25:1-3)

<u>Social Dignity</u> the right to be honored and safeguarded by society.

…if you buy a Hebrew slave, he is to serve for only six years. Set him free on the seventh year. (Exodus 21:2).

…if any of your relatives fall into poverty, support them and allow them to live with you. (Leviticus 25:35)

…the people of Israel must never be sold as slaves. (Leviticus 25:42)

…if any Israelite has not been redeemed by the time of the Year of the Jubilee, they and their children must be set free. (Leviticus 25:54)

…when you release a male servant, share with him some of your bounty. Don't send him away empty-handed. (Deuteronomy 15:13-14)

Family Solidity and Continuity the rights of inheritance.

...a *"kinsman redeemer"* assures the just sale of Israeli properties. *(Leviticus 25)*

...the Levitical pastureland may never be sold; it is their permanent, ancestral property *(Leviticus 25:34).*

...the Lord replied to Moses: the daughters of Zelophehad are right; you must give them an inheritance of land. *(Numbers 27:5)*

...none of the inherited land may be passed from tribe to tribe. *(Numbers 36:7*

Property rights:

.. you shall not steal *(Deuteronomy 5:19*

...if a thief is caught in the act of breaking into a house and is killed, the person who owns the house is not guilty *(Exodus 22:2)*

...do not use dishonest standards when measuring length, weight, or volume *(Leviticus 19:35)*

...if you see a neighbor's ox or sheep wandering away, take it back to its owner *(Deuteronomy 22:1)*

Rights of Workers

...always pay your hired workers promptly *(Leviticus 19:13)*

...never take advantage of a poor laborer *(Deuteronomy 24:14)*

<u>On Sharing Food:</u> rights of the hungry poor.

…let the poor among you harvest any crop that comes up… let the same apply for your vineyards and olive groves (Exodus 23:10-11)

…leave the extra grain and grapes for the poor and the foreigners (Leviticus 19:9-10)

…your hired servants and foreigners may eat the produce that grows naturally during the Sabbath year (Leviticus 25:6-7)

…bring the tithes of your crops to the Levities who have no inheritance as well as to the foreigners, orphan, and widows in your towns (Deuteronomy 14:28-29)

…when beat the olives from your olive trees, don't go over the boughs twice; leave some for the foreigners, widows, and orphans (Deuteronomy 24: 20)

<u>Honoring the Sabbath:</u> right for a seventh-day rest, gratitude, worship, and praise.

…set apart the Sabbath as holy and as a day of rest (Exodus 20:8-11)

….the Sabbath day must be dedicated to the Lord your God (Deuteronomy 5:12-15)

<u>Honoring Marriage:</u> society's right of inviolate, marital relationships.

…do not commit adultery (Exodus 20:14)

…do not practice homosexuality, it is a detestable sin (Leviticus 18:22)

<u>Right to a fair trial:</u> social justice is an ultimate, nonnegotiable entitlement.
…do not twist justice against people simply because they are poor (Exodus 23:6)
…take no bribes as it hurts the cause of the person who is in the right (Exodus 23:8)
…always judge your neighbor fairly, whether rich or poor (Leviticus 19:15)
…your Lord your God gives justice to orphans and widows (Deuteronomy 10:17-18)
…let justice prevail (Deuteronomy (!7:20)
…never convict anyone on the testimony of just one witness (Deuteronomy 19:15)

…a king must read a copy of the Law daily and obey all its terms (Deuteronomy 17:19)

<u>Animal Rights:</u>
…if you see an animal struggling under a load, stop and help it (Exodus 23:5)
…allow your livestock and wild animals to eat off the land's bounty (Leviticus 25:7)
…if you find a bird's nest on the ground with young ones, take the young. (Deuteronomy 21:6)

****

In support of the ideas of 21ˢᵗ century's democracy and by referencing and citing the five books of the Torah written by Moses before the birth of Jesus, this is what was preached during the ministry of the Messiah concerning the socio/political rights of persons. All truly democratic societies are premised upon the Mosaic/Jesus ideas of social/political justice.

- personal righteousness, love, and social justice are the ultimate, non-negotiable realities governing human life on Planet Earth; these are the overriding messages of the four Gospels of the NT.
- do not yield to evil temptations of injustice (See Matthew 4: 1-11)
- God blesses those nations which recognize their need for him (Matthew 5:3)
- Those who mourn will be comforted by God and community (See Matthew 5:4)
- God blesses the humble leaders of nations (See Matthew 5:5)
- Citizens who crave justice will be blessed by God (See Matthew 5:6)
- Societies which are merciful will receive mercy (See Matthew 5:7)
- The hearts of leaders must be pure (See Matthew 5:8)
- Striving for peace, forgiveness, and love of enemies ought to be the goal of just, legal proceedings (See Matthew 5:9; 43-48)
- Freedom from persecution must be assured by government (See Matthew 5:10)

- Democratic societies are the "salt and light" of the world (See Matthew 5:13-16)
- The Bill of Rights reflects, not rejects, the Mosaic Law (See Matthew 5: 17-20)
- Protection from murder, violence, and revenge is a primary task of free societies (See Matthew 5: 21-26; 38-42)
- Marriage and family are the building-blocks of free societies and must not be defiled by divorce and adultery (See Matthew 5:27-32)
- Democracies must be compassionate to the needy (See Matthew 6: 1-4)
- Public prayer by officials of free societies ought to be regularly scheduled (See Matthew 6: 5-13)
- Love of money is at the root of socio/political evils (See Matthew 6: 19-34)
- The Golden Rule, as Scripturally reflected in Court precedence, laws, rules, and regulations, ought to be the uppermost concern of democratic societies
- A democratic nation, which is premised upon the Mosaic/Christian ideal, will build, not on sand, but on the foundations of solid rock and deep roots (See Matthew 7: 24-27; Mark 4)

In succession and progression, from the Mosaic Law to the Magna Charta to the Declaration of Independence to the US Constitution to the United Nations Charter, 21st century's yet-evolving Mankind has etched within its socio/political consciousness the freedoms assured by the Bill of Rights, a Global commitment to universal human rights, the legal proceedings declaring civil rights for all, and an international marketplace dedicated to economic parity, barring none who dare apply.

Ergo; by way of the Revolutionary War, the American model of socio/political freedom tells us that democratic societies, at first, evolved as compassionate communities followed by the operational and legal mechanisms of free nations. In a variety of ways, and over 3000-years ago, the Mosaic Law was commissioned by God to bestow fundamental, socio/political rights upon the individual, human soul. Subsequently, about a thousand years later, the Hellenic Empire began to devise and formulate thoughts of democratic ways&means for the nations of Greece. By way of the enlightened scholarship of Aristotle, Socrates, Plato, and others, the notion of the "good and just Man" was introduced as the basis for a "good and just nation," that might be both free and compassionate.

After many centuries passed by, democratic ideas continued to evolve via the scholarship of the Renaissance (15th-16th centuries), the 18th century's Enlightenment, Common Law and the Magna Charter of England, along with the writers who fueled the French Revolution. However, the truly great experiment of a society bent on individual liberty became crystallized in the New World. Implausibly, the Founding Fathers of America, led by the spiritual character of George Washington, the classical persona of Thomas Jefferson, the legal/moral fiber of John Adams, the political charm of Benjamin Franklin, and the shrewd, sensible mind of James Madison put together a working model for a practical, democratic government. In a capsule, the US Constitution became a revised, enriched, and expanded replica of the Judeo/ Christian Code, which respected individual rights through a medium of social compassion. Within five decades prior to the 21st century, this socio/political experiment began to cascade across the governments of the family of nations. Both in style and substance, the US Constitution became the archetype for the world communities to emulate. A government of individual freedoms, universal human rights, civil liberties bar none, and the opportunities for economic parity for those who dare apply, became the inalienable touchstone for the five continents of the world. In truth although not trouble-free, the "noble struggle" for human dignity endowed by God for all nations, which thusfar only knew of their political traditions of central control, entrenched caste-systems, and military subjugation, is becoming brought to fruition across Planet Earth. Indeed, from the Mosaic Law as fulfilled by Jesus came the UN Charter of universal, human rights.

Alluding to the message of Sacred Scripture, our Founding Fathers understood:

> *...On the sacred rights of Mankind, these are written as a sunbeam in the whole volume of human nature, by the hand of Divinity itself; and can never be erased or obscured by mortal power. (Alexander Hamilton 1775 AD)*
> *...we hold these truths to be self-evident that all men are created equal and endowed*

by the Creator with certain unalienable rights. (The Declaration of Independence (1776 AD)

Such as:
- the right to free speech
- the right to worship freely
- the right to assemble
- the right of a free press
- the right to petition the government
- the right to bear arms
- the right for persons to be secure and equal
- the right to a fair trial
- the right to free and fair elections
- the right to life, liberty, and the pursuit of happiness.

In the 21st Century, we can expect to add Christian themes to the US Constitution with a Bill of Genetic Rights, a Bill of Patient Rights, along with a Bill of Victim Rights.

****

American Christianity and its democratic institutions move us into the fourth, reform stage of the Moral Evolution of Western Man. Christian denominations are numerous, yet their primary Christian beliefs are few. First, Evangelical Christians believe in the inerrancy and inspiration provided by the Bible, a book that ought to be read and/or studied daily. For these New World Christians, Scriptural reading on a daily basis becomes an interactive conduit between the personal soul reaching upward to a personal God. Secondly, American Christianity understands that it's all about Jesus, a living persona of the Divine, who protects, provides guides, loves unconditionally, and supplies the necessary grace/energy to make one's life meaningful. Accordingly, forgiveness of individual sin, repentance, salvation, and a commitment to a life of love, righteousness, and social justice in thought, word, and action, are the basic building-blocks of sanctification— assures eternity with God. Thirdly, American Christianity holds to the importance of honoring the Sabbath as an opportunity to praise and worship the One and only God, while offering gratitude for the many blessings of the past week. Lastly, the American Christian must look to the Holy Spirit for guidance and not trust the Old World, established authorities, i.e. the Papacy, the Patriarch, and/or the Church of England. All other theological issues, e.g. Baptism, Eucharist, etc, are worthy of spiritual speculation, but secondary to the entering of the Kingdom of God. These four, primary pillars of Christian belief are the commitments of the various, New World denominations of America, i.e. the Evangelical people of the Gospel.

Since the 17th century, the fourth stage of the Judeo/ Christian evolution and ongoing reform, aka American Christianity, experienced a number of "centennial steps" leading to the 21st century. Each hundred years or so, the socio/ political issues posed by "democracy vs religion" emerged and progressed in a parallel mode, linked together and energized by competition, contention, controversy, and compromise. Freedom of religion and the paradox of separation of Church

State, as realized by the denominations of the New World, challenged their parishioners to seek and rise to a higher level of Divine intimacy as they might pertain to a free society. By way of ideological and theological truths, democracy as conceived by God and as Evangelically been portrayed was forged by the Founding Fathers and the Magna Charter of England. It is a government steeped in the principles of Christianity and has socio/politically fashioned our 21st century society.

As early as the 17th century, by escaping the religious intolerance of the Old Euro/World, Puritans, Quakers, Congregationalists, Lutherans, Baptists, and Pilgrims, sought to disestablish themselves from the autocracy, corruption, false doctrine, and persecution of the Churches of Rome, England, and Constantinople. These pioneers relied upon the guidance of the Holy Spirit, an inerrant Bible, living a personal, loving, righteous, and just relationship with Jesus, and by honoring the Sabbath with praise, worship, and gratitude. In a capsule, American Christianity became a struggle between rational Enlightenment and spiritual Evangelism. This ideational stressor accounted for the formation of democratic institutions and its free society called the USA.

Roger Williams, a Puritan, brought the first Baptists to America in the early 17th century. A few decades later, these Puritans formed the Massachusetts Bay Colony, along with the Pilgrims' Plymouth Plantation. Both sects joined forces when they realized and decided that they held in-common political, social, economic, and spiritual freedoms. In chorus, they also resisted King Henry VIII's Presbyterians and Methodists, which were Old Euro/World, Church of England derivatives. Arriving Pilgrims and Puritans called themselves Congregationalists. Subsequently, later in the 18th century, persecuted immigrants from Switzerland, Holland, Hungary, and other Euro/countries also sailed to the New World to form Synods of North America. Simultaneously during this same period of time, the Quakers, who were persecuted in England, began to appear in the New World. They were disillusioned with the demeanor of the English Church, and its expanding ritualistic complexities, therefore they sought and opted for a simpler, more intimate, affiliation with God. This religious movement, the Quakers, blossomed in Boston, MA, yet the persecutions, whippings, incarcerations, and social expulsions continued to beleaguer them. Over the decades, their Christian values drew widespread, popular attention and climaxed the American "freedom mindset." Quakers stood for peace, civil rights, women's rights, the rights of Native Americans, voting rights, the Underground Railroad, and in the 20th century assisted the relocation of Jews. God's gift of socio/political freedom was embodied in the Quaker character. Indeed, Quakers became the prototype for the American democracy. Unquestionably, these persecuted, New World refugees were about to elevate the Christian Outlook up to a new stratum of political enlightenment.

The spiritual beliefs of the Founding Fathers of the USA typified the coming together of the American democracy with the New World version of Christianity. History has shown that their socio/spiritual "freedom thoughts" represented two sides of the same coin. No longer would Judeo/Christianity and a free society be ideationally compromised or politically disengaged. One without the other could never attain or gain or acquire historical significance or evolutionary justification. Freedom to believe devoid of established, Church authorities became the rallying cry of the New World American. Liberty to worship propelled their patriotic efforts and military sacrifices. Within this political context, each Founding Father referred to Providential Divinity. God the Father; Jesus, God the Son; and the guidance and inspiration offered by the Holy Spirit were often mentioned in both their oratory and writings. The Founding Fathers were all professing Christians of some sort, either openly like George Washington, John Jay, Alexander Hamilton, and James Madison or tangentially as Deists or Unitarians, like the other colonial leaders, such as Thomas Jefferson, John Adams, and Benjamin Franklin. In their writings and political activities, the Founding Fathers sought to advance the notion of liberty by way of the Christian message and by proselytizing both the Euro/loyalists and the Native American populace. Not unlike Emperor Constantine of the 4th century, the Founding Fathers too had to conceal their true, Christian beliefs so as to avoid the possibilities of negative, political spinoffs. As compelling anecdotes, Constantine was baptized on his deathbed, Alexander Hamilton died as a professing Anglican just prior to his demise. Within the political realm, it was difficult to reconcile openly one's, deeply-held, personal beliefs within the varying complexities of the political aura. On the message of Jesus, Franklin, Jefferson, and Adams agreed: *I think on morals and religion, as He left them to us, as the best the world has ever seen, or is likely to see.*

However, with freedom, whether spiritual or political, come the social evils of immoderation and lawlessness. Also, with political liberty comes economic freedom (or license), called capitalism or unbridled laissez faire. We find that in the late 20th century and early 21st century, the economic corruption of American Christianity has become endemic, especially in the mega-churches. It has been reported that Franklin Graham earns $800,000/yr and Rick Warren $900,000/yr. Widespread, all too many super large churches of both liberal and conservative persuasions, Old World or New World convictions, are misusing their stewardship, cooking their books, exploiting the congregation, and for some, outright corruption. By way of their tax-free status, which must demand a strict, Christian accountability of parishioner tithes and donations, the American "religious dishonesty" instead has become legally at risk. Jim Bakker, who misappropriated church funds, included the building of a carpeted, air conditioned doghouse, and Jimmy Swaggart, who used church funds to solicit prostitutes on a regular basis, are just a few egregious examples of the systemic corruption of modern-day Christianity. As well, there are a growing number of cases-in-point of capitalistic/felonies being committed daily in other mega-churches and tele/evangelistic ministries. Big-time Christianity has become big business perched upon the fulcrums of unethical illegality. In progress, the US Congress has been conducting investigations of a number of the major, television, Sunday-services, which are alleging as a legal defense for their financial lack of accountability, "separation of Church and State." In addition to their stealth, accounting practices, there are a number of ongoing, respectable churches who consider their congregations as a group of consumers, rather than souls to be spiritually nurtured.

Accordingly, perceived as customers, some pastors are paid obscene salaries plus outrageous perks. A number of these "capitalistic churches" have come out of the teaching traditions of Oral Roberts University. However, the most egregious of all churches operating within the American Christian marketplace is the Roman Catholic Church. It functions as an administratively/financial, secretive organization, filtered through with sexual perversion, steeped in socio/hypo racy, heretical, with its false doctrine, and rituals which only be described as idolatrous. Jesus and Sacred Scripture hold a low priority among the Roman clergy, which instead promotes the idolatry of "Pope worship" and the praying to/thru Mary and the saints. In a theological context, nothing good can come about without Divine grace. And, any believer in the Holy Spirit as the prime source of spiritual enlightenment would conclude that God has pulled His approving grace out of the sinews of the Roman Catholic Church.

In general, Catholics aren't encouraged to read the Bible daily, the Divine system of communication between a soul and God. Regularly, these Romans pray, not directly to Jesus, a living, personal God, but to/thru saints and Mary as their prime source of idol worship. They are told that the daily Mass is a sacrifice for daily sin, ignoring the theological factoid that

Jesus, as the ultimate sacrifice, already died for all human breaches of love, righteousness, and justice, in thoughts, words, and deeds. The Pope, who calls himself "His Holiness," is an affrontation to God, who is the one and only holy persona. The Pope is considered: (a) infallible under certain constraints; (b) one who claims to be able to forgive human sins via his priestly representatives; and (c) one who claims a legacy of continuity from Peter the apostle. According to Martin Luther, these conjectures are unfounded, theological fabrications. In fact, the Papacy is an administrative position, which was created on or about the 7th century AD, not in the 1st century AD, in order to meet the needs of the growing number of Christian churches. Sound Biblical scholarship tells us that only Jesus can forgive sin. Only God is holy. Only the guidance of the Holy Spirit is infallible. The primary mission of the Roman Church is not the salvation of the individual soul, but rather the expansion and maintenance of their Global "bondage politics." Their trumped-up theology is intended to control and exploit their Global constituency with fear, guilt, and institutional dependence. Ergo; the false doctrines of purgatory, limbo, mortal/venial sin, the tenuous character of salvation, Eucharistic transubstantiation, Gnostic self-hate as demonstrated by the life of St. Francis of Assisi, acceptable priestly sexual perversions, along with a range of pervasive, idolatrous practices all qualify the Roman Church as a Medieval cult with 21st century Global, political ambitions that finds itself emptied of God's grace and approval.

Yet in spite of the prevailing, fiscal corruption operating in a number of the American megachurches, which have become obscenely prosperous at the onset of the 21st century, there is an influential, commanding, honest&holy, evangelical movement that has become a pulsating feature to both the American democracy and its Christianity. These churches are large and small, coming out of a number of traditions, and as a composite represent the fastest growing, religious movement of the American spiritual and cultural life. They are the Evangelicals, the people of the Gospel, who believe and are dedicated to four, primary precepts. One, to read the inerrant and inspirational Bible daily. Two, to honor the Sabbath. Three, to seek their guidance from the Holy Spirit. And four, it's all about Jesus. Period. Some of these honest&holy churches come to us as tele/mega institutions directly out of the evangelical traditions of the mid-19th century. The Enlightenment and Great Awakenings of those times also produced and consolidated the Evangelical Movement that we find so robust in both in true democratic politics and within the religious lives of America of the 21st century. The supersized crusades of Billy Graham, who has been the spiritual advisor of most of the American Presidents of the 20th century; Robert Schuler, pastor of the Crystal Cathedral; Jerry Falwell, and his Moral Majority; Charles Stanley, an international tele-evangelist; John Hagee, and his political support for the Israeli link to the Judeo/Christian tradition; and Rick Warren, whose megachurch hosted the 2000 AD debates of the presidential candidates, all have their Christian roots set in the democratic processes. They carried forth the 19th Century's, Evangelical traditions of the American Enlightenment and the Great Awakenings initiated by Francis Willard (1839-1898), Wayne Wheeler (1869-1927), and Billy Sunday (1863-1935).

It's no wonder that Christianity has become the largest and fastest expanding religion in America and on Planet Earth. Jesus' message is compatible with all nations and communities that love the socio/politics of individual liberty. Even in India, a hardcore Hindu nation, there are twenty-one million Christians in its Southwest region, all part of the 1st century ministry of St. Thomas, one of Jesus' original apostles. Likewise, in Central and Southern Africa, Christian populations are exploding to new heights. South Korea too, since 1950 AD has megachurches with Christian congregations as large as 100,000. Similarly, once-Catholic, once-Orthodox Europe, which now professes to be part of a Post-Christian Era, i.e. secular humanism, is poised to redeem itself with a 21st century, spiritual revival. And, China, which has adopted Western capitalism, has a persecuted, underground Christian Church, numbering 60+ million believers. Indeed, Christianity and the politics of liberty have evolved to become two sides of the same coin.

CHAPTER 2

Freedom of the Seas and Commerce: Capitalism
The War of 1812

For Planet Earth, the American Revolutionary War pioneered the novel ideas of individual liberty and the socio/political ideals of God's gift of freedom. In this quest, during the next 250-years of American warfare, 218,000 soldiers, airmen, sailors, and marines have been buried in US cemeteries in foreign lands. Socio/political freedom includes....

- the right to free speech
- the right to worship freely
- the right to assemble
- the right of a free press
- the right to petition the government
- the right to bear arms
- the right for persons to be secure and equal
- the right to a fair trial

- the right to free and fair elections
- the right to life, liberty, and the pursuit of happiness.

Yet a second war in the year 1812 was needed to complete God's Will and gift to humankind of socio/political and individual freedoms. The Common Law of the English 10th century, along with the Declaration of Independence, and the US Constitution of the 18th century, fulfilled *Phase One* of this Divine Plan of universal liberty. While wading throughout the 8-years of the bloody Revolutionary War, what also had to be explored were the innovative ideas of: (a) natural rights as God-given; (b) government by the people and the laws enacted thereof, and not autocracy; (c) democratic, not regal, institutions; and (d) the limits of shared power between Sovereign States and the Federal government, i.e. Federalism.

Freedom, like holiness, justice, and love, are some of the major attributes of God's nature. Add to these, infinity and transcendence. Why so? God is love and love cannot be expressed without the freedom to choose love vs hate. Or, fairness vs injustice. Or, goodness vs. evil. On Planet Earth, either the presence of freedom, or its opposing counterpoint, bondage, seems to exist socio/spiritually as a fundamental, unending human struggle. Not vegetating inertly, all of the revealed "great ideas" of the Western World, via their history, have been freely ever-evolving and transcending toward an infinite solution. In toto, the Organic Realm, the laws of science and mathematics, travel options, military prowess, central banking, monetary and financial theories, transportation, info/technology, economic concepts, spiritual illumination, theological suppositions, the Moral Evolution of Western Man, along with democratic government and the free marketplace, i.e. capitalism; all have been dynamically surging to newer and higher levels of competency and fulfillment. Freedom or the pursuit of freedom has been the dynamic, driving the ideational evolution of humankind.

Be that as it may, early in the 19th century, what was yet to be accomplished was the absolute independence of America from the domination and exploitations of Mother England, along with, freedom of the seas, Global capitalism, i.e. the free market, and the integrity and full identity of a free, American nation, as later achieved by the colonial victory of the Indian Wars by General Andrew Jackson. Taken together, both the final results of the Revolutionary War and the War of 1812 came together to form a ***Revolutionary Epoch*** of American history. These two momentous, freedom events set the stage for the Wars of Manifest Destiny, the American Civil War, the Industrial Revolution of the late 19th century, the Modern Era of the 20th century, and the Post-Modern Era of the 21st century. In many ways, God's handprint could be found interceding throughout these war years from 1776 to the 21st century.

In Sacred Scripture the cause of ***freedom*** intermittently appears throughout its 1200 pages and 3500-years of God's involvement in Judeo/Christian history. In Exodus 6:6, "I am the Lord and I will free you from the slavery in Egypt." In the NT, Galatians 5:13: "For you have been called to live in freedom, not freedom to satisfy your sinful nature. But, freedom to sacrificially serve one another in love." John 8:36 tells us: "If the Son sets you free, you indeed will be free." In Galatians 2:4: "see our freedom in Christ Jesus" or in Galatians 5: 1 "so Christ has really set us free. Now make sure that you stay free." Romans 8:15 tells us: "So you should not be like cowering, fearful slaves, you should behave instead like God's own children." In Corinthian 3:17: "Now, the Lord is the Spirit and wherever the Spirit of the Lord is, he gives freedom." In a capsule, Sacred Scripture asks: from what are we to be set free from? From sin, fear, death, bondage, the Mosaic Law, and the world's allures (in Romans and Hebrews). Socio/spiritually, the blood shed by Americans in the pursuit of freedom has not been in vain.

Prior to the American ***Revolutionary Epoch***, *t*he free marketplace of capitalism and the liberation politics of democracy as practiced by the Empires of yore have been virtually nonexistent; a millstone inhibiting the ideational growth of economics and politics. The absolute rule of monarchies, oligarchies, Church Establishments, Islam, and in the 20th century, Nazism/Communism/Fascism, composed the socio/political and economic styles of human societies. Yet, God wanted it otherwise. If so, then the imperative, deeply-seated debate facing and challenging the "survival status" of 21st century's humanity must address the theoretical, theological, and political concerns of the ongoing threats of social and individual bondage.

One might ask: does the human species deserve extinction in the context of these Global holocausts of yore? As prophesized in Revelation, ought the highly vulnerable, unstable, Galactic tenure of our unique, Planet Earth be terminated by the full wrath of God? Should God forgive and forget these mass, wanton murders of innocence committed throughout history by England, Germany, Russia, Italy, China, Central Africa, Cambodia, Estonia, Spain, Hungary, Austria, Romania, and Japan? As Scripture tells it, to re-establish the integrity of His Divine Nature, via His Creation and Redemption Plans, will God seek vengeance and demand atonement and repentance from this array of morally accountable, guilt-soaked nations? If truth were told, the genocidal urges of kings, despots, tyrants, Imans, and established clergy, can be spiritually understood as a rejection by Man of God's desires for free and just, democratic nations, along with free and fair, marketplace of capitalism.

The *Revolutionary Epoch* in American history was not completed with the British surrender at Yorktown in the year 1781. At this location, historians tell us that the British force, blockaded by the French Armada prevented the escape by sea. Cornwallis' troop size was much smaller than the American force at Yorktown, VA. General Cornwallis' decision to surrender and end the Revolutionary War was caused by these two Divinely-endorsed, unexpected conditions. Prior to his defeat, Cornwallis realized that his ocean escape was futile so he tried to retreat across a river to Gloucester. However a Divinely generated thunderstorm, not unlike that at Bunker Hill in 1776, prevented his flight. This victory by George

Washington meant the end of fighting. Lord Cornwallis became war-weary and did not want his troops slaughtered, so he ordered them to lay down their arms. After 8-years of battle the English economic attrition drained the land. Military resources at the homeland became depleted causing the British defeat to become inevitable. As negotiators, John Adams, Benjamin Franklin, and John Jay, drafted a peace accord, i.e. Treaty of Paris, which assured the American independence, along with, setting the border between the USA and Canada, and the withdrawal of all British troops from the American mainland. King George III accepted the full blame for the English defeat and accepted the conditions of the Treaty of Paris. Seen as traitors with little socio/economic choices, over 100,000 Loyalists to the Crown, i.e. Tories, fled America for England, or settled in Nova Scotia, other parts of Canada, and/or the West Indies. In Philadelphia, July of 1787 a Constitutional Convention convened to approve the US Constitution and the fashioning of the foundation for a permanent American government.

Yet within a few years as ravenous predators, four formidable Euro/nations saw the prospects to militarily stake-out and geo/exploit sections of the New World. The British and French vied for Canadian lands. The Germans sought lands to assure their religious freedom. Spaniards staked-out Florida and other parts of the Southwest. The Dutch eyed Pennsylvania for settlements. And, twenty-seven Russian counties sought fur-seeking by inhabiting California and Alaska. To assure their conquests, these Euro/explorers dispatched their military assets to a vulnerable, yet-amorphous New World. Motivating the Kings of these Euro/nations was the notion that they were not convinced that the Yorktown surrender was due to a strategic, American victory over England, but simply an inadvertent, temporary militarysetback. As expected, the British, still the greatest sea power in the world, was humiliated and dishonored by their tactical defeat by weak and disorganized colonies. Due to the harsh, unpredictable terrain of the New World the British generals became convinced that they had no hope for further land warfare wirhin the American New World. The terms of the Treaty of Paris that ended the Revolutionary War was considered honorable, ordered to be respected, and kept sacrosanct by King George III. So in the year 1812, the British began to revive and revise the American conflict both on non-colonial lands in the New World and on the seas so as to thwart free commerce with their impressive fleet of battleships. As a two-front strategy, the British and the French targeted Canada as their New World sphere of influence. Similarly, Florida became in Spain's domain. Parts of the unchartered West and Alaska were also colonized by the fur-seeking Russians. And just prior, Pennsylvania became settled by the Germans and Dutch. America was being inundated from all sides by European predators. As a result, to protect the socio/political and religious freedoms gained by a new concept of governing, a declaration of war was passed by the Continental Congress that began the War of 1812. First, against the commanding British Navy which impressments of sailors from American ships became intolerable and secondly, in reaction to the loss of Global commercial revenue from incessant, British sea attacks. As spiritual documents, God-scripted, the

Declaration of Independence and the US Constitution, which assured socio/political and religious freedoms, were not to be Divinely compromised by this post-Revolutionary aggression. Historically, the War of 1812 became Part II of the American Revolutionary Era.

Ever since the Year 1807, as their new strategy to defeat the colonies the British periodically launched attacks on the United States by killing, wounding, and impressing sailors. First, on the Chesapeake. These Treaty offences went on for five years until the Congressional war hawks from the South and West insisted on a Declaration of War against England on June 19th, 1812. The discernible issues to justify war included the impressment of American sailors and attacks on American shipping to impede free commerce. For Americans, the preservation of additional freedoms became the national inspiration for this war because after the Revolutionary War over 2500 American sailors were impressed by British war ships. Now-President Jefferson tried to invoke diplomacy to avoid another rivalry with England, but to no avail. The British wanted to continue the War. Accordingly, Congress had to prepare the nation to thwart the array of Euro/ predators eyeing the bounty of the New World by issuing a million dollar bond campaign to attract 100,000 soldiers and sailors with pay incentives. Prior in the year 1791, six new Man-of Wars were commissioned by a prophetic Congress to be included to the United States Navy. The now-famed, USS Constitution, with its 44 guns, called Old Iron Sides had a sister ship the USS United States. In 1797, the USS Constellation with 37 guns was added to the fleet. The land

and sea encounters of the War of 1812 took many turns, both defeats and victories, to-and-fro ranging from the land battles in Canada to the British landing at Fort McHenry and the burning down of Washington DC. On Christmas Eve 1814, in Ghett, Belgium, England became drained of its war resources across the Atlantic and agreed to a treaty with America to end the War of 1812.

To God, universal freedom has a number of cultural and spiritual facets that must be reconciled. Freedom is a foremost attribute of the Divine that eventually had to be replicated along the future chronicles of Mankind. As lore throughout the history of Humankind, the control of the seas always has been pursued by autocrats seeking Global bondage. So as to subjugate the vulnerable, smaller, and weaker nations, he British followed suit along with a number of predator Empires of yore. Defeated after the Revolutionary War with the signing of the Treaty of Paris, which assured the American independence and the removal of all British troops from the colonies, England substituted sea battles for land battles in order to win back and continue to exploit the American colonies. Hence, the War of 1812 became a carry-over of the War for American independence. When socio/political and religious freedoms become etched upon the souls of men, the shedding of the blood of soldiers and sailors in the hallowed pursuit of freedom of the seas becomes defensible. For this reason the sea battle on Lake Erie was the first defeat and capture of a British fleet in their entire history. On September 10th, 1813 during this Battle of Lake Erie the American Commander, Perry, conquered intact a substantial portion of the British Armada. During one of these firefights, Perry became known for his inspirational message to the American generals on land: *"We have met the enemy and they are ours."* This communiqué was iterated during a number of sea and land battles throughout the American war history. Alone, yet spiritually inspired, Commander Perry, who courageously directed fire from a sole rowboat off his flagship, the Lawrence, broke the British lines and their will to continue fighting. His bravery and leadership was responsible for the crippling of two British warships, the Detroit and Queen Charlotte. Likewise a month prior, the famed American Man of War, the USS Constitution, won a major victory for the fresh and yet-untested American Navy by blowing the British frigate, Guerriere, plumb out of the water. The Guerrere was so badly damaged that it burned and sank in the St. Lawrence Waterway leaving 75 dead and wounded. The USS Constitution, along with the American Navy, no longer became a military prey on the high seas. They now became a marauder that humiliated the Royal Navy with better tactics and more accurate gunfire. Throughout the War of 1812, the USS Constitution, the USS United States, and the USS Wasp continued to distinguish themselves in a number of memorable sea battles. Accordingly as God intended for America, "freedom of the seas and Global commerce" joined "freedom of religion" and "socio/political liberties."

Still, the Brits carried on with their Global aggression against the colonies. To regain full control over the New World while honoring the Treaty of Paris, England hypocritically added to their Post Revolutionary strategy greater disruption, diminishing both America's Global imports and exports. The British harassment of the Global free market, i.e. capitalism, arose to become the foreboding and economic concerns of President Madison and the Continental Congress. International capitalism was being violated by the Royal Navy which further gave rise to the declaration of the War in 1812. America's Congressional leadership knew that the new British strategy would ultimately win out, thereby shrinking and limiting economic growth. Along with their Divine aspirations for a set-apart nation based on law, freedom, and the will of the people, the American leadership opined: a robust and freely expanding commerce was considered indispensable to maintain the "freedom gains" made during the past few decades. Socio/political freedom, the freedom of religion, freedom of the seas, and the unity and integrity of a free and independent USA; all are based upon a Global free market and the dynamics of fair competition among all nations. Furthermore, America's resolve in the early 19th century to expand in all geo/directions of the New World was highly depended upon the freedom of Global trade. Soon the Louisiana Purchase bought from Napoleon by the wiles of Thomas Jefferson doubled the geographic size of America and its economic potential. In the South, the annexation of Florida from Spain gave the colonies a North/South reach. After a number of encounters on the seas, the American leadership decided to convincingly challenge the British Navy and the British strategy to weaken America by naval means. Protecting its economic base and the socio/spiritual promise of America became a major Congressional issue. For this reason, to continue to maintain full control over their colonies in the New World, America's War of 1812 fought for Global economic freedom reached a critical mass, a point of no return, in Anglo/American relationships.

As early as 1813 AD, confidently hoping to suppress America's Global commerce, the British military strategists, having failed to totally win the land wars in the New World and the conflicts on the seas, frantically decided to make military use of the countless Indian tribes, who hated the colonists for taking and occupying their lands. Tactically, with Indian participation the British expectation was to undermine, weaken, and overwhelm both the Continental Army and the State militia. Yet irrespective of copious Indian tribes, which could be found throughout all geographic regions of the New World, Native Americans as a integrated fighting force remained disunited and of little military use to the British military plans. The DNA tells it all. Genetically the White Man's survival skills, when compared to the Hybrid Asians, i.e. North American Indians, proved to be superior and exceptional. Evidently, the DNA of the Natives had limited socio/survival skills. These Asian Hybrids crossed the Bering Straits over a 12,000-year period during a melting Ice Age chasing mammoths for food, fur clothing, and bones for their arrows. But unlike the pioneers of the 17th century, who prospered without much delay, the Natives failed to become conceptually aware of the plentiful, potential, and natural bounty of North America. Generally, most Native Indians lived marginally, died young, and suffered through the harsh weather across these 12,000 years. As contrast, the Caucasian pioneer descending from the Neanderthal, Cro Magnon, and

Viking genes evolved into Scandinavians, Northern Germans, Northern French, and those of the British Isles. These were the American pioneers who were better able to fashion the intellectual/survival adaptations fit for a livable and free New World nation. Colonists suffering through many forms of hardships while seeking the gift of Divine liberty, both the freedoms won-over in both the Revolutionary War and the War of 1812 finalized, unified, and added a spiritual integrity to the landmass of America; a Divine nation set-apart and devoted exclusively to God's gift of freedom.

At the close of the War of 1812, it seemed that the Indian wars would overcome America's fortitude and return the colonies back to British domination. However, like the many battles almost lost in the Revolutionary War, God intervened again and commissioned President James Madison and Colonel Andrew Jackson, an Indian fighter, to save the Union and consummate the Revolutionary Period in American history. Not unlike George Washington and the Founding Fathers, who were also handpicked by God, now-President Andrew Jackson selected, tailored, and targeted by Deity as the man who must save the American union to fulfill the Divine Will of a set-apart, free nation. But at first the Indian War took many twists and turns. Prior to the War of 1812 as far back as August 31st, 1803 Thomas Jefferson, now President, sent Lewis and Clark Westward to explore the land beyond the Mississippi River. In preparation, this voyage proceeded from Pittsburgh PA to Louisville KY to St. Louis, MO. At the same time, President Jefferson sent James Monroe to Paris to meet with Napoleon to purchase the French territory for 80,000 francs. This vast landscape, later known as the Louisiana Purchase, geo/politically doubled the size of the American territory. Enroute, the Indians encountered by Lewis and Clark played a mixed role, some, the Sioux and Blackfoot, were unfriendly, some, the Shoshone, were helpful. The Indian teenage wife of one of the explorers, a Shoshone squaw, played a key role in the success of this mission. She acted as a translator. On November 7th 1805, after a death-defying journey of a year and a half and over 4000 miles, the Lewis and Clark expedition reached the Pacific Ocean and opened up all kinds of economic and political possibilities for the soon-to-be manifest destiny of a bulging nation.

For the sake of their protection and survival, all Indians were considered by the frontiersmen as British spies and military envoys. Tecumseh, a Shawnee Indian Chief and his brother, The Prophet, assembled over 10,000 warriors ready to fight for the British. These warriors lived west of the Mississippi River. The British military mission for these tribes was to thwart the expansion of the White Man's intrusion in into Indian Territory. With irony, North American Natives had no concept of personal ownership of land. Otherwise the Western tradition as far back as the Ancient Hebrews cherished the ownership of personal property as protected by the force of law. By the early 19th century, over 30-million acres of Indian lands were seized and annexed over a decade by the White Man's seductions by treaty, with whiskey, and gun power. Then, ordered by

President Jefferson, General Harrison was commissioned to defeat the Shawnee nation at the Battle of Tippecanoe in Indiana, marking the worse bloody conflict since the year 1791 between Americans and Indians. A series of battles between frontiersmen and Indians took place at different locations. In Frenchtown, Michigan, the British with 6000 soldiers and hundreds of Indians ambushed a 1000 Kentuckians with the element of surprise and targeted cannon fire. Hundreds on both sides were taken prisoners and hundreds more were killed. Likewise in the Mississippi territory, the Creek nation with Chief Red Eagle's warriors massacred over 500 settlers. In reply, both Davy Crockett and General Andrew Jackson retaliated and killed many hundreds of Indians, taking their women and children as captives. In due course, General Andrew Jackson signed a treaty with the Creeks and was able to acquire 23 million acres for the USA. The famished Creeks, formally allied with the British, were starving and accepted the feeble terms offered them. Moreover, within the context of the Louisiana Purchase and treaties from 1802 to1809, General Harrison stole, captured, and pacified Indian tribes, while seizing their lands. The famed Shawnee Chief, Tecumseh, led the disunited tribes into their last great battle against the Americans, promising his warriors immunity against bullets. As expected these delusional, dancing Indians were shot, killed, routed, and had their tepees burned down.

Yet for the colonists, it was the famed Indian fighter, Andrew Jackson, who finalized the Revolutionary Period in American history. He preserved the Union as an incorporated, undivided free nation, being liberated of British, European, and Indian threats and coercion. Andrew Jackson (1767-1845), was a hard-hitting, hot-headed Irishman, who became a US Senator, a Superior Judge, a Major General, and later the 7th President of the USA. He was born in South Carolina and orphaned at 14-years of age. Now alone in life, he joined the Continental Army, fought against the British and became a POW. He learned to hate the British when they slashed his face with a sabre. In 1787 after the Revolutionary War Jackson became a lawyer and was appointed as a prosecutor in the State of Tennessee. His successful law practice and land speculations made him a wealthy husband. Never a "legal intellectual," yet angrily opposed all forms of unjust disputes, Jackson devoted his life to action, not philosophical discourse. Then the War of 1812 broke out Major General Jackson offered the Tennessee Militia to the Federal government. His military reputation soared as an Indian fighter after he led triumphant campaigns against the Creek Indians, along with defeating the Seminole nation in Spanish Florida. After the War of 1812 he lived the life of a country gentleman in his life-long home, now-famed Hermitage in Nashville TN. Although an iconic hero, who won military campaign after campaign, yet his signature conquest was against the British in New Orleans. Henceforth, British/Indian military alliance and influence waned and became permanently shattered causing the American Union to become forever Divinely sealed, signed, and delivered. This final battle marked the end of America's **Revolutionary Epoch**, as God intended and planned for the freedom of a set-apart nation, America.

Freedom and its 21ˢᵗ Century Consequences

Both the Revolutionary War and the War of 1812 had far-reaching, profound consequences for the scholarship of theology and political philosophy. With little doubt, the root causes of Global mayhems seem to be related to the evil inroads pursued by power-hungry godless leaders, as they justified, manifested, and were bolstered by the flawed theories of social suppression. If historic truth be told, what were installed by evil-possessed leaders were the ideologically immoral, predatory dogmas, coupled with the spiritual collapse of compassionate religions. In tandem, African primitivism, the bizarre Hindu-derived religions of Central Asia, and the hardcore atheism of China, inadvertently collaborating with the "class struggle" thesis, affixing impiously a socio/political agenda to the life of a soul. This world-stage led directly to the Global, genocidal slaughter of innocence. Indeed, the standard models of the past, whether economic, political, socio/psychological, military, or evil, charismatic leadership, will never lead to an understanding or explanation of the causes of these "holocausts" of yore. In the 21ˢᵗ century, our survival and intellectual enlightenment must point us elsewhere. Perhaps the telling of other factors that better describe, explain and predict the course and causes of past genocides. Also perhaps, the genetic realm and its Divine dynamics, aka as the bio/spiritual factor, underlies the motivational course of evil history. And perhaps, scholars ought to be rethinking the Philosophy of Man by including the underlying scientific workings of the Human Genome in conjunction with the theological forces of the soul. And perhaps, the DNA and the human spirit are the sole, designated carriers of the metaphysical attributes of existential life. Simply stated, the genes and the attributes of the human souls are the true carriers of the paradox of righteousness (vs evil), love (vs hate), justice (vs unfairness), the intelligence of adaptation (vs the irrational and insanity), and *freedom* (vs bondage). As set within the Creation and Redemption Plans, these five bio/spiritual dimensions carry the existential building-blocks of organic life on Planet Earth. God's Nature spans from the far-reaches of Outer Space to the specks of the individual, human souls. By complementing the specifications of the Creation Plan, the spiritual factors also are part of the human equation.

When viewed from the Divinely decreed, Judeo/Christian, Redemption Plan, i.e. the message of Jesus, the sinister code of godless, tyrannical leadership suggest that the leading, contentions facing the enlightenment of Mankind is bio/spiritual. Will the ultimate resolution to this ideational leap solve the mystery of the meaningless slaughter of millions of humans occurring across the Epochs?

Undeniably, the leap of ideational evolution triggered by the domino effects of both the Revolutionary War and the War of 1812 were sweeping. A better understanding of the dynamics of the Human Genome as it interacts with the human Spirit fused together as an inseparable unit, also can direct our socio/politics. As a corollary, won't all other paradigms employed throughout the Ages be overrated as predictors of past and upcoming human events? Haven't economic models failed to account for the presence of barbaric rule? Haven't the military accounts of history failed to explain why the "weak will inherit the Earth," thereby negating the British obsessive lust for world domination? What has been patently missing in the ideational folly of the socio/politics of the 18th-19th centuries has been inconsistent with the God of History. Why has Secular Socialism been anchored to the momentary and transitional circumstances of life&love? Or 8th century Islam which has been committed to the corrupted belief of human bondage and the immorality of jihadist hate? All in all, only a spiritually-based science of the Genome, as guided by the message of Jesus, is capable of illuminating and propelling the insights of the 21st century. Only the economic/political "freedom derivatives" of bio/spiritual factors will "capitalism and democracy," be able stand tall against human chaos and its cruelty. Yet, at the cusp of the potentials posed by a New World Renaissance, America the Beautiful has introduced via Warfare the rewards of free market capitalism and Constitutional democracy. Will humanity be able to avoid a steep, cultural decline triggered by the ideology of the 2008-2014 elections? Already this turndown of national character has produced: (a) diminished, economic vitality; (b) vacillating adherence to the rule of law; (c) scarcity of political integrity; and (d) lack of cultural moral fiber. Instead, under the insurgency of the Obama administration, America, once the last and only hope for the freedoms for the human race, seems to have chosen socialism and neo/Bolshevism; a European style government for its future. The Left-winged lunacy of Liberal government has put forward: (a) the acceptance of cultural depravity; (b) ideological bias from the mainstream Media; (c) politically tainted, University education that teaches hatred for God and country; (d) the immorality of millions of abortions of defenseless prebabies,; (e) legalized drug usage: (f) a 50% divorce rate that has shredded the fabric of the natural family: (g) children born and raised in single-parent and same-sex homes: (h) capricious lawsuits by predatory trial lawyers,; (i) high rates of urban crime and contempt for police officers; (j) chronic educational failures in the inner cities; (k) the decadence of entertainment and its pseudo/art forms; and (l) the ungodliness of thwarting religious expressions. In toto, these destructive conditions describe the State of the American Union in the year 2016.

These 2008-2014, national elections and its choice of the "Chicago mob" as a socialist model has revealed that the American electorate no longer cares about the relevance of candidate experience, past accomplishments, current character, Liberal leanings, or valid, religious choices. It is becoming politically noticeable during the presidential terms that Obama is governing as a hardcore Globalist who hates America and Christianity. By exploiting his left-winged, power base, Obama is bent on destroying capitalism and Constitutional democracy fought for in both the Revolutionary War and the War of 1812. His political strategy has been to overwhelm the American economy with gargantuan debt and massive entitlement spending, far beyond our national capacity to pay within the current intake of revenue. The American debt and deficit levels rely principally upon the borrowing from China, Japan, and Europe. With the true, unemployment rate as of 2014 well over 14%, soon we can expect social chaos erupting in most major cities. As his veiled intentions, Obama knows that these anti Christ activities are certain to destabilize the States, cities, and townships at the very heart of America. Indirectly, by encouraging violence through "class struggle," the stealth, sinister goals that Obama acquired from his Chicago upbringing and mentoring by Professors Cloward&Piven while studying at Columbia University in New York City during the year 1983 AD, has fueled his vitriolic rhetoric with hopes to control America by transforming the USA from a creditor to a debtor nation. Over the past five decades, this duplicitous political strategy has been well-documented by the historical analyses by expert scholars who have studied the theories originally proposed by most autocrats. Although President Barak Obama with his keen mind, charismatically honed by an Ivy League, law degree and glib charm has duped the electorate again in the year 2012.

This next Presidential election of 2016 AD should tell the world and the American citizenry whether the Divine/American ideal of socioindividual freedom and a free marketplace, as expressed in our capitalistic democracy for many years, ought to be restored, or not. Or, whether America has already reached a point of no return and headed toward the cynical road toward Euro/Socialism. Will our nation be able to recommit to its traditional principles of Constitutional Conservatism? Will the detrimental, entrenched Liberals in the mainstream Media, the University, and the Liberal Churches professing "liberation theology," be exposed and fade away in influence as socio/spiritual, authorities? Or, will America continue to drift headlong into a Euro/

Socialist transformation consisting of big government, high taxes, fiscal irresponsibility, class warfare, and the ebbing of individual and business freedoms? As well as, eventually to succumb to a godless, military dictatorship as witnessed in the past across the Eras. No doubt, in America there is a political conspiracy taking place led by an anti-freedom Democratic President. Voted in, by a "racially compassionate," mostly Caucasian, independent electorate that was duped by political, charismatic deception, of which its paramount goals were to destroy the American capitalistic, democratic, and cultural fabric. To believe otherwise is tantamount to seditious "ostrich politics," naïve and unworthy of a history of American freedom, bravery, and exceptionalism.

Covertly, to carry out his plan to deceive and destroy America the once-Beautiful, President Barack Obama has been proposing a full range of socialist legislation that is destined to be repealed after the Presidential election in 2016 AD. His opening volley was passed by bribery and "Chicago mob" politics. At the very start of his presidential term, it was his ***universal health care law*** that reeked with hyper-Liberalism. The huge increase in health costs beyond our fiscal capacity was intended in due course to overwhelm, make dependent, and control the health of the American citizenry with centralized, single-payer rule. This terror tactic of socio/dependency on State governments also was part of the British strategy in the 17th-19th centuries to gain total jurisdiction over colonial commerce. Today, the governmental approval or denial of health care availabilities holds considerable incentives for any family concerned for its elderly and children. The rationing of health care can be a strong deterrent against civil protest. This type of legislation parallels the intentions of the King George III administration with his dictatorship of the early 18ᵗʰ century. As compared to the American tradition of pioneer and immigration history that featured a robust, independent living. Today a political angst, fear-provoking anger, and citizen-guilt is sweeping across the nation for handing over their beloved country over to the most Liberal Congress in American history, Once in accord, now beset and divided by class warfare, American families of all races, ethnics, gender, and national origin have become deeply concerned about the future of their children and grandchildren. Have we betrayed the freedoms fought for in both the Revolutionary War and War of 1812?

In addition to his health-care fiasco, Obama was able to pass-on a useless economic **stimulus package** of a trillion dollars allegedly to create jobs for a soaring unemployment rate. After eight years, this expenditure, which failed to improve the job-creating potential of the private sector, has been enlarged and made most lucrative for the employee coffers of the public sector. It was a massive "give away program" that worsened the fiscal standing of the Federal Treasury that required more and more borrowing from China and Japan. In order to avoid a national bankruptcy, Obama's "hate America" governing style, through corruption, abuse of authority, and exploitation of his Presidential powers, proposed the raising of taxes on the middle-class, small businesses, the well-to-do, and the private corporate job-creators. In concert with contempt for the Bourgeois, who owned the means of production, and who rivaled the Proletariat workers, Obama attacks on the wealthy and successful, high-income earners, whose success within the American Dream wasn't deserving of a mega/tax hike. Deja vu, the expropriation of the wealth from the prosperous to finance Liberal causes and redistribution of wealth came out of the "political abhorrence" for the American democracy and its free market. Obama, not unlike the despots of the past, is reliving the failures of most of the societies of yore. Soon, the calamitous, fiscal consequences of exorbitant interest paid on the American, foreign debt are expected to absorb most of the revenue intake of the USA. Add to these two, fiscally disastrous, budget-busting, socialist programs is the ***cap and trade*** proposal that is designed to control the energy needs of all businesses and private homes. In combination, health care rationing, high and higher deficit spending, and staged energy needs, have been alluded to control the means of production. Yet as economic fact, energy-legislation that simply raises taxes has nothing to do with global warming, but all to do with payoff: (a) to the Liberal, mainstream Media; (b) to General Electric Corporation; (c) to unions: (d) for the redistribution of wealth; and (e) by adding of substantial wealth to the coffers of the Democratic Party. Hopefully, not to be trusted energy legislation will become tabled or defeated by Congress by way of the "political demolition" of the Democratic Party as polled for the 2016 AD elections.

As an assault against God's hopes for freedom living for humans, the socio/political attacks against the American economic and cultural institutions in order to assure a Democratic Party victory in 2016 AD has been sustained as an appeal to Black racism, illegal Hispanic border-crossings, and Puerto Rican Statehood. With 90% of Afro/Blacks "yet living on the plantation" by voting for "uncaring Democrats" election after election, one wonders whether most "Black Americans" can be truly represented in a free government or even fit for democratic/capitalistic living? Likewise as well might be said of the island politics of Puerto Ricans who clearly resist Statehood by preferring economic and political slavery? What could this Island-bound, Hispanic ethnicity truly contribute to the American Dream of freedom and prosperity? Add to these uncanny Liberal causes: (a) the policies that endorse open borders in the Southwest; (b) amnesty for illegal immigrants; and (c) the redistribution of wealth by way of educational, medical, and law&order policies. With satirical sarcasm, many are wondering: do our domestic politics and international performances reflect some sort of a revengeful, stealth-hatred for the USA and Caucasians-at-large?

Freedom, a Godly "existential certainty" for life on Planet Earth, always has been one of the issues-at-hand. In both political theory and military encounters, compassionate capitalism and enlightened democracy only can be understood as two sides of the same coin of liberty. Freedom, along with goodness, justice, and love, is a fundamental component highlighted and installed both in the Divine Creation and Redemption Plans. Accordingly, freedom in governing and in the marketplace are consistent with the universal, human plea to God: *"give us this day our daily bread."* In this Scriptural context, it becomes apparent that the bondage of socialism and autocracy of any form are evil expressions and perverse to God's Will. The horrors and terror committed during the Ages by godless Empires that detested and violated socio/political freedom will be pondered and adjudicated as wicked by all future historians, scholars, and theologians. In the course of history, as the transcendent dynamics of freedom governing and its management of free wealth have been unfolding and heavily debated across the Eras, yet somehow, Mankind continues to be straddling on a tottering fulcrum of skepticism and doubt regarding the actual implementation of national freedoms. Philosophically, this central concept, i.e. liberty vs bondage, has been tossed-about aimlessly, both intellectually and spiritually as a Divine command for organic life. *De facto*, all conditions and events within the human circumstance have been freely evolving, together with human, morphological features, physiological subsystems, the psyche, the sociology of politics, banking practices, art forms, military prowess, geo/explorations, economic paradigms, transportation options, along with the full range of ever-advancing technologies. Truly, freedom is an essential dynamic needed for the evolution of human life. Always, the freedom to grow and improve readily can be identified everywhere within the human ambiance. As theologically represented in the Will of the Divine, this existential vibrancy can be found in the economic/political, "freedom model," as time-honored in American life. The human bondage of socialism and dictatorship are the cruel antithesis of liberty. Nowhere on the Globe is political liberty and market freedoms better represented than in the USA. Our capitalism, set within the context of risk and Christlike compassion, is premised upon the trust of the individual to God, along with the assurance that private business-owners are capable of making the best and most profitable business decisions needed for profit or prosperity. As near-certainty, the trade and industrial evidence of this robust expression of market liberty regularly can be verified by the reduction of unemployment statistics. Is it any wonder, that all other forms of governments never entrust economic judgments to individual entrepreneurs. As scholarly scripted from Ancient to Modern China, a nation that has become the archetype of economic failures, has had a 6000-year traditional history contingent upon the whims of hyper-centralized, corruption, and authoritarian regimes. Why does this mega-ideational dispute, i.e. liberty vs bondage, which refuses to abate or disappear from the front-burner of philosophical discourse, remain an enigma?

Both the notions of capitalism and democracy have been evolving since the days of the Ancient world. In half steps, scholars have pinpointed traces of freedom expressions in economic and political institutions for centuries. Even curtailed paradigms of the rights of private property and the marketplace can be detected in the Ancient, Classical, Medieval, and Renaissance Eras. Only in the latter years of the Gothic period of the late, Medieval Era up to the 18th century do we see the slow but accelerating evolution of both capitalism and democracy. Adam Smith's thesis, *The Wealth of Nations*, solidified the economic notion of *laissez faire*, and its implications in support of the free, political society. Indeed, freedom in the marketplace and freedom in government are two sides of the same coinage that have been formalized by the bloodshed of the Revolutionary War and the War of 1812 From their history as a traditional, Asian nation, the separation of economic freedom from political liberty might be noted in 21st century Singapore, where capitalism seems to thrive set in a highly oppressive, authoritative politic. In addition as a sidebar issue, what can't be ignored is the influence of an evolving technology on the styles of governments and the marketplace. In the Industrial Revolution of the 19th century, a surplus of goods and services, along with credit availabilities for the small business and higher employment, directly caused large and small firms to grow and prosper. With paradox, this "manufacturing revolution" during the Industrial Revolution also gave worker credence to Marxism and unionism a new meaning. Yet, none of these prosperous, economic effects can be indirectly attributed to the tenets of socialism and fascism. Godless, political schemes, which seek power and privilege for the few in Oligarchies, lack the spiritual energy for true achievement. When taken at the P&L bottom-line, the central control of production and consumption by way of military terror was maximized across the Epochs, which became responsible for the creation of slave-labor and the eventual slaughter of many, innocent lives. Since Adam Smith, both capitalism and democracy received the "grace approval" within the Divine Creation Plan. *Genetic exceptionalism* has been the hallmark of Americans, mostly Caucasian, who created the concepts of capitalism and democracy for a great nation-to-be. In the year 2016 AD, both the Presidential and Congressional elections will determine the direction and continuity of the American Dream of individual freedom-for-all or the inevitable extinction of the American Dream. Concisely, Humankind can no longer "spiritually absorb" and replicate the mass atrocities being committed by the bondage of flawed socio/politics.

As appended to the workings of the Natural Order, *freedom,* granted to all expressions of Creation has been ordained by an awesome God. If "God is Love" then the freedom-to-love must have been a basic specification of the Divine blueprint. He has extended this attribute of "existential liberty" to all facets of his organic handiwork. Even the vast, physical and chemical array of the Universe, with its lawful scientific and mathematical constraints, have been set-free to function and evolve from its hydrogen base to an oxygen enveloped Planet Earth that was destined to encompass and sustain organic life. Socio/spiritually, human freedom, which also came about from the neuro/evolution of the brain's, frontal lobes, became a decisive feature of both an individual's socio/political and eternal life. The free-will mechanism of each soul enables each of us to choose daily "righteousness and social justice" vs. "evil and immorality." The contemptible record of the Empires of yore vs democratic-living has confirmed the magnitude of this noble standard of freedom. So too, the freedom to choose an intimate relationship with our personal God, Jesus, also impacts our eternal destiny. Godlessness and oppressive socio/politics is a toxic, lethal mixture, sure to result in the extinction of the human race. The dictatorial atheism of many societies of yore, ought to stand forever as a paradigm of socio/political insanity never to be replicated again. God in his wisdom has set our consciousness, i.e. soul, with the freedom to choose the good vs. evil, both individually and collectively. To God, these are non-negotiable options demanded for both our daily lives and governing styles. While bad choices are forgivable, they are never Divinely sanctioned. Why! Simply, because we have been made to His image and likeness whose Divine Nature is good, holy, and just; hence, righteous and loving.

On the other hand, the evil of bondage is universally counter-evolutionary that acquires its energy and density out of Global, human sin, i.e. bad moral choices. Evil is the reverse replica of goodness. God created neither existential evil nor the evil of choosing hell. In this regard, God never sends anyone to hell. In lieu of an intimacy with God through eternity, many humans foolishly choose to be marooned in the Outer Darkness, surrounded by weeping and gnashing of teeth, forever. Out of His "love Nature," God allowed socio/political wickedness to challenge the human soul by offering it the opportunity to share and choose his majesty. To partake in His Nature and to earn His protection, guidance, love, predestined grace, and providence, every soul has the power to seek and choose salvation, repentance, justification, and sanctification, rather than being marooned in the Outer Darkness, surrounded by weeping and gnashing of teeth, forever. Truly, salvation is a "freedom option" which ought not to be refused.

In many ways awaiting our future, emerging out of the seven building-blocks that define our very existence both on and out of Planet Earth, enlightened, compassionate, democratic societies will be legislating within a bio/socio/

spiritual context. Thomas Jefferson alluded that in a democracy each generation must launch the next, ideational level of illumination. To be sure, the "genetic vision," along with its bio/spiritual and socio/political consequences, will be the next mega-innovation of note. The constraints of the *Moral Evolution of Western Man*, i.e. Judeo/Christianity, will muffle the bondage ideologies and all its repercussions causing Man to develop: (a) the sagacious DNA/management of *Criminal Justice;* (b) the scripting of *Bio/spiritual History;* (c) the revealing of the neo/scientific, theological principles of *Bio/Anthropology;* (d) the featuring of the spiritual dynamics of *Bio/Social Diversity* and their *Sociobiology* fit for speciated humans; (e) the religious methodology appended to *Pedagogical Genetics;* (f) the moral fairness of *Industrial Eugenics* and its *Free Marketplace;* along with (g) the politics of an *Upgraded Democracy*, which will surely include Bills of Genetic, Victim, and Patient Rights.

All this and more under the shroud of Divine freedom.

Think 21st Century: Not unlike the Homo Sapien, all higher mammals are capable of expressing: (a) the spiritual dynamics of love, in lieu of pointless violence; (b) intelligence, as in adaptation and fulfillment; (c) the beauty of their own existence; (d) the existential choice to be; (e) goodness, as in parental responsibility; (f) the dynamics of transcendent evolution and (g) freedom, in lieu of bondage. These metaphysical traits are carried and transmitted by their species-specific genomes.

In sum, America, a struggling, free nation still has time to operationally define itself culturally, economically, theologically, politically, and socially. Asking, how should the powers be allotted between the Federal government and the States? Can the colonial passion for a Global "manifest destiny" justify its foreign policies? Not unlike the Ancient Hebrews under Joshua who conquered Canaan as a Divine destiny? Should we be isolationists? What about race and ethic relations? Will the cultural and technological advances from the 19th century to the 21st century set the stage for a manifest destiny, a new Industrial Revolution, a Modern Age, and Post-Modern Era?

CHAPTER 3

God's Westward Movement

The American Wars of Manifest Destiny

By the mid-19th century, America became a legitimate nation devoted to freedom with a Divine destiny to spread the democratic idea and ideal across the Globe. Its ***Revolutionary Epoch*** was complete. As proof-positive that God has been obliquely involved in the "freedom history" of His set-apart nation, America, comes to us from the year 1845 AD to the beginning of the Civil War. These two, 19th century decades that followed the Revolutionary "freedom Epoch" of American history was the primary spiritual inspiration gripping the souls and mindset of colonists and frontiersmen was the irrepressible idea of moving westward as its promise land on to the Pacific Ocean as the Will of God. This was America's "manifest destiny," not unlike the Israelites of 1350 BC, who were commanded by God to take Canaan, the promised Holy Land. With a delay of 40 years living in the desert under the leadership of Joshua the Divine summon for a manifest destiny toward a land of milk and honey inspired the Hebrews. Déjà vu, the Americans took their promised land westward to the Pacific Ocean placing them in a land bountiful and overflowing with abundance and economic potential. God's intentions were obvious, plain as the nose on your face. The Ancient Hebrews were selected to be the first humans who interrelated directly with God while defining His Moral Order all the while the first Americans were Divinely commissioned to pursue the socio/political and spiritual meanings of God's gift of freedom.

In Sacred Scripture, the book of Joshua was an account of invasion and rewarded promise by God to His set-apart people to inhabit Canaan, the Holy Land. The twelve tribes of Israel reached the Jordon River with a Divine charge to move forward into Canaan, God's land. This became Israel's manifest destiny. Almost three thousand years later, America acted likewise in response to God's gift of freedom under the leadership of President James Polk and his military confidant Andrew Jackson. Thus began the American westward movement, both toward the Southwest and Northwest, to take over God's land in the New World up to the Pacific Ocean. As well, this was the American manifest destiny that was driven by a national, spiritual fervor, which neither could be repressed nor suppressed. While the Israelites had to do battle with the Hittites, Amorites Moab, Midianites, and dozens of Kings from smaller villages, the Americans had to militarily and diplomatically deal with isolated, roving Indians bands, Mexicans in the Southwest and California, along with, the English and the Russians in the Northwest.

In both these Ancient and Modern events God always was available to intervene to fulfill His Will to promote the Moral Order and His gift of freedom.

Biblically, in the book of Joshua God said:

> *Now that my servant Moses is dead, you must lead my people across the JordanRiver into the land I'm giving them—from the Negev desert in the South to the Lebanon Mountains in the north, from the Euphrates River to the east of the Mediterranean Sea on the west ad all the land of the Hittites. No one will be able to stand their ground against you as long as you live. For I will be with you, as I was with Moses. I will not fail you or abandon you.*

In America, it was President James Polk, a deeply religious Christian, who led God's manifest destiny in the middle of the 19th century AD. It was he who politically transformed and doubled the landscape of America. James Polk and his wife, Sarah, were staunch bible-reading Presbyterians who honored the Sabbath above politics. Polk was raised on the frontier in Columbus, Tennessee just south of Nashville. As a young boy he suffered a serious urinary, aliment and remained childless. Polk frequently referred to God when making difficult political decisions. One of his closest friends was Andrew Jackson who helped him spark the manifest destiny theme that became Polk's signature accomplishment. James Polk died a month after his one-term Presidential tenure ended. Sarah, his wife, lived as a widow on their Hermitage plantation in Nashville TN for 42 more years. As a ardent "manifest destiny" proponent, President Polk, who occupied the White House for only one term from 1845-1849, added Texas to the Union, diplomatically outfoxed the British and Russians out of the Oregon territory, and gained California as well as most of the Southwest during the Mexican War. These annexations of the West awakened the travel urge for thousands of settlers to relocate by way of the Oregon and Santa Fe Trails, extending from Independence, Missouri to the Columbia River in Oregon, and south toward New Mexico. To this day, it remains an historic enigma that President Polk is considered one of the most underrated Presidents in American history.

On May 13th, 1846, Polk assured by a national zeal and a joint resolution by Congress pretextually declared war on Mexico. He knew that it was a widely held belief among Texans, Southerners, and Westerners that it was America's future to govern this part of the New World. Polk's declaration of war produced a full-scale aggression that quickly broke-out between Mexicans and American forces. Initially, four thousand troops under General Zachary Taylor were ordered by President Polk to move immediately to the Rio Grande River. Although outmanned by 6000 to 2200 General Taylor tactically surprised the Mexicans and gained a victory. A cavalry charge by American forces routed the Mexican infantry to panic and stampede in retreat. On Christmas Day, 1846, the conquest of New Mexico at Las Cruces came shortly thereafter under Colonel Doniphan with 800 American infantrymen and cavalry. In early 1847, the Northern Mexican campaign began. Santa Ana, the Mexican commander with 15,000 troops surrounded 5000 Americans who were then rescued by the famed General William Tecumseh Sherman's artillery barrage. This American victory marked the end of the war in Northern Mexico. On January 13th, 1847, Captain John Fremont ended a quarter of a century of Mexican reign in California by accepting their honorable surrender, further abating the hostilities in the West. In Los Angles, Mexican Captain Jose Flores with 450 troops refused to surrender, but was repelled by an American force of 400 dragoons, sailors, and marines. California now became a territory of the USA.

President Polk's home State, Tennessee, fully supported the Wars of Manifest Destiny. In the Southwest, on behalf of Texas independence, 39,000 volunteers offered themselves to the Federal Government to fight, if called upon. Three decades prior, Tennesseans also volunteered to fight in both in the Mexican War and the Creek Indian War under Andrew Jackson. As history has a way of lingering, today in the 21st century the State of Tennessee and its sports teams became known as "Volunteers."

With California and Northern Mexico militarily secured, the fighting moved inland toward Mexico City. On the Gulf of Mexico, Vera Cruz was a well-fortified city protecting the direct route to Mexico City. Here Santa Ana held the high ground making it almost impossible for the American forces to scale. As a result, General Winfield Scott, the American Supreme Commander, who led an armada of over 200 ships that carried 10,000 troops, brought in mountain soldiers from New England to conduct a bayonet charge to the top of the Mexican stronghold. Again and again, American imaginative, war tactics and troop bravery won its battles. Facing 12,000 Mexicans with only 8500 troops, General Scott called on his big naval guns, the most powerful artillery ever conceived, to date. The Mexicans became militarily traumatized by the naval guns. Acquiring valuable military experiences, Ulysses S. Grant and Robert E Lee were junior officers during this Vera Cruz campaign on a road leading directly to Mexico City. Thus the route was now opened to American forces after taking full command of the Mexican stronghold in Vera Cruz. The human price tag was 400 dead Americans and 3400 dead and captured Mexicans. After this decisive defeat, Santa Ana was nowhere to be found. His army was in full retreat.

During the 300-mile trek from the heights of Vera Cruz to Mexico City, a number of skirmishes produced another thousand American casualties, while Santa Ana lost over 30% of his Army. After a number of turbulent battles against Santa Ana's 25,000 troops plus his battalion of 200 American deserters manning 100's of cannons, General Scott's 10,000 soldiers triumphed causing Santa Ana to shift his tactics from offense to defense. Both the American well-placed, highly adept artillery coupled with daring infantry charges resulted in Santa Ana's surrender and the American flag to be unfurled over the National Palace in Mexico City. The Mexican War virtually ended on October 12th, 1847. In a capsule, the large Mexican armies fought defensively and passively, and lost; the smaller American units fought fiercely and spiritually inspired to fulfill God's mandate of manifest destiny. The Americans, who fought proactively offensively and bravely, annexed Texas, California, Arizona, and New Mexico. In the pursuit of a manifest destiny, thirteen thousand Americans lost their lives in combat or disease with an additional 4000 wounded. Then, President Polk proclaimed a landmark treaty on July 4th 1848.

To this very day, the valiant defeat of the American-held Alamo, which was a crucial holding tactic awaiting the army of Sam Houston, stands as a signature victory for both the American "manifest destiny" and the Monroe Doctrine as mandates of American spiritual destiny. On March 6th, 1836, at this small village location, a century old mission with adobe walls, about 200 Americans commanded by William Travis, Davy Crockett, and James Bowie waited a dozen days for Santa Ana's 3000 man army to arrive and attack. After three attempts at the Alamo, Santa Ana finally succeeded and defeated the Americans who were mutilated and burned in a pile. Arriving soon thereafter, April 22nd was Sam Houston and his army who surprised and defeated Santa Ana, now captured and forced to sign over his entire army by conceding the full independence of Texas.

Sacred Scripture tells us in the book of Joshua:

> *Today, I will begin to make you great... now they will know that I am with you, just as I was with Moses. Today you will know that the Living God is with you.*

Also as part of the American "manifest destiny" awaited the Oregon territory to become fully annexed. In tandem, these geo/expansive wars were carried-out in two regions, the Southwest and the Northwest. A shooting campaign was conducted in the Southwest, known as the Mexican War, while the Northwestern conflict against Britain and Russia, which lasted for over a decade, was confined to a cold war of diplomatic disagreements within the context of a series of multiple interactive treaties. Wisely, Polk didn't want to fight a shooting war on two fronts so he kept the Oregon campaign mostly political and diplomatic. On August 14th 1848, President Polk signed a bill establishing the American territory of Oregon. Polk and his wife Sarah retired in Nashville, where he soon died from an epidemic disease. His manifest destiny was now completed. While later, on November 7th 1848 Zacchary Taylor, who was elected President, fully supported the political implications of the victories that led America to the Pacific Ocean.

God's Military Strategy

God's plan was a covenant of Global righteousness that would come about with the fulfillment of four Divine factors. *One*, with set-apart people in set-apart nations that were purposely chosen to actualize God's will. *Two*, with the Divine approval of spiritually inspired wars set chronologically. *Three*, through the selection of endowed and capable leaders especially targeted and tailored for any particular mission at hand. Surely, who would expect that George Washington praying on his knees in Mount Vernon for God's providence and who commanded a ragtail army and independent militias, would defeat the most powerful country in the world? Or, a Thomas Jefferson who spent his lifetime fighting for freedom of religion? Or a John Adams, who came from a Puritan/ Quaker heritage and who with James Madison would make possible the crafting of the Constitutional workings of a democracy, while refusing to own slaves? Or, the political talents of a Alexander Hamilton, James Polk, and Andrew Jackson?

Add, Divine factor *four*; with God's involvement, as warranted by specific battle conditions or diplomatic encounters. Such as, the Battle of Bunker Hill, the heroics of Valley Forge, the Mexican encounters, President Polk's treaties, the Indian Wars in the mid-19th century and/or Perry's naval battle on Lake Erie. While the Revolutionary War, paired together with the War of 1812, gave humanity the hope of freedom in a number of ways, the scripting by God of the US Constitution gave Mankind the hope of socio/ political liberties. The Bill of Rights, also scripted by God, gave us freedom of religion. And, as Divinely inspired, the Declaration of Independence gave us the freedom from outside, autocratic domination and its social bondage. Add the War of 1812 when the American Navy gave us the freedom of the seas. The American privateers gave us the assurance of Global capitalism as freedom of commerce. And Andrew Jackson, the famed Indian fighter, who afforded us the integrity and unity of a nation fully committed to the defense of freedom. No doubt, the *Revolutionary Epoch* in American history, which included both the Revolutionary War and the War of

1812, was God's initial handprint in His plan to free Planet Earth from its moral and social bondage.

Portrait of an Emerging Free Nation

Soon thereafter, both the wars of "manifest destiny" (1844-1849) when paired with the American Civil War (1960-1865) gave America a complete nation with a steadfast geo/horizontal and geo/vertical landscape. In view of these two wars, America became a powerful nation protected by the natural borders of the Atlantic and Pacific Oceans. This new country and its now-sizeable terrain was overflowing with God's bounty of trees, oil, ores, water, ideal climate, land fit for planting, deep rivers and harbors to navigate, and an edible wildlife. Biblically, a lamd of milk and honey.

So as to preclude the extinction of humanity, 75-years after these wars of the mid-19th century, God was able to assemble the only nation on the face of the Earth that would be capable of doing battle with the Global, godless evil brought about by Nazism, Communism, Fascism, and the crimes against humanity committed by the militarism of Japan. The same four Divine factors held true for the wars of the 20th and 21st centuries. Not unlike the Revolutionary War coupled with the War of 1812 that introduced freedom to the nations on Planet Earth, the Divine victories of the wars of "manifest destiny" and the beginning of the American Civil War set the socio/political, military, technological, and cultural ambiance for the Industrial Revolution of the late 19th century, along with, the Modern and Neo/Modern Ages of the 20th and 21st centuries.

Steadily a new, but troublesome, *Age of Bio/Cultural Freedom* descended upon our national consciousness. With paradox, this Age which is bound to usher-in both hope&conflict can become an Era of dreams fulfilled, as courted by the longings of the Statue of Liberty. Yet what could not be avoided were the threatening, disrupting, societal dissonance, bound to disturb the peace with momentous events that mightsporadically bubble-up as civil and criminal disobedience. With the various modes of terrorism defining the times, the "bio/freedom injunction" of the future surely would outpace the turmoils that even occurred during the Revolutionary Wars 225-years prior--as experienced by both America and France alike. During those 18th century years, the French sought freedom, apart from religious inspiration; while otherwise, the colonists were motivated to fight and die for their freedom by clinging to and trusting the insights of Sacred Scripture. As a prophetic anecdote, many Americans concluded that the natural deaths of Thomas Jefferson and John Adams, both occurring on July 4th during the same year, couldn't have been happenstance events--but rather signs ordained by the Divine Creator of democracy--the God of History. War&peace which characterizes all revolutions can never be deferred because of the moral nobility inherent in the struggles for independence and liberty. Out of the DNA of discovery, liberty, and neighborly love came forth our socio/political aspirations. Hope of freedom from tribal conflicts, infectious maladies, and slow-paced starvation became the American mandate; lest mass extinction via the Malthusian Stalker occurs in the morally impoverished lands. By way of our DNA/building blocks as God intended, our chromosomal "pioneer edifice" judicated justly by US Constitutional precedencies has been constructed out of the basic "bio/social personality" of two compatible human mutants--the Viking&Mediterranean Genomes. When all this theory becomes jam-packed, streamlined, and stylized in a bio/historical nutshell, most likely its theory will become recapped as follows: *"...what bio/social, compassionate America has been all about is the "personality grit" of the Viking Genome, acting in alliance with the "creative insights" of the inhabitants who bordered the Mediterranean Sea.* Of which, the outcome of this genetic miracle has created the unique politics of Americana and its worldwide contributions to the ideational evolution of the Homo Sapien.

Thomas Jefferson tells us:
> *...with a firm reliance on the protection of the Divine Provenience, we mutually pledge to each other our lives, our fortunes, and our sacred honor.*

Thomas Payne tells u:
> *Heaven knows how put a price upon its goods and it would be strange indeed if so celestial an article as freedom should not be highly rated.*

John Quincy Adams tells us:
*You will never know how much it has cost
my generation to preserve your freedom.*

Freedom Politics Designed for America's Diversity

The Wars of Manifest Destiny of the mid-19th century, fortified with the assurances of freedom won-over by both the Revolutionary War and the War of 1812, set the geo/horisantal landscape for a later-to-be diverse nation to come into fruition needed for the onset of the challenges and confrontatons of the Modern Age. The spiritual favor of the American, Westward Movement, along with the spiritual fervor supplied by Moses and Joshua to take the Holy Land at Canaan was God's Plan for the future safeguard, survival, and fullfillment of Mankind. In biblical truth both the Wars of Manifest Destiny of Israel and those of the USA were existentially and theologically consequential; painting the initial portraits of two set-apart nations as freedom persona.

Verily, the ideological and technological discoveries up to the 21st century might very well divulge that the American cultural diversity eventually will consist of a dozen, discernible bio/breeds of the American citizenry; all seeking socio/political freedoms and a greater prosperity. Sooner than imagined, bio/technologists might find revealing patterns of gene clusters which clearly identify: (1) the Euro/Viking; (2) Mediterranean Man/Woman; (3) Euro/Asian Hybrid; (4) Purer Mongol; (5) Hybrid/Asian; (6) Afro/Black; (7) Euro/Black; (8) Iberian; (9)

Hispanic/Indian; (10) Afro/Hispanic; (11) Native Amerindian; and (12) the Aborigine. Eugenically, over the span of thousands of years these subspecies of Humankind have been tailored to live-and-love via their particular behavioral patterns, such as: (a) cultural, community, and family lifestyles; (b) choices of religious media; (c) potential effectiveness, or likely less-effectiveness, or totally ineptitude, in dealing with the socio/political demands of democratic living; (d) gradations of formal, educational proficiencies; (e) success levels operating in a free-market milieu; (f) metabolic and immunity, disease propensities; (g) crime rates; and (h) the tendency to resist (or welcome) the learning (or use) of the most effective language ever devised by Mankind, i.e. English. Accordingly, within this complex socio/anthropology of a single species, i.e. the Homo Sapien, the 19th century political stage has been set for the emergence of a new nation that will form the framework of a 21st Century democracy. Indeed the Divine annexing of the lands of the West has been Divinely planned and in harmony with Moses and Joshua's annexing the Holy Land thousands of years prior.

Via the astonishing brilliance of the US Constitution, as conceived and scripted by the Divinely inspired, Founding Fathers, as never before experienced in the political and theological history of Mankind, the unique tenets of governing by both Israel and America have become distinguishable both by bio/spiritual style and bio/political substance. These two nations set forth both the legal guidance&mandates for: (a) individualized, political liberty; (b) freedom in the marketplace; (c) copious generosity for the downtrodden; (d) for the "traditionally oppressed," along with the emancipation of females and minorities; and (e) for the large and small nations hovering within the vast landmasses of Asia; all gift-wrapped with Godly ideas and axioms of knowledge; such as, high-mathematics, high-science, high-technology, the economics of capitalism; along with the insights of socio/behavioral sciences and modern education; (f) the theorems and procedures of participative government; and (g) for SubSaharan Africans and their marginal existence and the plight of the Aboriginal Class with the Divine hope of emancipation from slavery, disease, famine, and war. In toto, these socio/spiritual guidelines personified the human aspirations of both a Hebrew nation and America-the-Beautiful.

Surely, some critical thinking is indicated for the ideational and demographic clusters for the 19th to the 21st centuries frames of mind. What needs to be added to our political lore is greater, scientific knowledge of our bio/social qualities--by individual, gender, and ethnic groupings. We ought to be inquiring via the election booth: *"..what role has theDivine handprint been playing in our democratic politics?"* Are the dynamics of the soul and its politics intertwined and correlated with the daily experiences and cicumstances of the individual citizen? What political implications have become revealed by the dissimilarity of the bio/social natures of Americans--who happen to be Black, Asian, Amerindian, Caucasian, or Hispanic? Truly in the context of today's, bio/technological revolution, which is now taking place within the background of an accelerated, evolutionary setting, raises vital, political questions which call for a resolution within the tenured timeline of the 19th-21st centuries. By looking back in the contentious, war history of freedom ideas, first arising out of the 18th century enlightenment up to the nature/nurture debate as it pertains to democratic politics in the 21st century, the legislative goals of such "freedom knowledge" might be to: (a) tag differences of bio/psychological agility; (b) reconcile the disparities of inheritable, educational success-rates; (c) identify an assortment of political communities by voting records; (d) scrutinize the bio/spiritual rationale underlying religious styles and preferences; (e) acquire a peek at the medley of our cultural aesthetics, as emitted by the our traditional expressions; (f) account for the medical variations of disease incidences and treatments of our subpopulations; along with (g) to formally acknowledge the forces of "industrial eugenics" that underlie the free-market proficiencies of individuals and their cultural subgroups. In potential, this direction of knowledge might further the course of democracy by better explaining the anthropological differences underlying the decomposing&chaotic, effects of unrestrained cultural diversity.

Global Spinoffs from America's Manifest Destiny

As the artifacts of prehistory and the scripts of war history have illumed scholars from the single-cell to the complex human brain, the bio/spiritual forces driving all of Earth's lifeforms that also includes the Homo Sapien who likewise has been responding bio/socially to a wide range of geo/survival forcefields; thereby ultimately becoming "tribally variegated" by virtue of physical, physiological, and socio/political modes and preferences. These etched patterns of the human species that seek to live in a democracy would include styles of mating, family, nesting, food-gathering, protection of territory, gender roles, and freedom-seeking. In the future as deciphered for democratic politics, these evolutionary processes propelled by the principles of "organic sociology" must be insinuating that a bio/spiritual diversity, not a socio/cultural diversity, must have been operating in America and Isreal. Truly, it would be highly tangential to surmise that America's Global composition of citizenry, which is being mislabeled by political correctness as a socio/cultural diversity, actually reflects the multi/breeds of Man, by race, gender, and ethnic origin. If so, mightn't this bio/behavioral truism also lie at the root for our continuing, political challenges of trying to implement our democratic ideas and ideals of freedom, tolerance, and equality for all? Only when the freedom principle becomes legitimate and politically internalized will the efforts of the Westward Movement of the 19th century be able to deal with the social realities of citizen-based differences? Governing the 12/DNA tribes of Americana, within a community context of universal human-rights, equal civil rights, and economic parity of opportunity, must be produced by the force of war that is governed by Divine fiat. Only then will the ways&means of these neo/politics reconcile "rights and bio/ differencess." This reconcilation would be socio/upgrading, socio/intensifying, and socio/thickening the density of our democratic consciousness; accordingly in a practical mode by setting into motion a radical shift in legislative priorities and redirecting the war struggles of the 19th century on to the civilizations of the 21st century.

Will our syllogistic untruths concerning the adaptive parity of *"Democratic Man,"* as believed at this very instant be confused with the equivalent freedom rights of *"Non-Adaptive Man?"* Ultimately, to become clarified, conciliated, reconciled, and illuminating for a 21st century version of society-large? If so, then out of the now-cascading "freedom vision" an assortment of racial/ethnics consisting of possibly, twelve DNA-tribes soon will consume the political attentions of our national consciousness. In support of this conjecture, a recent study published on 12/20/02 in *Science* reported that DNA markers indicate that modern humans fall into five categories. Worldwide, this study utilized 52 human groups and convincingly "factor analyzed" the Homo Sapien, i.e. Modern Man, into Africans, Europeans, Asians, Melanesians, and Americans—all seeking freedom. Morality-seeking Hebrews and freedom-seeking Americans have been the Divinely set-aparet people derived as DNA/Man. In the Western Hemisphere, a new "race" of human life has been formed with a new set of DNA/credentials; those which have become reconstituted via 4000-years of manifest destiny to either Canaan or the New World by Euro/pioneers. In Europe today, surprisingly depleted out of the best-of-the-best of Mother Europe's population, the forces of "genetic exhaustion" seems to have replaced the Euro/vitality of its genetic/spiritual enrichment. Sadly, now Europe has become no more than a museum of the Western World; a pagan Continent, cult-committed to secular humanism, espousing a value system which worships Man, State, and reasoning, not the faith in God. Seeking socio/bondage, not freedom for all, the spiritually debased nations of Europe Proper comprise a land that has been responsible for the innocent, horrific slaughter of over a 100 million innocent people in the 20th century.

Truly, a new Age of Ethnographic Bio/technology seems to be rapping at America's "democratic door" marked with: *"...enter here ye for a lifetime of greater freedom and opportunity."* And its corollary: *"...enter here ye for a lifetime of less disease, less poverty, less famine, and greater, individual liberty."* It's no chance happenstance that so many of the world's communities and Islam are jealously resentful and hateful toward Israel and America. Surely with political courage&integrity embracing the contentions of the Global socio/politics, a better understanding of the underlying, human condition that promises a citizenry less suffering and greater well-being for all, voter discourse, and future freedom legislation. This socio/spiritual perspective of political realities will be stretching our Jeffersonian imagination to seek-out many freedom prospects of governmental modes.

Consider as analogies these God-centered, historic events. Since the 16th century, the hereditary building-blocks of Euro/America have been formed, marshaled, and operationalized as a result of the interactions of the inherant character of two, dominant and ascendant subspecies of the Homo Sapien. Mainly, via a medley of personality attributes exuded by the **Viking Genome**, in partnership with the intellectual ingenuity percolating out of the **Mediterranean people,** eventually hatched new freedom customs by which societies ought to conduct themselves socio/politically. Throughout the 19th century, while the Viking bio/persona may have contributed to the "skeletal&operational" structure of our democracy; lying fallow in-wait lay the Mediterranean cultures that fleshed-out to more fully dilated the "great notions" needed for a free-society. With this legacy of "great ideas" in-hand, America slowly matured up to the ***Wars of Manifest Destiny*** to eventually to become the "great empire" of the Western World. In partnership, it took both the Viking and Mediterranean cultures, which were DNA compatible, to synthesize the attributes needed to accomplish a Divinely-inspired, Jeffersonian "feat of feats"—America the Beautiful.

Geographically by region, the "mutational components" of both these ethnic clusters can be more or less identified and mapped-out by land-sectors on any world map. Chiefly, the Viking communities initially evolved out of the icy-regions of Northern Europe; which included: Scandinavia, the communities bordering the uppermost coastline of this same Euro/Continent, along with the array of British Isles. For tens of thousands of years, these hardy people, originally the Cro Magnon mutant, seem to have been derived out of the many generations of inbreeding steming from their "original Adam;" who with mutational brilliance, suddenly appeared on Earth's landscape with physical, neuro/psychological, and sociological attributes, which according to anthropological speculation heretofore have never existed within the realm of the Organic Realm. The living Swedes. Norwegians. Danes. Prussian Germans and Northern French, abiding in the cities and townships on the northern rim of the English Channel seemed to have been all chromosomally related, that is, of

Viking bloodlines." So too, the British, Irish, Scots, and Welsh probably are also Cro Magnon derivatives. From the 16th century AD this precise Euro/ancestry both explored and organized the pioneering efforts of North American communities as they trekked toward a Westward Movement from the Atlantic to the Pacific Oceans, across the New World's hills&vales, deserts, and mountain ranges. Still as the wiles of Mother Nature always creates a special-case exception appearing to countermand her generalized rules of evolution.

For example as a bio/social paradox, today's Basque people, straddling France and Spain, somehow seem to have become "genetically closeted" apart from the archetypal, Viking Genome; sort of a Caucasion mutation arising out of, or perhaps incised out of the Viking mainline. Even in this day of national socio/volatility, the Basque style of society has proven to be self-protective, traditionally stable, and resolute. Culturally unchanging as a enclosed, Basque nation, this sub-tribe of the Northern Caucasoid continues to fiercely protect its borders, by narrowly defining its traditional identity by preserving its unique language, all the while practicing an ultraconservative religion. With violence if need be, the policies of the Basque leadership have opted to remain nationally set-apart, pure and persevered. One might ask: Why? Where lies the compelling, scholarly evidence to support such a outlandish conjecture of an autonomous, Caucasian bio/breed? Indeed so, there is such evidence available. DNA studies by linguists, who were seeking an explanation for the uniqueness of the Basque language. They have confirmed that these people carry genetic, language markers, distinguishably apart from the mainstream, Euro/Northern Caucasian. Hair samples from their teenagers were part of the research employed in these scholarly language studies. With little doubt via probability mathematics what had to be concluded must be: "...the Basque language isn't derived from the Euro/language family, hence, perhaps these people ought to be considered as a hermetically sealed subspecies of the Caucasian race." Eureka! out of this Basque, bio/political supposition it would also seem scientifically proper to eugenically extrapolate further. Such as, in combination does the Viking/Mediterranean Genome possess the compatible, chromosomal ingredients that have accounted for the "political handprint" of the United States? Furthermore, proven to endure the slings and arrows that have assailed the USA, the oldest Constitution in the history of Mankind continues to profess the freedom theme. Verily predestined by the universal dignity of Man, this land of the brave and home of the free has been selected by "Divine fiat" to govern the most "vulnerable and volatile" segments of human life. Indeed, most all of American politics has been biblical and Christ-like, loving the lame, the last, the least of us, and those spiritually lost.

Today abiding in diversified America, as an bordered and bonded, national portrait, we must ask: who are the twelve tribes of DNA-Americana? In addition to the Viking/Mediterranean Genomes, there might be ten, additional discernible, bio/social clusters which share the American, freedom landscape. Eager for digestible answers by the common taxpayer, what must be ascertained by both scientific and socio/political efforts are the bio/geological and behavioral inclinations of the non-Caucasoid; that is, as measured by their territorial impulses, metabolic endurance, immunity against disease, family and mating styles, abstract/brain faculties, and food/chain effectiveness. For its continuing survival, America can only thrive by knowing and dealing with the results of these survival differences. We must be willing to ask and know: how did the neuro/psychology, socio/traditions, and racial/ethnic cultures of Black/Brown/Yellow/Hybrid races develop? How well will these non-Caucasoids function in an highly competitive, freedom/oriented, American nest? Other than the SubSaharan who has been living in America for 400+ years, how rapidly can we expect the neo/immigrant, whether legal or illegal, to be absorbed and assimilated into our vibrant, eco/energized, self-sufficient society? Our nation composed of confederated States, each of which will be demanding that the individual's **net input** must total-up *greater than* the sum of their **output**, as the defining test of democratic freedom. As a matter of economic fact, Capitalistic America always has been a nation which consists of social elements which add-up greater than the sum of its citizenry. Moreover in this regard our demographics will be able to learn the "curricula ways" of the White Man's schooling. Will the genes of the non-Caucasian permit him/her to thrive with self-reliance within the educational/freemarket constraints of the American pantry? If so, soon in the light of the inescapable research conducted and composed by the cross-cultural bio/technologists, the DNA/character of the twelve breeds of the American citizenry will become ostensibly featured; first by sci-fi writers, followed by the polling musings of the respectable Media, then via scientific numerics, and lastly, being legislated according to the expressed, social power of the electorate. Indeed, within the human, social consciousness lies a genetic-based democracy enroute from the 18ᵗʰ century wars of freedom to the 19ᵗʰ century wars of of manifest destiny.

Yet in spite of everything "said and spun" by statesmen and politicians concerning the freedom events and ideas of the 18ᵗʰ-19ᵗʰ centuries, the proceedings of world politics has shown. *"...it takes more than the social grit of a democratic personality to implement the full dynamics of a truly free-society."* For example, Russians have Viking-esque grit, but never had a workable democracy. Why so? Even in this day of in-vogue, political emancipation, Russians and Chinese continue to crave a strong, centralized leadership. Consequently, even after the implosion of the USSR in the early 1990s, this multiplex society still finds itself in a meltdown mode, plagued by rampant alcoholism, unchecked drug-abuse, unbridled corruption, a pandemic of AIDs, runaway crime, a high suicide rate, a two-class, rich or poor economy, and stress-related diseases most-common even to the ordinary citizen. A democratic society based on individual choices tends to better solve these sociatal threats. For hundreds of years most Russians still cling to the longing for the alledged predictability of an autocratic regime. In bondage, the Russian population has been experiencing a precipitous decline both in conviction and hope, not unlike the "great plagues" of the 1300s AD, or as in China which is dabbling with and counting on the axioms of marketplace freedom, in lieu of political liberties, for its future stamina and survival. Both Russia and China fail to understand that freedom priorities is what could ultimately give them a civilized society which they can't seem to attain. Mainland, modern China, not unlike the Mongol Khans, when evaluated by political perspicacity, rather than by economic phantasm, have entrenched leaderships which always seem to revert to their ugly, bio/genetic, barbarian ways. Otherwise America prizes true liberty, whereby political power is diffuse, shared, and replaced as needed; as deemed by citizens where true freedom is viewed primarily as a Divine gift of social righteousness. Traditional America isn't bolstered by an inflated, ballooned, stretched-thin economy, or a veiled, contrived despotism--as in China and Russia. Verily, liberty requires risk-taking, not the CYA startle-reflexes of a bureaucratic, totalitarian government.

Similarly in Asia, a candid, close-up view of India's bloated, pseudo/democracy will reveal its true caricature; an ancient land, which elections are regularly bribed events and party-determined, with little-to-non voter input nor social power by the individual citizen. India is not a democracy. It has no elementary, public-educational system. No democracy can exist or thrive within a milieu of grassroots ignorance. Without universal, primary, public education no nation can claim to be a free society. Most all of India's, rural children are illiterate and are expected to earn a meager income and die at a very, young age. For any true democracy to exist, reading and writing must be deemed most-basic, fundamental and unconditionally vital for freedom living. Although as politically spun, the facts indicate that India is not the world's, largest democracy. Otherwisw, it's the

Global.s largest, sham-democracy. The differences between China/Russia/India, and the USA is somehow related to the national wars of ots original 18th century pioneers. So too, it might be said that without direct Euro/supervision, Dark Africa doesn't even approach the starting-line of a racial/ societal survival or medical civility. The SubSaharan region of this lush, rich continent, filled with all the natural resources available for prosperity, always has been more tribal than civilized. Strewed across the Globe, the SubSaharan has failed to mutate for freedom living. Its aura reiterates slavery, famine, tribal warfare, and deadly infectious diseases. In all history and prehistory there has never been a workable, civilized Black society.

In order to flourish, any true democracy requires the interactions of exceptional, socio/political/spiritual attributes; those built into the individual character of both its leadership and citizenry. These fundamentals of existential life is what makes for a true democracy. This is what the lifelines and lifeblood of freedon-living rely upon. Upfront at its cornerstone, any true democracy requires the "know-how" to self-reliantly and cerebrally acquire an *economic surplus*. In Asia, Central America, most of South America, and Africa to accrue and assure a livable warehouse of foodstuffs for their *entire* populations seems near impossible. Secondly, true democracies require *formalized education* in order to institutionalize, operationalize, protect, and maintain the tenets of freedom. Freedom comes at a hogh price.

At its societal roots and since its alledged independence the policies of India's ruling, corrupt governments remain ignorant and backward. By "politically ignoring" the outward flow of its societal talent, i.e. brain drain, India's customary depletion of its human capital has caused an ever-emigrating tradition of its cerebral elite. Democracies, unlike dictatorships, monarchies, oligarchies, and theocracies, retain, not lose, their "cerebral elite." Hence, India's multi-billion populace is assured of a continuing wretchedness. For this reason, it seems more and more likely that only within the dynamics of 40,000 or so genes per cell, which dwell mysteriously nestled upon the DNA/ribbon, can the fruition of socio/economic liberty yield digestible answers to these Global, demographic riddles. In a nutshell, lying fallow within the singular units of human tissue abide the creative, innate attributes and ideational traditions of any people or "genetically compatible" either with the Viking/Mediterranean Genome or its tribal derivatives. As 18th-19th century America has shown the world, by acting in partnership, the national moral fiber of the British, Prussian Germans, Coastline French and the Scandinavian; when complemented with the bio/mindset of the Mediterranean inhabitants, can and will ultimately produce a democratic personality for a free society. Later in history when the annals of recorded time become reinterpreted, Mankind will realize that the political personalities of the Euro/Northmen/ women have been necessary, although not sufficient, to the fashioning of the true, Americana. The Anglos, Normans, Teutonics and Scandia tribes actually constituted only part of the American Saga. This epic, political voyage has been augmented by the demographic, puzzle pieces of the DNA/

brilliance of the Mediterranean Man/Woman. The nations bordering the Roman Mare with their unique blend of cerebrals have added the integrated "democratic persona" of explorative grit and ingenious thoughts which emerged out of their mutations of yore--from the Ancient World, to the Renaissance, to the Enlightenment, to Modern Europa on to the New World. Bio/socially this chromosomal blend paints a fuller American portrait, as embellished by the resourceful character of the Ellis Island immigrants of the late/19th thru early/20th centuryies

The Italians from the Mezzogiorno Region, Christian Poles, Jewish Russians, and sundry Slavs, motivated by the innate thrust of their dauntless determination, bravely sought freedom and opportunity away from the oppressions of Southern and Eastern Europe. Truly the bio/history of America has been a "Divine miracle," when DNA/ingredients Divinely converged in time beyond all human expectations. Today, those who chose to remain in their Motherlands, in lieu of emigrating in the search for greater freedom and greater financial opportunity, comprise a Old Euro/Western Asia/Northern Africa composite, which social aura can best be described as abiding in a depleted "DNA/museum of yore."

Viking/Classical Roots of Freedom Living

Across the timelines and through the prisms of enlightened, ideational speculation, some humanoid scientists have mulled about America's, demographic portrait as a genetic trail left behind: (a) by first the Cro Magnon; (b) then the Scandinavian

Viking; (c) followed by, the conquests of the British/French/ German Euro/piomeers; and (d) ultimately by the 18th century, New World Americans. Indeed, the survival traits of this remarkable "New Man," a "New World Caucasoid," can be subsumed by both the Scandinavian traces of its prehistory and history alike. Prior to the 10th century, the Viking was an enterprising, socially aggressive, often brutal, always explorative, and ideationally inquisitive prototype of the Homo Sapien. Seemingly this Northman, no different than the Cro Magnon, also became dynamically curious of the workings of his spacious surroundings. Later on in prehistoric evolution and history itself, the Early Americans have been described in a similar fashion by both friend, competitor, and foe. Soon by bio/historical portrayal, the comparison of this particular lineage of societal communities, ranging from the **Cro to the Euro to the Yankee**, will confirm a bio/ cultural resemblance. Vikings, the alleged descendants of the Cro Magnon, have been known to seek socio/political freedom by forming tight and efficient settlements, whether by plunder, extortion, raid, slave-trade, while terrorizing their neighbors. Similar to: the adventurisms of the British Empire which sun almost never set. And, similar to the conquests of the French, Napoleonic Era. Or, Joshua's Hebrews who conquered Canaan. Or, the expansionism of the America's "manifest destiny," which proceeded to gobble-up Indian lands with its Western Movement.

On the genetic downside, the Prussian tribes which accounted for: (a) the fall of Rome by the Teutonic Visogoths; (b) European militarism for centuries; and even (c) the horrific extremisms spawned by the Nazi, Fascist, godless elitism, and years later, Communist evil socio/politics. All this must be included as part of this Caucasoid lineage. Interestingly as a compare, contrast, and historic generalization, the Black&Brown Races of Planet Earth haven't regularly sought to invade the remote lands of their neighbors. Only the Caucasian and the Mongol have had a resolute history of colonial expansionism, which for the White Race now includes the conquest of Outer Space. Earlier as time flew by, the Mongol and its hybrids have become "geographically contained," along with the Caucasian hybrids of Euro/Asia, who although culturally geo/localized, were nations with ever-shifting borders. In themselves with thoughtful reasoning, the Discovery Explorations of yore must point to the nature of the tribal heredity of territorial aggressors. With ever-decreasing doubt, scholars are earnestly wondering if and how the Cro Magnon Mutant begot the Viking, who begot the Northern Europeans, which helped inspire the socio/political, "Constitutional imagery" of first, the Greco/Roman, then British, French, on to the USA's pioneer. Were these historical trends mustered about the roots of Western Man bio/socially actuated and guided by freedom impulses? In a nutshell, has this pedigree, which initially consisted a of roving Cro, then invading barbarians, also became the scholarly messengers and socio/political stewards of the "great societies?" With little doubt as noted throughout the history of the Western World weere the DNA/behaviors of the Modern Caucasian. They have been the dynamics of an amazingly fertile "freedom"legacy;" along with lamentably, with traces of a "chromosomal darkside" and stimulants that sired the genocides of yore.

Prior to the 19th century, by way of their pioneer immigration to the New World, the Viking derivative, i.e. the English, Scots, Welch, French, German, and Irish, in alliance with the Danes, Swedes, and Norwegians, initiated the exploration and shaping of the social and political contract of the American Portrait. Add to these converging, Northland émigrés, the communal remnants of the Ancient and Classical Worlds, which peopled the inspirational coastlines of the Mediterranean Lakeline and became the complementary, demographic puzzle-pieces needed to flesh-out the accomplishments of the Neo/Viking society--we now call America-the-Beautiful.

Yet, as historians remind us, it took a timeline and much warfare for the "democratic idea and ideal" to ripen. Before the 20th century the United States was still a minor, world power and industrial fledgling with a predestiny was yet to be fulfilled. It took the bloodshed of a number of Divinely inspired wars for the Divine gift of freedom to create a modern-day democracy. Be that as it may, it now seems self-evident that during the 20th century, it took the input of the humanizing/ intellectual identity of the: (a) fleeing hordes of Southern/ Mediterranean's immigrants; (b) cogitating traditions of the Jewish escapees; in combination with, (c) the fortitude of the Eastern European newcomers, to consummate, so as to actualize, the true American Portrait. Surely, this newly admixed demographic made the USA a world contender based fully on freeddom-living. In that, it took the bio/social sinews of the Viking Genome to construct a stable, self-reliant, dominant, and cerebrally self-reflective free-society when affiliated with the compassionate/democratic ideas inspired by the genius of the aesthetic surroundings of the Sea of Rome for America to emerge and blossom. In real time, out of the Mediterranean Genome came the fuller development of the "democratic conviction" of freedom for all. Over the centuries, this radical, political notion has been spoon-fed to the modern world; first by Pericles, Aristotle, Socratis, and Cicero; all notable, Classical characters on the early stage of the Western tradition. Later on, the paradoxical principles of both national stability and national liberty became the Machiavellian contribution awaiting Viking-esque society, which was to be named in the 16th century after Americus Vespucci. Verily, America is a beauteous, Italian/Renaissance word; a national designation echoing the ideas of Locke's concept of a "social contract." And which, subsequently influenced the 18th century theories of Montesquieu; Rousseau; Jefferson; and Kant. As a radical idea for the socio/political life of a nation, this new American homeland was to be based upon the force of law, not violence, along with the force of universal human-rights, not the fiats of autocracy. Thus beginning with those times, a revolutionary compilation of democratic ways&means, began to be proposed, form, gel, and cascade. Such as: the defense of freedom; the social origin of liberty; the natural rights of Man; along with the peaceful implementation of demographic pluralism, a.k.a. culturally expressive diversity. These were novel theories that had to be executed by an enlightened, Sovereign, confederated, 13-State system. Moreover, these became ideational roots, which were originally planted by the Ancient and Classical Worlds, and which later grew and were nourished in a post-Renaissance Europe; then eventually amplified by the judicial thought-process into the Anglo/American system of government. Across the years, America became the treasured society to be emulated by the full family-of-nation.

In the light of this impending New-Age, we ought to be asking: was it chance happenstance that the American Portrait began to blossom-out after the swarm of Southern and Eastern European immigrants who invaded the shores of the American, Neo/Viking World? By fate, weren't these Euro/peoples "latently poised" to boot-up and embellish the doctrines of democratic politics? By lot, weren't they enticed by the prospects of freedom and its prosperity by way of the axioms of capitalism? Was it a fluke that these immigrants of the late/18th and early/20th centuries adapted easily to American lifestyle *in just one generation*? For sure, this "one generation turnaround" must have been induced by some expression of "chromosomal identity," and not by their capricious cultures. While others; ghetto Blacks, reservation Amerindians, and barrio Hispanics haven't been able to adequately absorb, assimilate, and implement the American Dream for their offspring across multi-generations. Today we find it strange that even during booming years both America's conventional and newly arriving minorities, whether arriving legally or illegally, are still struggling both with the national identification and the cultural digestion of the ways&means of the USA. Instead, the underclasses of innercity's disadvantaged find themselves clinging to the addictions of social dependency and/or political detachment from the American mainstream. Might these maladaptive, social conditions be caused and manifested as follows: *"..the enormous inoculations of taxpayer fundings for compensatory and retributional programs have been mainly and mostly ineffective, due primarily to the socially-indisposed, nonWhite minorities."*

As a Malthusian skit, although fitted for cold climates the Neanderthal required just a 2% higher, reproductive, survival rate to be viable today; however love and sex alone, which poets tell us transcend all other considerations, somehow failed this primitive, archetype of Man. As archeological proof in support of these conjectures come from the relics of both the Neanderthal and the half-breed Cro which relics have been excavated in Iberia and the Balkans. Archeologists tell us that without competitors the Cro Magnon ultimately became free to fine-tune his/hers: (a) food-gathering skills; (b) rituals and mythologies associated with mating, family-life and spiritual glimpses of Creation; (c) territorial and travel imperatives; in conjunction with, (d) intertribal relationships. As the millennia drifted by, a direct line of Caucasian inheritance expanded upward, forward, and outward throughout the European/Asian/North African landscapes.

So where does the antidote lie? How do we reconcile the tripart, inherent contradictions of our Globalized "cultural diversity," which tells us that: (1) *all* are rights-protected; (2) *all* are free to express their uplifting, religious and cultural life-and-love styles; but (3) *all* individuals and groups are *not* equally DNA/endowed to fully appreciate the freedom mechanics and perks of the Viking/Mediterranean nest, now known as democratic America. Yet somewhere somehow, the antidote does exist for the solutions to this socio/political dilemma. Indeed the invasion of Mexicans, Asians, and Central Americans across the porous borders of the Southwest should be telling us that the very survival of the American Dream is dependent upon the politics of the genetic vision. But for sure elsewhere, apart from the "social correctness" bequeath us by the philosophical fallacies of the Liberal powers that be. Elsewhere for sure, not in today's Left-winged, political models. Nor, in unrestrained, classical capitalism. Nor, within the tenets of military dominance. Nor in the sentimentalisms of psycho/educational theories. Nor, in the misguided pseudo-axioms of cultural anthropology. So where then? Where can we find the palatables digestible to the disillusioned, but acutely inquiring, mindset of the 21st century electorate? Possibly, via the R&D of the American Genome. Possibly, with scientific creativity and wisdom by which the systematic bio/excavation of the chromosomes might unmask the "black box" secrets of the behaviors of the diverse bio/breeds of Mankind, abiding in the deep&dark urban cores. Focused and floating within the singular cell-tissue, the genes clinging to the intertwining ribbons of free-floating DNA is where the bio/behavioral research centers must seek-out the answers. With well-designed, cross-species studies it may be possible to seek-out the micro-correlations of genes-to-acts, genes-to-social preferences, genes-to-emotions and genes-to-spirit. After which, charged with these mathematical insights of genetic microanalyses, a mapping of the bio/anthropological DNA/structure of the Cro Magnon ought to come into view. Yet today, blindly infected by the dogmatically orthodox, American, political mythology, we are relying heavily upon the superstitious belief and trust in an all-inclusive, aspiring and transcendent socio/cultural diversity. In one form or another, this American folklore has been portrayed for 200+ years as an idea and the ideal of a free society and free marketplace; which as this myth posits: ***"...by way of Jeffersonian erudition a rainbow of essential goodness exists for the totality of Mankind which will eventually deliver the human desire for a democratic utopia."*** In the context of the "genetic vision," this view is mythological superstition which must be challenged and upgraded. In the 21st century, to a great degree the hopes of this political dream-state already has been materializing. Yet, who can deny that there are still glaring gaps in the workings of our egalitariat Republic. Soberly, as objective, program evaluations insist on pointing-out: what has been, and continues to be documented, are forewarning flags of democratic insufficiency threatening its collapse. These flags caution: ***"...beware, there are deep pitfalls lurking within the ways&means of our Liberal agendas andits practices."*** Indeed there are pitfalls; as activist judges legislate from their once "interpretative benches." As, the Media offering ideological opinions masked as editorial judgments, not facts. As, lawyering has become a predatory euphemism causing the piecemeal destruction of our institutional, rule-of-law. And, as election politics are driven by the greed of Liberal money, not ideas and ideals. From all this and more, shouldn't the electorate be concerned that their revered "American premises" are spinning their wheels, burning rubber, while hanging in limbo slowing twisting in the perilous winds of Global contentions? Can part of the core problem to our democracy be related to our flawed perception of our cultural diversity, which is being thought of with an all-inclusive supposition of equality. Perhaps, the DNA/elements of our basic biology are demanding higher standards for our political institutions? Perhaps, a genetic forcefield is trying to solicit legislative policies of socio/exclusivity, rather than socio/inclusivit? And perhaps conceptually, the bio/adaptive repertoires of the various racial/ethnics ought to be described as multi-tiered and not as a level, playing-field? Still further; while the bio/social implications of the democratic voyage have been "not fable," but authentic, relevant, and valid, the American mythology of freedom and equal opportunity seems to be more applicable for the Caucasian migrants of the late-18th to the early-20th centuries--than to the "people of color" whose diversity has been confounding and confronting us for the past 5-decades? In many ways at the onset of the 21st century, we're discovering that for the conventional, minority subpopulations, Afro/Blacks, Hispanics, and Amerindians alike, the generous offerings of "blank checks" by political fiat, guaranteeing an aura of freedom and opportunity for all, doesn't work as well as ought to be expected. This American "political naiveté" hasn't produced the comparable socio/psyche results for the nonWhite citizen, as it did for the Euro/Caucasian who graced our shores via Ellis Island 150-years ago. Or for that matter, for those original pioneers who migrated to our New World over 300-years ago. If these observational premises are trustworthy, ***then logically, there must be DNA-components which separate the proactive from the reactive migrant.*** Only an intellectual lightweight would disclaim that in the main, the eugenics which shaped the American Portrait, forced or otherwise, of Blacks, Hispanics, and Amerindians have been *reactive* experiences, as compared to the freedom-seeking Caucasian, who clearly has been engaging the American challenges *proactively.* Accordingly, these bio/social differences must be politically relevant and compelling. These differences ought to be cause-enough to reroute our political discourse toward a genetic-based society, at the very least, to better-utilize the limitations of our tax-funds. Partially justified, granted although misguided, the case might be made that our national commitment to "citizen nurturing" as a principal key to equal freedom and opportunity has worked only in some degree. Rightly so, in that for over 5-decades legislators have been only fractionally successful injecting "monied fuel," by firing the social ignitions of the disadvantaged, hoping to spark a fuller, democratic participation of its full citizenry. Yes, in part there were some successful polities and programs. However unrightfully so, these fundings have failed to meet the reasonable marks of bottomline productivity and/or profitability; those factors which a free nation demands from its citizenry in order to thrive and survive. As a matter of statistical fact, neither community peace nor innercity prosperity have been sufficiently attained by those programs of big government for; (a) the homeless; (b) the hungry; (c) the underclass; (d) the low/voting constitiencies; (e) the high incidence, heinous criminals, nor, in the urban schools which have failed; (e) the minimum standards of educational basics required for even marginal, democratic living. Even within a reasonable time period as the modulator, both the "selfless and selfish" efforts of left-winged legislators have failed to deliver the Liberal dogma as an all/inclusive, national policy. Why so? Liberalism, as a euphemism for true democracy, has proven to be narrow-in-scope, evil, and riddled with socio/political non-sequiturs. In reaction, prophetic, more conservative, political logic lurking in the wings of Jeffersonian postulates are about to ambush the flimsy, liberal theorems of the 21st century. Today in the colleges there are conservative, student movements which are exposing the political conspiracies of overpaid and under-worked "academic professors." The ideas gone-by contending with the ideas staged-to-be are about to jolt the complacent, dogmatic, socio/political delusions-of-the-day. Verily, the "freedom dynamics" of our national community may have been wrongly depicted as materializing out of a idyllic mold of a socio/cultural diversity. And, not out of a bio/cultural population. A 21st century corollary to this political fantasy ought to declare: ***the political nurturing of our diverse citizenry, while ignoring its bio/social nature, has to be considered the cardinal, ideational fallacy of Modern America.***

Somehow and in some way, the bio/diverse natures of our American demography must be permitted entry into the legislative arena. And, allowed to play a major, decisive role in our democratic agenda. ***First***, we must continue to solidify our democratic principles. Unequivocally, our laws, executive fiats, and court proceedings must address, clarify, as well as continue to institutionalize the universal tenets of fundamental freedoms. Human rights, civil liberties, social justice, and the equal opportunity for economic parity ought to blanket the gamut of freedom's tones and timbres. These political/spiritual rights account for the very justification of any open society and its free marketplace. ***Secondly***, with equal fervor and tolerance, a multi/racial/ethnic democracy must respect and protect all uplifting forms of cultural imagery and practices, along with their mythologies of beauty, language, foods, traditions, and religion. Always, the expressive ways&means of races, nationals, and ethnics must acquire the same standing as the basic rights of Mankind. Especially, the expressive utterances of speech and it's First Amendment rights guaranteed to each and all of a citizenry. In a genetic-based democracy, the Bill-of-Rights, including freedom of expression, must continue to be considered nonnegotiable and irreversible. As a sidebar, from a political perspective Jesus was crucified because of "freedom of speech." By looking back into antiquity and as a defining antecedent for societal freedom, it might be noteworthy to point out that at the Scriptural/ political level the prophetic heroes of our Judeo/Christian tradition were summarily executed when they dared express their freedom of oration. Many of the OT prophets and NT apostles and disciples alike, who propelled the Moral Evolution of Western Man, were brutalized and executed by the State (Roman or Israeli) because they dared talk openly about the new thoughts of Mankind's socio/Spirit. Jesus was crucified by the Jewish and Roman establishments irrespective of his inalienable right of free expression of new ideas on how men could and should conduct themselves. Moreover, the High Priest of the Ancient Temple, who argued that to kill someone for the sake of the community is OK, inadvertently set the stage for a "Western metaphor" pinpointing the sacred right of free speech and due process for all. What would the world be like today without the guidance of Judeo/Christian tutoring? Would the "great ideas" of the Western World, which emanated obliquely out of the aura of the Abrahamic/ Mosaic Law, be available, coveted, and embraced by today's, full family of nations--whether Hindu, Moslem, or Buddhist?

No doubt, America is one nation under God. Our socio/ political foundations stand as a firm bedrock of treasured, biblical values. Our national creation has been incomparable. Our system of self-government by the consent of those governed with checks and balances by the force of law can't be found throughout the history of Mankind. As an expression of political/Christian ideals, America gives us the freedom of religion, not the freedom from religion, mainly with legislation of social love. It took the Divine scripting of the US Constitution and the Declaration of Independence for this miracle to have happened. For political efficiency, America became a republic, not a democracy. We are represented by those we choose to elect with the aid of the US Constitution that was designed to perpetuate the Judeo/Christian Code. Jesus brought us a true freedom, not the bondage to idols, false doctrine, drugs, alcohol, immoral sexuality, wealth, or positions of power. In the famed Supreme Court decision in the year 1892, it was ruled that our laws and institutions must be based upon the teachings of our Lord and Savior. Our national anthem and our flag embody the democratic values of our nation. Accordingly, American exceptionalism of its original citizenry that came initially from its pioneer Viking DNA database gave us both the self-disciple and self-reliance needed for socio/political freedom, the moral rule of law, and the institutions fit for a democracy. When the Pilgrims landed in Plymouth in 1620 AD, they were Christians who laid the groundwork for a moral democracy that would endure for time without end. As Separatists fleeing the Church of England they chose to live in the New World wilderness where the could worship God according to Sacred Scripture. From this year to 1776 AD, these evangelical set-apart people were forced to fight wars to defend God's gift of freedom. Indeed, the handprint of God, via the bloodshed of warfare, was defining, sculpting, and refining America the Beautiful.

Thomas Jefferson tells us:
My God how little my countrymen know what precious blessing they possess.

CHAPTER 4

God Halts Human Bondage by Saving the Union
The American Civil War

The second pair of American wars in defense of God's gift of freedom and His covenant of Global righteousness includes the American Wars of Manifest Destiny (1845-1849) and the American Civil War (1860-1865). These two major conflicts expanded the American territory from the Atlantic to the Pacific Oceans, along with, assuring that the full Union would be preserved, rather than be divided as two separate nations across the North/South, Mason/Dixon Line. God's selection of Abraham Lincoln became His set-apart spiritual leader during this Civil War; a series of brutal battles that claimed 600,000 lives. Again, just like the Revolutionary War when paired with the War of 1812 gave us a nation committed to individual and socio/political freedoms, so too God chose the Wars of Manifest Destiny paired with the American Civil War to create a large and powerful set-apart nation, America, capable of defeating the future enemies on two fronts. The repulsive, hideous, godless, macabre evil soon-to-be during the **Modern Age of Human Carnage** (1930-1945) threatened the very survival of Humankind. Clearly, God was thinking ahead when the eradication and extinction of freedom and justice were at stake.

> *Isaiah tells us....*
> *My purpose will stand...What I have*
> *planned that I will do.*

> *President James Madison told us...*
> *Only the people who govern themselves*
> *using the 10-Commandments will retain*
> *their liberties.*

In the year 1860 the Congressional House was divided North/South. This nation could not possibly stand intact. Soon Abraham Lincoln was elected President causing the South to dismiss the notion that the political conflicts between the North and South might be resolved in peaceful ways. They knew that Lincoln was fully committed to the abolition of slavery. As political positions hardened between the North and South and the threat of further separation prevailed, compromise virtually became impossible. The cultural divide between an agrarian and industrial community was too great. In reaction, the armed forces of the Confederate States of America opened fire on Fort Sumter in South Carolina, an installation controlled by the Federal government. When compared to the South, the North had vastly superior technology, a firmer economic base, a much larger population base, a stable financial position, and a greater industrial capacity. Yet the South insisted on maintaining its class-based demographics and its agricultural, slave-based economy. Within this political reality, the American Civil War had two Divine goals. *One*, to eliminate the horrors of slavery and declare freedom for all humans. *Two*, to prepare a unified and powerful union to do battle with the soon-to-come WW II and its Modern Age of Human Carnage (1930-1945). This well-built nation could have prevented the extinction of the human race and an evil Planet that could never have survived unscathed in the Galaxy.

Abraham Lincoln was determined to save the Union at any cost. In 1863 his spiritual goals were Divinely realized. The greatest battle in the Civil War was fought with God's intervention at Gettysburg, PA that resulted in a Northern victory. A few months later in the town of Vicksburg, Mississippi, the Confederacy was cut in half resulting in the unconditional surrender of its forces. Many important battles were yet to be fought during the next two years; however the superior manpower and firepower of the North eventually wore out the South's resistance. As the Confederate forces became decimated, on April 9th, 1865 at Appomattox, Virginia, Robert E. Lee formally surrendered to Ulysses S. Grant. About two weeks later the Confederate General Joseph Johnson admitted defeat and presented his Southern Army to General William Tecumseh Sherman in North Carolina. This virtually ended the American Civil War that saved the Union and began to abolish slavery in the USA. Again, God's

Will triumphed. Prophetically, two years prior on January 1st, 1863, Lincoln issued the ***Emancipation Proclamation*** declaring the beginning of the end of slavery with the 13th Amendment being added to the US Constitution, officially passed by Congress in the year 1865.

The Civil War issue of slavery and its abolition took a number of step-by-step transformations. As early as September 18th, 1850 President Fillmore signed the ***Fugitive Slave Bill*** that returned runaway slaves back to their Southern masters, who first had to prove ownership. This Federal Law also applied to free States. Fugitive slaves were denied trial by jury and the right to be a witness in a court room. Caucasians who helped runaway slaves were imprisoned or heavily fined. As expected, this clause was opposed by the North, but fully endorsed by the slave-owner. As art precedes ideas, in the year 1852 Harriet Beecher Stowe published her novel, ***Uncle Tom's Cabin*** that sold over 300,000 copies. This novel was a heart-rending story of a Christian slave who rescued a white child and then was sold to a sadistic slave master, who had him flogged to death. This book became so popular that it became converted into a play that ran locally for many months before being performed in the National Theatre. Stowe's work re-energized the anti-slave movement across the country. In reaction to the continuing bloodshed between abolitionists and slave owners Congress repealed the Missouri Compromise of 1820 that made Maine a free State and Missouri a slave State. Congress also passed the ***Kansas/Nebraska Act*** that authorized settlers to chose between slave and free. This caused the territory of Kansas to be politically separated into two governments. Then, Congressman Abraham Lincoln condemned the Kansas/Nebraska Act and called for the full emancipation of all slaves. He said: ***No man is good enough to govern another man without the other's consent.*** In Kansas, abolitionists became victims to murder, mutilation, and beheading, while their Senators were beaten right in their chambers.

God's plan to deliver freedom and justice of all sorts to His beloved souls took the form of the American Civil War, whereby the freeing of slaves and the preservation of the Union became His principal objectives. Indeed, God is all-knowing. God is all-mighty. God is ever-present. God is fully righteous. God is freedom and just. Henceforth, both slavery and later the shameless evil of the Modern Age of Human Carnage (1930-1945) that threatened the very survival of the human race would never be ignored by Him. With the blood of 600,000 Civil War casualties, God avenged the cruelty of human bondage imposed on the Black Race and others. As a result, with the American Union now intact, 75-years later God would be avenging the slaughter of 100 million innocent men, women, and children during the godless reigns of Western Europe and Asia. If truth be told by historians and theologians, the American Civil War (1860-1865), when coupled with Wars of Manifest Destiny (1844-1849) had far-reaching theological and spiritual implications and international consequences. God's plan of a Global Covenant of Righteousness had to include His gift of freedom and justice, even at the cost of substantial human bloodshed.

During the Civil War the preserving of the Union and the freeing of human bondage took seventeen major battles. Unyielding, the Deep South with its agri-based cotton economy needed slave labor to prosper. The cultural market south of the Mason/Dixon line was premised upon the aristocracy of the wealthy planter. He was a cotton-king who was chivalrous and committed to a spurious Code of Honor. In real time, the North and South were two dissimilar societies, with diverse outlooks, with diametrically opposed values and unlike cultural needs. Primarily in the North business wasn't agricultural, but industrial. Here, a web of railroads emerged that carried finished goods to numerous Northern marketplaces. As justification for pursuing the bloody Civil War, this fundamental industrial disparity accounted for the passion and fury felt on both sides of the Mason/Dixon line. As far back as the year 1619 AD, the first Black Africans arrived to work the Caribbean fields. Some, both Blacks and poor Whites, were treated kindly as paternal offspring; yet some were overworked and ruthlessly supervised. While the North made use of labor-saving mechanics, techniques, and procedures, the South exploited exhausted slaves for greater and greater profit. In the North, the mills in Massachusetts, the coal and oil fields in Pennsylvania, and the railroad yards in Illinois formed an industrial core that prospered this Northern region. Yet, violence in the industrial cities, public drunkenness, and labor riots were not only immoral and against God' intentions, but also questioned the precarious and unsafe living conditions of any industrial society. Within this backdrop, in the year 1860, Abraham Lincoln, without any formal education, who failed to make a workable living in a number of business and political attempts, became elected as President of the USA. Somehow, the electoral system and not by popular vote, Lincoln became Divinely chosen to lead a nation in a Civil War.

At once, South Carolina withdrew from the Union by declaring that the United States of America has now been dissolved. Both the bondage of slavery and the preservation of the American Union needed to thwart the contemptible evil of the Modern Age of Human Carnage (1940-1945) became the two Divine freedom concerns of the American Civil War. Also, in the middle of his presidential term, Lincoln demonstrated his long-term wisdom by signing the Land Grant Act that gave each State 30,000 acres to set up colleges in agriculture, engineering, and military science. Today in the 21st century the 50 States boast of the best colleges in technology, agri/science, space science, and research. The war to preserve the Union began at Fort Sumter, an island Federal installation off the harbor of Charleston. Lincoln declared that the States have no right to secede and was determined to defend all Federal properties.

Seventy-three Federal soldiers were prepared to fight for the Fort but had to surrender to the South Carolinian militia and the Confederacy. One day later, President Lincoln called for 75,000 troops to reverse this insurrection. Steadily, the Southern States joined the Confederacy. Tennessee, Mississippi, Georgia, Alabama, Louisiana, along with Texas, Virginia, Arkansas, and North Carolina that followed suit. The battle lines were positioned and drawn with 23 Northern

States opposed to 11 Southern States. Jefferson Davis, an aristocratic West Point graduate was elected as the President of the Confederacy. He was an honorable person, able speaker, and very brainy. On March 3rd 1861, under many threats of assassination, Lincoln arrived by secret train to Washington for his Inaugural Address declaring his commitment to preserve the Union. Within six months, the North began to blockade with naval artillery the Southern ports. The Union had 90 gunboats. The fluctuating disposition of this War became apparent in three major battles. In his attempt to control Western Virginia, General Robert E, Lee was summarily defeated. In turn, on the banks of the Potomac the Union was crushed at Bulls Bluff. On November 7th, General Ulysses S Grant was victorious in Missouri on the banks of the Mississippi River. Both West Point graduates, Confederate General Lee and Union General McClellan faced each other with sizeable forces. At the major battle of Bull Run in Virginia, the capital of the Confederacy, Richmond, 34,000 Union troops were routed and forced in a orderly retreat back to Washington. The Civil War battles, both victory and defeat, continued to seesaw for both Southerners and Northerners.

The spiritual/military genius of President Lincoln was repeatedly demonstrated by his selection and promotion of aggressive "fighting Generals" and the removal of passive "spineless Generals," who delayed decisive fighting in the heat of battle. General McClellan was a coward and proven by history to be militarily incompetent. He kept asking Lincoln for additional troops to assure his personal safety. In battle, McClellan moved his troops by the half-step causing Lincoln to relieve him of his post as General-in-Chief of all US forces. Out of political expediency Lincoln appointed General McClellan to Command the Army of the Potomac. Otherwise, by his aggressive, bold and assertive tactics, General Ulysses S. Grant over and over again became victorious in battle. On April, 1862, during the first land victory for the Union, Grant with 17,000 men captured a key Confederate Fort on the Cumberland River in Kentucky. Instantly, he was promoted to Major General. Soon thereafter without delay Grant took Fort Henry and demanded its unconditional surrender. At the Battle of Shiloh, Tennessee both armies fought to a standstill in a long and bloody engagement. General Grant proved his tactical skills by outmaneuvering 40,000 Confederate troops to a military draw. Yet his battle toll was 2000 Yankees captured, with 13,000 casualties. The South lost 10,000 men including its General Johnson. General Robert E. Lee took Johnson's place. The Christian song, ***Battle Hymn of the Republic***, was composed as a tribute to this battle. Meanwhile, at the Confederate Capitol, in Richmond Virginia, the Army of the Potomac under General McClellan met in battle with General Lee and proved that the selection of Richmond as the Confederate capital was a colossal, tactical mistake. For a number of military reasons, choosing Charleston, South Carolina would have better served the South. Again the Northern General proved timid and incompetent. McClellan forces moved unhurriedly, waiting for the artillery to arrive with its big guns, allowing General Lee to move his troops speedily away from the Union forces. At Richmond, the Union casualties were high. McClellan took a severe hammering and barely escaped with his life. Lincoln was displeased with McClellan's excuses, always asking for a justification of his unwise delays. Once more Lincoln had to remove McClellan from command. When he was in a favorable position to win a key battle, McClellan failed again to defeat the Army of Northern Virginia. At Antietam it was his unwillingness to seize the initiative. McClellan's military cowardice turned a sure victory into a stalemate. No doubt, history will show that McClellan was both a pompous coward and highly incompetent. Not unlike the reason for this command replacement, General Ambrose also was cowardly defeated at Fredericksburg by General Robert E. Lee. Add, General Burnside, who was defeated as a "combat inept" officer who led his troops into deep mud caused by torrential rains. Burnside, not unlike McClellan, was also instantly relived of command duty. All in all, Lincoln's forte as Commander-in-Chief was his expertise to judge and promptly act upon the military performances of his General corps. No doubt, the saving of the Union had long-term implications for God's gift of freedom. It meant the very survival of the human race 75-years later during the Bondage Era of the Modern Age of Human Carnage (1930-1945). This evil threat to both democracy and God's gift of freedom by Nazism, Communism, Fascism, and the crimes against humanity by Red China and Japan required a strong and powerful "righteous nation," like America, to conquer the enveloping wickedness gripping Planet Earth. So too, the bondage of slavery was of deep Divine concern that was forthright addressed during the American Civil War. Abraham Lincoln, a deeply religious Judeo/Christian, was chosen by God to spiritually lead and manage both the bondage issues of slavery and the extinction of humanity.

On January 1st, 1863 in Washington DC President Lincoln signed the ***Emancipation Proclamation*** freeing all slaves in the South. This Act validated God's intention to free all humans from socio/political bondage. To Lincoln, the old ways of the South must be declared obsolete and give way to new ways. This G0d-scripted proclamation, not unlike the Declaration of Independence and the US Constitution, which caused jubilation to spread across many parts of the land especially in churches, declared that America has become the land of the free and just and the home of the brave. It was estimated that between 2-3 million slaves were set free by this decree. Seeking liberty, what began to take place was an exodus from the Black South to the North by land and sea. Three weeks later the first Black military unit was officially formed and armed to fight for the Union. Black militia sprung up in Kansas, Louisiana, and South Carolina already having incurring death and battle wounds. Soon thereafter, July of 1863, the most noteworthy battle of the Civil War took place at Gettysburg, located in South Central Pennsylvania, a small town with ten roads leading into it. Here it was General Robert E. Lee's intention to take the fight to the North with three corps, I, II, and III. It was a brilliant military plan. However, here God's involvement could readily be seen in the bravery and tactics countered by the Northern troops. At this location in central Pennsylvania, despite the decisive military advantage of the Confederacy, after three days of rivers of bloodshed, the Northern Army of the Potomac ultimately defeated the Southern Army of Northern Virginia commanded by General Robert E. Lee's 14,000 troops. Even after the infamous charge by the South's General Pickett coupled with the artillery exchange by North and South, historians wondered how the North ever gained such a a victory. God's handprint was clearly visible at this decisive battle. As General Pickett foolishly formed a single line a mile long caused the Union troops to shred it with swords and bayonets. General Lee screamed-out repeatedly "it's all my fault" and submitted his resignation to President Jefferson Davis, who refused to accept it. During this 3-day unstoppable battle, the North and South each lost 20,000 + men. General Meade, who was loyal to Grant, his commander-in-chief, and who headed the Army of the Potomac never panicked, used excellent military judgment in deploying his men, and delivered troops as needed to vulnerable targets. His reputation as a fierce fighter caught the attention of Lincoln. Meade became a true hero of Gettysburg, a war-defining battle. Today, a tourist visiting Gettysburg is sure to experience a spiritual sensation of the unresolved souls of the dead soldiers. To fight another day General Robert E. Lee with his tail tucked between his legs led a 17-long wagon train filled with Confederate casualties and wounded to safer locations in the South.

A few months later on November 29th at Gettysburg President Lincoln inspired by the Holy Spirit understood his destiny and drafted a speech to deliver his celebrated **Gettysburg Address**. Lincoln elevated the War to a higher moral level to a crowd numbered about 15,000, which listened intently to the message of his speech. It read: *Fourscore and seven years ago our fathers brought forth upon this continent a new nation conceived in liberty.... a final resting place of those who have given their lives that a nation might...that the nation under God shall have a new birth of freedom...and that the government of the people, by the people, for the people shall not perish from the Earth.*

Meanwhile General Ulysses S Grant, who was never accepted or respected by his military colleagues, those pompous West Point General Corps, continued to win difficult battles. President Lincoln had to politically protect General Grant for his assertive and fearless tactics that produced his back-to-back military victories. On July 4th, 1863 at Vicksburg, Mississippi the Confederate General unconditionally surrendered to Grant. It was a catastrophic, emotional defeat for Southerners in a war that conquered the South by denying them the needed war resources, giving the Union absolute control over north/south waterways. It was the strategic Union plan to cut off the Confederacy from the outside world with a blockade of the Atlantic Ocean and the Gulf of Mexico; while intersecting the Mississippi River. This Union strategic Plan plus General Grant's tactics proved brilliant. Later on November 25th 1863, Grant, with an infantry charge, drove the finest soldiers of the Confederacy off the high ground in Chattanooga, Tennessee. The South was swept off Missionary Hill while Grant's troops wildly celebrated victory. On May 6th 1864 in the Virginian backwoods, both Generals, Grant and Lee, both claimed victory after a turbulent battle, whereby the Union lost 17,000 men and the South 8000. Now as a Lieutenant General, Grant became almost as popular as President Lincoln, who issued a blank check to Grant to devise the necessary strategic plans to win and end the Civil War. Now Grant had full command of the Army of the Potomac and requested and was granted 500,000 additional troops. By the close of the Civil War, General Grant became the most notable commander in the Union and became President of the USA in 1868.

Another distinguished military officer serving under General Grant was General William Tecumseh Sherman. He was a Captain in the Wars of Manifest Destiny. His signature victory that leveled Atlanta, Georgia into ashes came about after many months of artillery bombing and battle skirmishes. Sherman ordered the total burning down of the City of Atlanta, Georgia and continued to march eastward to Savannah. On Christmas Eve, Sherman telegraphed Lincoln with a holiday gift of a total victory over Savannah that yielded a bounty of captured 150 heavy guns and ammunition plus 25,000 bales of cotton. These Confederate defeats virtually ended the ante-bellum culture of the South and the freeing of thousands of slaves. Sherman was accused by the Southern press corps and the Southern elite of crimes against humanity. Yet otherwise was true. As Sherman's Generals approached the Atlanta in three directions and destroyed everything in its path by first warning residents to evacuate, Northern reporters considered Sherman's tactics humane and the best way to gut the Confederate's power to desist and to quickly end the war. Likewise, he was cherished by his troops and accepted as a great military strategist. For the next two centuries Sherman's philosophy of battle has been emulated in military colleges, and widely both in WWII and in the Israeli/Palestinian Wars.

After the defeats in both Nashville and Shenandoah, General Lee met with General Grant at the Appomattox Courthouse and surrendered his Army of Northern Virginia thereby ending the American Civil War. Sworn in as President of a second term, Lincoln said it was God's Will and Providence to forgive his enemies "with malice toward none and charity for all." Lincoln was hailed as the Man of all Ages. Yet, at the altar of freedom and the sacrifice of 600,000 dead in battle proved to be costly. The devastation incurred in the American Civil War left the Southern half the nation in ruins and with a multitude of casualties. For the civilian populace-at-large: to grasp the true devastation of war occurred when for the first time in history photos were produced that revealed the horrors of battle. This reality left President Lincoln in a deep, irrevocable, emotional depression. It has been said by theologians that God and His mercy, love, and compassion allowed John Wilkes Booth, a demon-possessed actor, to assassinate the President. Now in heaven, President Lincoln fulfilled his destiny to promote God's gift of freedom by freeing the slaves and preserving the Union for later wars. On December 18th 1865 the 13th Amendment was added to the US Constitution declaring that neither slavery nor involuntary servitude shall be allowed to exist in America. Three years later the 14th Amendment further added that Blacks were full citizens.

<u>*The New Ideas generated by the Post-Civil War*</u>

First and foremost, all "politics" is a territorial expression. This human endeavor is articulated by all of humanity as neuro/framed with words and symbols. It would be naive to assume that the art of community inter-communications and governance is primarily resolved by way of the conditioning to external/enviromental stimuli. Democraatic politics, as usually implemented by natural leadership, are survival alternatives offered by the effort to those ruled, not rulers. As a key, historical example, the universal, insatiable thirst for citizen emancipation can't be indefinitely oppressed by the politics of tyranny. Accordingly we can expect that for any true democracy, the principles of **Bio/Politics** will be discoursed, enacted, and embraced by its citizenry; when viewed as the next higher plane of socio/political enlightenment. In the immediate future, America, as the beacon of Global, ideational illumination, ought to consider making additional modifications to its US Constitution via Amendments; such as with a Bill of Genetic Rights, primarily addressing educational and job issues, a Bill of Victim Rights, addressing law&order, and a Bill of Patient Rights, addressing the infectious diseases arising out of the assorted metabolics and immunities found within a cultural diversity.

Our modern-day politics, via our territorial urges, cover more than just the possession of land and property rights. As anciently institutionalized by formal Codes, e.g. Hammarabic and Mosaic, tribalisms have been translated as the prescripts of economic affluence and governing Power. The drive to explore, property rights, inheritances, rule of law, and the military defense of borders, because of its terretorial commonality among and across tribes, range from the aboriginal clan to the larger and/or most civilized of nation/states. Most probably, the DNA of territoriality is fundamentally imprinted within our "genetic motherboard." However it is important to note that this same tribal DNA is only partially related to our bonding urges. Political behavior is different than intra-species "bonding." While the former is impersonally related to the more-remote, territorial matters, the latter addresses the intimate conditions which remain person-to-person. Within a wide-range of living styles; courting, mating, sexuality, family modes, and nesting all are potentially identifiable as components of social bonding. For science with a phylogenetic perspective, the bio/social studies of the ***Political Genome vs the Bonding Genome*** ought to be researched as separate systems with separate subsystems. Likewise out of a bigger picture, bio/political science ought to devote itself to the study of the perennial macro-plagues of Humankind that include modern warfare (law&order), pandemic disease (health and longevity), along with starvation (poverty and capitalism). These Malthusian Threats might be alleviated or forestalled with a deeper knowledge of Bio/Politics and its allied manifestations of Bio/Bonding.

It isn't chance happenstance that after the Civil War and at the onset of the Modern Era the full-family of nations craves the territorial successes of Western democracies and their free marketplaces. This covetness includes an orbit of ideas which underlie the: (a) structure of government; (b) course of practical politics; (c) economic capitalism; (d) reliance on science; (e) use of higher mathematics and data processing; (e) implementation of human rights; (f) ongoing R&D of technology; all as modulated by (g) the roots of the Judeo/Christian Code, which serves as the "vagus nerve" of these "great ideas." Regrettably, while all can partake in these great thoughts, not all human bio/breeds seem neuro/equipped with equal proficiency to live-out the ambitions and aspirations of the American type of transcendent society. Hence an axiom emerges: *living successfully in a free and just society seems to require the fuller, neuro/genetic "tribal development" of its composite cortex.* This yet-arguable theorem of future bio/science holds true both for individuals and the diverse bio/breeds of Mankind. In potential, this principle would compose a political platform for a truer, cultural diversity for future democratic governance. We now know beyond the shadow of doubt that the psyche level of the lobes and tissues of the brain of the Homo Sapien delivers to democratic communities: (a) greater self-control; (b) better judgment; (c) socio/appropriate emotions; (d) organizational efficiency; and (e) the neuro/delay mechanisms to assure more, adaptive self-reliance and decision-making. Indded, democracy only can be fashioned out of a unique Political Genome. Without eugenic intercession, not all the bio/breeds of Mankind are fully capable of supplying these socio/political qualities for freedom living. Moreover as the floundering United Nations has verified, as we continue to tread laterally in either a politically conservative or liberal direction, there remain to be few, useful solutions for the upgrading of the territorial plights of Humankind. Via Global politics; war, disease, bondage, and starvation continue to bludgeon the human condition. Indeed, the political sidestepping of the UN are taking us nowhere. So too in the USA, whether Democrat, Republican, Independent, Left, Right, or Center, the entire political spectrum has become stalemated and "politically inert." Similarly in the world context, national relationships have become weary, dreary, confrontational, and idling by the babble of spewing spin-masters of leadership. No matter how hard they try with "slipping and sliding," stuck-in-the-mud bromides regurgitated by pundits of the international Media, all the while the insights needed for a more wholesome, less vitriolic, democracy yet-remains Globally unattainable. Why so? Plainly, what is needed by the international politics-of-the-day is the acceptance of a bold thrust of "vertical launches" of neo/ideas. At the bottom of it, diplomatic discussions must be rotated and pointed vertically, "upward," away from the "lateral now" of politics-as-usual. Only by veering our "Global mindset" in this upturn mode will we be able to "find and fulfill" the designs and intents of the wars of freedom. Verily as an historical simile, liken to the great, oceanic explorations of the 15th-16th centuries, only the freeing-up of our "political ships of state" willing to sail assuredly in unchartered waters, can America and the world become and able to discover the more useful answers to our socio/cultural challenges, dilemmas, and contentions. The "freedom vision" promises a progressive thrust away from the stale ideas of the times—whether the politics are Left or Right or Centrist.

As a start to the inclusion of bio/politics into our governmental, educational, industrial, and medical instiutions, the sketching via "DNA/bar-coding" of targeted citizens with our known bio/technology (e.g. criminals, émigrés, students, teachers, business managers, and/or police) should be able to provide us with a "political peek" into the "black box" of our subGenomes. By correlating freedom issues with bio/social merit these "genetic shadows" reflect the composite Political Genome of humanity, which could reveal the secrets of a truer, Jeffersonian democracy. As failed alternatives to democracy; the conventional dictatorships; oligarchies, monarchies, fascisms, Nazism, and Communism, all have been forever discredited as valid territorial options by the unrelenting, evolutionary forces of neuro/history. Why so? Perhaps in concert, these "politically premature" models of government have been behaving overly centralized and cruel; therefore, neuro/spiritually unacceptable. Or, perhaps the unacceptance of a fuller participation of democratic ways&means, either by the common folks, illegal immigrants, or the cloistered minorities, is related to the prefrontal evolution of the brain structure. If so, then for the neuro/political scientist, it ought to seem evident that irrespective of cultural orientation or the universalality of human-rights, only a bio/amended democracy is capable of pacifying the hearts-and-souls of nations. All in all, this proposition should be telling us that we need a closer, bio/scientific peek at the territorial DNA/ mechanisms underlying our political theories.

No doubt, the micro-examination of the Political Genome will have to become the foremost challenge for any governmental progress to occur. Thusfar, over the centuries we've learned that any political revolution is a process, not an event. During the next, few decades, what will unfold is the onset of a *3ʳᵈ American Revolution*. Surely, this promising new-era of American life is confronting us; energized as a counterpoint in defiance to the fading, but yet-entrenched, liberal/secular decadence of the past century. In support of this conjecture, in his book, *From Dawn to Decadence,* Jacques Barzun, a noted and highly respected historian of France, tells us that from the 15ᵗʰ century through the end of the 20ᵗʰ century marked a distinct Era of human enlightenment. It might be called the Renaissance Era--as contrasted to the Renaissance Period of the 14ᵗʰ thru the 16ᵗʰ centuries. American politicians ought to carefully note the implications of Barzun's insights. What he submitted was that the Age of the Western World, including the American Empire, are soon to become yesterday's history. The forces of Malthusian decadence, which is defiling the most-civilized segment of the Globe, i.e. the West, has caught up with the progressive thrust of our ideo/techno contributions, thereby inverting the positive momentum of future, civilized advancement. If so, will the USA, which launched the human-rights movements for the Global communities to politically emulate and absorb, be remembered *only* as the great emancipator of human freedom? Or for its future, will the USA move-on to incorporate the upcoming ideas of greater relevancy; such as, by incorporating the politics of the DNA into its US Constitution? If we bravely accomplish this daring step-forward, our democratic politics also would be launching a new era of human evolution by assuring the continuation of our world leadership of ideas, prosperity, and tech/customs.

Chronologically recorded as the original, American Revolution, the first colonial uprising occurred long *before* the year 1776 AD. From the latter part of the 17th century to this watershed year, historians have been telling us that there were a number of socio/political metamorphoses erupting within the New World. Our Northern Hemisphere, bubbling as a "communal caldron" between the years 1680 to 1776 AD was consumed with passion and a burning desire for freedom designed for an autonomous, national citizenry. This patriotic mood-state engulfed the psyche of the American Colonies. As a counterpoint to the Euro/Anglo "status-quo," the political cravings of a maturing, post-adolescent America bitterly resented the arduous controls and exploitations by Mother England. Over the decades of bitter strife, driven by the wars of ideas, the American yearnings for national liberty continued to foment throughout our cities, towns, and rural countryside. Accordingly, an emotionally charged, revolutionary script began to compose a national drama calling for a new type of governing politic. These writings, now encased in the National Archives in Washington DC, were being intuited and shaped, pointing to an accelerated, spirit-of-freedom which spread like wildfire across the far-and-near localities of our original, coastal landscape. Psycho/philosophically, these communal mood-states, which targeted religious, economic, and political emancipation, erupted out-of our existential DNA/nature, as motivated by the magnetism of "love." ***Indeed for each of us, our thirst for God's freedom is the most-basic, operational component of love.*** Creation is love. Politics is (or ought to be) love motivated. Love doesn't and can't exist without the freedom to love. Accordingly, the spiritual yearnings for "political freedom" must be viewed as an irrepressible component of our very innate existence. As a matter of simple deduction, the genes have been the carriers of our appetites for freedom. Thus with paradox, "compassionate America" after the Civil War eventually became a novel society that emerged out-of a series of failed, governing experiments of the yore of Europe, probably Asia, and as likely, Africa. In the 21st century we must think that what was once unthinkable prowling below the subteranean core of our political subconscious was the "communal gene" of the Northland People of Europe/Asia Proper who played the determinant role in the fashioning of our embryonic Nation. Demographically in the 18th century AD a confederated Northern, Euro/American diversity unified, gelled, and amplified as a national community, driven by the special ingredients of Old World British, Irish, Welch, Skandia, Germans, Scots, and some Huguenots. Out of this Northern/Euro "genomal cauldron" bubbled-up-and-out a bio/cultural merging of Americana with the territorial covetness and the militant vibrancy of the Viking DNA/stock. While at the same time, the military/territorial influences of the Spanish, Southern French, and Portuguese ceded, subsided, and drifted apart and away from this momentous, American-eugenic miracle.

Proverbially our next insurrection, ***The Second American Revolution,*** began as a crystallized, political event on or about the year 1776 AD. It's rallying banner extolled the importance for any nation to recognize two, novel, political parameters. *One,* that all men are created equal and should be treated accordingly. *Two,* that by providing this "equality of experience" all citizens should be afforded the maximal opportunity for life, liberty, and the pursuit of happiness- -only if they dare choose and petition. Over the years as Americans, we have been able to institutionalize, both for our nation and for much of the world-at-large, the tangible and politically palatable, legal expressions of human rights, civil liberty, social justice, and equal opportunity for economic parity. To date, these political achievement have been the crowning, Divine gift shared with its citizenry, with the family of nations, and with the future of an ever-evolving Homo Sapien. Truly as ordained by God, America the Beautiful should be proud of its human rights accomplishments. The Civil War with its 600,000 casulties can best be understood within the spiritual importance of treedom, justice and with the blood shed by Jesus at His death on the cross.

However, just like the 1st American Revolution, i.e. pre-1776 AD, which set the stage for the scripting of the Declaration of Independence and the US Constitution, the 2nd American Revolution, i.e. post-1776 AD, both modeled and broadened the American Dream for universal, socio/ political freedom. For the past 240-years, from 1776 to the year 2016, our nation has been arduously hammering-out the legal latticework needed for a fuller-bodied democracy. Thus in the fullness of time, all Americans have been afforded the governmental options of an unimpeded free-citizenry. Nonetheless for the 21st century as the proceedings of the past four decades have shown, this remarkable, 18th century epoch of political freedom has been steadily running-out of relevance. Why so? Have our ideas and ideals been merely "pie-in-the-sky" delusions? Or, unattainable, unreachable, unfeasible goals? Day by day, our seemingly noble, set-in-stone, governing axioms are proving to be immoderate;, lacking coherence, inconsistent, and politically incomplete, wanting of clearer spiritual reasoning. Since the late-20th century, the American paradigm has been methodically cracking under the weight of overtaxed irrelevancy; a nation being dissipated by self-serving cultural-politics seeking socio/dependency and exploitation; rather than, being emboldened by the "colonial Viking-character" of self-reliance. Simply stated, we're slowly discovering that there are glaring cracks and instabilities to our political structure. America has been walking on the edge of a fulcrum, trying to straddle the merits of a "laudable democracy" with the socio/predatory demands of its culturally maladaptive, conventional, legal and illegal, minorities. Conspicuously, there are major puzzle-pieces missing in our democratic game-plan. Also noticeably, the pistons of our "national goodwill" are misfiring, stalling-out the social engines of our earned and established freedoms. What is wanting? Is the human spirit so potentially corruptible that it should be expected to inevitably degrade the common-good?

Many leading Muslims are claiming that Western Democracy is dead. Maybe Americans haven't been paying close-enough attention to the instructive forces of history; being deluded by the ideological blinders of political correctness. And perhaps we, not unlike all the past revolutions of all sorts, have been lulled into thinking the myth that the driving force of our ideals have been eternally assimilated, ever-consummated, totally actualized in perpetuity, and set-in-stone fulfilled.

With much electoral dissonance in the presidential elections of the years 2000, 2004, and soon to be 2016 AD, the American citizenry has been expecting and seeking better, political answers to their tenuous circumstances. Right-reasoning and responsible voters have been whispering: why haven't the tensions among the subgroups of the American diversity subsided? Why has there been so little progress in reversing the undesirable predicaments of inner-city residents? What should we do about the growing number of unassimilated and illegal immigrants who really don't care about America as an incorporated community; e.g. those recent arrivals who seem motivated more so by a socio/psychology of exploitation of America's resources, than by their sacrifices indispensably needed for their children's future? Why do the self-serving, overstated cries of "racism," "sexism" "elderism," "anti-Semitism," anti-immigrant, and "wealth redistribution," linger-on as political ploys; slowly hanging and twisting our nation in the winds of uncertainty; seeking to divide and fragment us, rather than unite us all as Americans? Why have our Washingtonian politics been so log-jammed, inert, and stalemated by career legislators? Why are we slipping and sliding sideways, *ad nausea,* from conservative to liberal, from Democrat to Republican, from majority to minority, as if there are no other directions or solutions left to a more-viable, political lifestyle? What has dropped-out of America's 240-years of nonstop, democratic feats for human dignity?

For sure, throwing tax-monies at our socio/political enigmas hasn't and will not do the trick.

Is there any upside, glimmer of hope peeking and perking out of our political obscurity? Or as yet, are the contents of the "black box" of differences in a cultural diversity incapable of being scientifically deciphered? In many ways, what is becoming apparent is that the American Zeitgeist is being handcuffed by the joint effects of our *"Dark Age of Egalitarism"* interacting concurrently with our *"Age of Cultural Diversity."* Both "Ages" are telling us: *"....at its most fundamental level, our governments, Federal, State and Local alike, have been wrongfully pursuing the tenets of nurture in lieu of freedom from nature.* Thereby, due to the fallacies borne-out of this ideational inversion, the bio/social robustness of our originally formulated politics has been degrading, deflating, and demeaning to our personal citizenship. Can this Malthusian Forcefield, which threatens our democratic survival, be confronted and rescued politically by the inclusion of the sociology of genetics?

What is shaping is a neo/modern caste system in America. The rich are getting richer, the poor, poorer. For sooner than imagined, the work of the bio/technologists will reveal a plausible answer: *the common cause of all tyrannies seems to be based upon the exclusion of the natural-law principles of bio/behavior apart from the established, political thought systems*. As we know it today, the openhandedness of the American democracy hasn't been able to eradicate the lingering caste-system within its Social Order; especially that which has been tenaciously separating the affluent from the underclasses. Although erroneous, the hard-core socialists and Neo/Marxists have been claiming that capitalism within a democracy in time will erect a neo/caste system. In retort, bio/political scientists will be contending that it's the "territorial genes" of human bio/breeds, which are producing either affluence or poverty; irrespective and independent of the axioms of civil liberties and trade practices of the open marketplace. In view of this, are we admitting that our political/economic theories are running short-of-the-mark? Or, hypocritically are predatory? Or at the root-level, are we no more than the monarchies of old, which had feudal, class systems separating their nobility from their peons? Aren't the original tenets of free-societies and free marketplaces supposed to be compatible, compassionate, and provide all with the opportunities at a level-playing field by not fragmenting its citizenry. America certainly is unlike Nazism, which had its racial definitions of privilege as Caucasian vs the rest of the world. Nor are we like WWII's Italian and Japanese brands of fascism, which attempted to justify their tyrannies with convoluted views of national separation from "inferior peoples." So too might be argued for Socialism, Communism, and even their residue, Fidel's Cuba. De facto and in common, all these 20th century despotisms, which America has forcefully renounced, have favored their party-faithful with economic privilege, while depriving others of the same political rights and economic occasions. One ought to wonder: are the modern-day democracies also culpable and capable of these same inequities, especially when State-sponsored, reverse bigotry prevails, denying the natural, genetic rights of the most-capable of its citizenry?

With a continuing exposition of its political spin-offs, the philosophical acceptance of the "genetic vision" can be sustained only by the revealing breakthroughs of the feats of the dehuminizing mega-technologies. Especially as they are related to: (a) the output accretions by gigga-bite computers which are capable of extracting-out voluminous, yet-hidden DNA-patterns; (b) a fuller array of elements located within the genetic cosmos, which moght be gauged and revealed by bar-coding micro/technology; and (c) the potential amplification by scholars and mathematicians of bio/genetic theories. Moreover acting as a counterweight, delicately balanced upon a fulcrum, these "equations of change" will be: (a) offsetting the "dollar failures" of today's socio/political programs; (b) neutralizing the disillusionments of the non-sequiturs of legal events; and (c) welcoming the differential, performance expectations of our cultural diversity. Axiomatically, true revolutions of thought always consist of positive and negative valances trying to tip-over the fulcrum of progress. This repositioning of the human mind will be creating a new Philosophy of Governing; mainly *The Age of Bio/Politics* that will constitute the leading focus of governance. With this new scholarship, along with the searching-out of the mathematical relationships of territorial genes, via bio/technology, the sifting among the DNA building-blocks, known as the A, T, C, G, along with the billions of combinations and permutations which they generate, migbt come the in-vogue science for a new millennium. Verily, the *Age of Bio/Behavior* has descended upon us. Moreover in support of the workings of the Political Genome, the most-modern principles of chemistry, biology, and physics will be called-upon to help solve the enigmas generated by the falsehoods of the psychological, sociological, anthropological, and political establishments. All of which in common, have been zealously and incorrectly committed to the efficacy of the "unit of experience." With the aid of future mega-computers, which already are capable of generating trillions of calculations per gigga/second, the technological progress for these scientific efforts will be at first a trickle, slowly accelerating, then snowballing, so as to push Mankind's "envelope of insights" out to a higher orbit; thereby cueing politicians that a new Era of scientific and philosophical enlightenment is on-hand. With carefully worded hypotheses emanating out of the results of integrated, multi-science inquiries, scientists of both the hard and soft persuasions, will be able to better account for the puzzling array of complex, human behavior, including our politics. Eureka: the understanding, control of, and forecasting of bio/political events will be conceptually italicized by this new, bio/social philosophy of Humankind.

By way of a Bill of Patient Rights, a new ***Bio/Social Medicine*** will be the first to hatch out of the "genetic vision." This surge of bio/theory will cause the creation and funding of differential, treatment options for ethnics, genders, races, the young turks, and old bulls. Tactically, physicians will be basing their diagnostics/therapeutics/prognoses upon the images of DNA bar-codes. So too, medical insurance providers will follow suit by funding targeted, tailored services for the multiplicity of bio/social groups, and no longer for humans-in-general.

For example, what will appear are Centers for the Bio/Propensities of Afro/diseases, specializing in the accounting and treatment of the higher-incidences of their race-specific, medical problems. Likewise the same would hold true for the Hispanic/Indian, Mediterranean, Asian, Afro/Hispanic and Viking-esque maladies. Along with; the diseases of females, ailments of males, maladies striking the young, and afflictions of the elderly. With proper consultation Congress will respond legislatively, hopefully out of scientific wisdom and not by minority coercion or political correctness, which reflexively has tended to claim victim, retributional guilt. By partially and gradually shifting our vast, research entitlements from drug to gene interventions, from universal to targeted medical care, from general to specialized hospitals and Centers, the citizen tax-dollar burdens should be better served and more-lightly borne.

In addition to medical genetics, which will be committed to the practice of bio/social care, an unprecedented political focus on the "DNA of crime" will materialize and be repositioned as high-priority for our law&order policies. Sooner than imagined also as part of the Political Genome, the field of **Genetic Criminology** in many ways will be able to identify asocial and antisocial DNA/propensities, according to demographic groups, pre-parents, children, and even in fetuses. In general we now know, these kinds of criminal anomalies are personality bio/types; some who feel little-to-none, bonded affiliation toward neighbors. With convoluted thinking, these aberrant, asocial-types tend to rationalize: "...*why not* act-out with violence, abuse, or exploitation of others for immediate, personal gratification and monetary gain." For these bio/abnormalities, the "emotions of neighboring," which has been a non-negotiable, critical pillar for civilization, evokes little-to-nothing feelings of human identification. So goes the twisted reasoning of criminal bio/types. They, although accounting for only 1%-2% of the general population, are irredeemable, irreversible DNA/outlaws, who remain unduly troublesome and costly to 98% of the more, responsible citizenry. Indeed in the politics of the future, the time has come for recidivist DNA/offenders to be socially identified and contained through the efforts of the hard, biological sciences and their allied technologies, always as modulated by the dictates of compassionate law-enforcement and universal human rights.

Other than world-terrorism, who would deny that today's rate of bio/criminal behaviors has become an "unacceptable obscenity" to a free society. Especially, at an incidence-level which seems destined to encumber a nation finding itself at the cutting edge of human evolution. As national policy committed to credible&just DNA/blueprinting, criminals who have relied on evading the technological limitations of law-enforcement, will quickly lose their sinister edge. The shroud of secrecy, which has been shielding the "dispassionate criminal," will be shredded and torn-away from their moorings of "bio/social hate." The "temptations of crime," when cleverly marketed by law-enforcement, would cause the potential perpetrators to realize that they run a high, personal risk of near-immediate identification, near-certain capture, along with, inevitable, long-term incarceration--or as some have suggested, more ideally, "public reckoning." Ideally as a political goal for the near future, heinous crime in a Jeffersonian democracy ought to be pegged at a trickle. The national crime-rate, estimated between 1%-2% of the general population, should strive to be at least at par with the dubious, zero-tolerance of dictatorships. Then, and only then, will the dreams of our Founding Fathers approach their wishes for a transcending society laced with communities liberated from heinous behaviors. Freedom-based societies are always undully victimized by the henious criminal. For society-at-large, genetically generated, asocial and antisocial personalities account for most of the heinous, horrific, and flagrant crimes against life's, vulnerable innocence--whether by individual, within the community, or against humanity-at-large. With DNA research, it becomes possible to see the dispositions toward bio/crime can be first identified, computer cataloged, and then, within the code of human rights and liberties, eugenically backbred out of the evolutionary chain. As a birthright, citizens living in democratic societies deserve the political intervention of this line of tax-sponsored bio/ research. How so? First, to identify and integrate the genetic factor in crime management within a US Constitutional Amendment which formally recognizes the *rights of victims*. Only then, with the knowledge gained from these DNA studies of *lawbreakers*, might a number of creative, legislative bills be proposed and enacted by *lawmakers* of all party and ideological affiliations. Concomitantly, preventive programs also are urgently needed via the enactment of DNA/counseling centers, in which their basic objective ought to be to avert the escalation of the interbreeding of criminal genes. To boot, instead of the hideous practices of abortion clinics, a number of preventive "eugenic hubs" of planned parenthood might be organized so as to advise childless couples, both pre-wed and newlywed adults, of their gene composition. With time and legislative wisdom as partners along with the DNA/ control of bio/criminal behavior, the appalling outcomes of impersonal evildoing are bound to wane. Especially, those sexual predators who victimize children by snuffing-out the beauty of their innocence. With DNA-based, law enforcement the rate of incarcerations ought to tumble.

In addition to the genetic-based inroads made into the food, crime, and health-care fields, also to be considered as part of the Political Genome will be the pivotal issues which daily impact the formal education of our offspring, along with the decision-making in the business sector. Surely, formal education and practical business go hand-in-hand. Primed and nudged to the forefront of political awareness, we can expect a flip-flop shifting in pedagogical and corporate theories to veer away from the coddling of over-nurtured pupils and employees--on to the tough-love funneling of bio/performance talents, via the intercessions of the DNA. Specifically what will be seen is the ebbing of "acquisition principles" of human behavior, which have been over-featuring:(1) psychological conditioning; (2) expectancy training; and (3) socio/ cognitive brainwashing. With the piecemeal reorientation of classroom and workplace methodologies, the fanning-out of the *Learning Genome* will cause both the school and working milieu to take-on a new erudition and new criteria for performances. First, as workshops to aid teachers and managers to train on the principles of bio/performance. Followed by, coursework in the Schools of Education and Business on the bio/nature of learning, as networked with the DNA/paradigms of basic, intellectual skills; that is, the innate, fundamental talents of language, space, and number. When tailored for a bio/curricula, by way of the elements of the Learning Genome, this re-teaching by way of trainer seminars will cause the fields of both ***Pedagogical Genetics*** and ***Industrial Eugenics*** to flourish, thereby taking-on identities of their own. Politically, the real-world successes from these efforts then will be submitted as planks to the platforms of National, State, and Local, political conventions. Thus in time, the ideational balance of "nature vs nurture" will prevail to disperse and replace the wobbling, learning tenets employed during the past decades. In the future classroom "no child (or worker) will be left behind" as they have been in the inner-city schools. Moreover the ruminations by Liberal educators and managers, which have been taunting and tainting our performance environments for many years, will become permanently scrapped in the junk-yards of ideas gone by.

In the recent past, across the educational/industrial establishment, the three principles of psychological learning, i.e. conditioning, expectancy learning, and socio/cognitive brainwashing, have been touted and misapplied as the cardinal tools-of-the-trade. However at the crux of the next phase of educational/industrial evolution, the conversion of our mindset orientation from nurture-to-nature will override this faulted triad of failed, Liberal, tutorial techniques. Accordingly as a radical harvest in America-at-large, a new breed of educator/manager will be mandated to retire the past and introduce the future to a ***genetic-based democracy.*** Alike as camp-followers in the search for a higher truth, a new cadre of bio/political historians will find themselves in a position to better appraise the diminished outcomes tolerated by our current, post Cival War democracy, while simultaneously evaluating the potential merits of rising ideas, such as the socio/political instruments of bio/performances. By legislative fiat, the "genetic vision" will introduce new tech/ concepts to both pedagogy and industry alike, as devised to yield more-reliable and more-valid "decision indicators" for teachers, managers, parents, and legislators. Accordingly, b***io/ psychometric evaluations*** will be devised to crosssectionally assay the complex ratios of bio/potential inheritances as numerically related into classroom/workplace performances. For the schools, ***"talent contours"*** would be formulated to identify a broad range of innate, learning functions--ranging from precocity to normal to retardation to anomaly. And for corporate settings, if and when made "politically palatable" for our current-day, culturally correct society, ***brain scans*** too might be utilized to identify the adaptive capacities of the dozen or so bio/breeds who labor within our demographically diverse workplaces. Hopefully with these types of bio/ scientific clarity, the cluster-patterning of student and worker adroitness as composed to appear on computer monitors, the cerebral talents (and/or defects) which regulate a wide range of expressions will become visible; such as, music; art; language;

gross motor movements, as in sport; spatial; mathematical; leadership; finer-motor dexterity; along with the wide-orbit of communicative proficiencies Then, these profiles could be made available to teachers, managers, and/or political leaders.

For the State-funding of socio/political DNA/policies, what this might mean for the real-world education of "preschools for tots" lies the socio/value of a universal system of bio/education, possibly ala the Montessori Method. She, born in the 19th century, was an Italian visionary for the future of 21 century education. Dr. Maria Montessori, with her avant-garde theories, sought to *unfold* a child's "bio/capacites," rather than educationally *intrude upon* this same natural capacity. Undoubtedly a century ahead of her time, Maria's basic principles of early education pointed inadvertently to the functioning of the innate, individual genes. In support, since the 1960s AD the extensive body of work conducted by neuro/psychological scientists has alluded the validity of the Montessorian notions of bio/education. These scientists in their research have revealed that the early, developmental stages, i.e. 2-5 years, are capable of accelerated, neurological growth, which is self-networking and highly sensitive to a time-factor. Maria intuited that during a handful of these critical, preschool years, the "nerves" mesh "adaptively and meaningfully" via the stimuli of enriched, concept-oriented experiences. Since, we have learned that for each human life a well-targeted, preschool setting can become irreversibly crucial, thus optional for the ideal and maximal development. Also Montessorian is the principle that after these preschool years, i.e. the primary grades from the ages 6 thru 11, the installation of a school curriculum, which features the more-definable, bio/aptitudes is urgent for healthy neuro/growth. Bio/education in the primary grades can be the key which unlocks and deepens the role of the genes for later, adult bio/performances. At the root-level, we know that the faculties of the mind come to us in a "cerebral packet" as threefold functions: language skills; quantitative skills; and spatial skills. In some way, most all of human thought is dependent upon this neuro/psychological triad. Both preschool and primary bio/education tend to approach the outer-limits of genetic potential; thus providing the preteen years with greater capacities to: (a) numerically count; (b) symbolically communicate; and (c) effectively perceive the tangible and intangible surroundings. These key, cerebral attributes can be maximally cultivated via an integrated program which *features the role of bio/inheritance--by individual and/or by racial/ethnic/gender groupings.* Hence, by highlighting the genetics of the pre-and grade-school years, the adaptive capacities of the brain become amplified, optimized and maximized; thereby setting the stage for more-advanced bio/education in the high-schools, colleges, technical schools, and in-house industrial settings. Truly irrevocably intertwined via the freedoms of bio/politics, the proper funding of bio/education by democratic governments becomes a big-time payback for a national citizenry.

In a freedom-based, genetic-based democracy, following the formal bio/education of students and as managed by human-resources professionals, the principles of *industrial eugenics* ought to be incorporated within the constraints of today's, standard, employment paradigms. A *tri-part, bio/commercialized system* would be able to furnish both program guidance and curricula direction to secondary-schools and University counselors. In *Part One* of this industrial-eugenics program, the planning and funding for the "academic colleges" should be designed to train and educate about 30% of the student population; that is, those students who have demonstrated the natural aptitudes as needed for the intellectual positions of society, whether college-level, corporate-level, or as practicing professionals. A bio/elite corps becomes an non-negotiable imperative to any high/tech/info democracy. Through a specialized, rigorous curricula devised for the approximate top-third of the student corps, as separate from the lower 60%; the positions of management, faculties, and tech/sciences can be filled with a modicum of certainty.

In *Part Two* of a bio/educational program, the lower 60% of the student body are those who most likely would be job-functioning in manufacturing, maintenance, and service industries.

Cascading in political awareness and its allied funding are the ever-expanding "Community Colleges" which are currently operating in many cities and counties. Federal, State, and Local legislators ought to be focusing upon the interactive processes of real-world jobs with bio/enhanced schooling as they might pertain to the free marketplace. These student/workers, a segment comprising 60% of the general population, would be offered a targeted, classroom education plus hands-on training, as selected according to "non-abstract," intellectual assessments; such as; with serviceable projects; problem-solving; along with, those skills needed for customer-service interactions. In partnership as consistent with the principles of pedagogical/industrial genetics, the 30% plus 60% of a general population would be earmarked as ***educable*** for the mainstream job-market; as apart from those solely ***trainable***, i.e. intellectually, physically, and or emotionally disadvantaged. These latter citizens, the remaining 10% who are "genetically challenged" and who happen to be inflicted with marginally adaptive neuro/capacities and/or with neurological damage, would constitute the bottom rung of a learning/ eugenic program. In a compassionate democracy committed to the Judeo/Christian Code, they must be teacher-managed with a ***Part Three***, amply-funded, educational program. In a nutshell, ***"intellectually deprived" students must be afforded meaningful, trainable instruction, rather than pointless, formal, classroom experiences.*** With great care and empathy mandated by legal authority, the bottom 10% rung of the student/worker ladder ought to have access to the full exposure of rights-oriented, humane, "survival training." Long-term, it would well-serve a Christian free-society if the bottom tenth of non-pliant genes (not people) become pre-parenting identified, then made extinct over a number of generations with physician administered, eugnic counseling. Socio/spiritually, the adoption of children in lieu of the abortion of fetuses has mighty, moral implications. Jesus loves the lame, the last, the least of us, and these spiritually lost. And for the many sectors within our neo/immigrant diversity, an ***"educational/employment scale"*** combined with, a ***"coefficient of democratic potential"*** can be utilized to measure the varying levels of effective, psycho/social functioning, which might be made useful to fiscal policies within an open-Agora; thereby solving the riddle as to why most of the conventional immigrants and other minorities continue to resist their full-assimilation and absorption into the American, economic schema. However, *inalienably, the bio/education of a Political Genome must be implemented sternly within the moral order and full-complement of human rights, civil liberties, social justice and with job opportunity for all, who dare apply.* God;s gift of freedom would require that these socio/political factors become part of our democrstic processes, as pre-ransomed by the 600,000 casulties of the Civil War.

In summary, with each passing day the bio/behavioral revelations of the DNA by the bio/tech labs; those who may be specifically tied to the *Political Genome*, are strongly pointing to a "freedom linkage," which in the past tainted the proceedings of the 2nd American Revolution. When this notion of political frreedom of nature vs nurture takes root with legislators and historians, a *3rd American Revolution,* by way of the inew deas of a Post-Civil War, will be perceived as a reality-in-progress, causing America to take-on the political aura of a full-bodied, freedom-based democracy. Thus for the new electorate, a higher, socio/political norm will loom which says: *"... in a cultural diversity, the 'demographic character' of an individual citizen and/or that of any subgroup affiliation will be expected to strive to become greater than the sum of its parts."* Indeed the *Dark Age of Egalitariat America,* which has been foisted upon us by the Liberal mindset now has been spawning and spiraling us into a *Dark Age of Politically Correct Cultural Diversity*. Hopefully soon, this plummeting socio/political ambiance will find itself replaced with the luminosity of the *Age of Bio/ Politics*.

CHAPTER 5

The Rise of Dehumanizing Technology
America's Industrial Revolution

The Industrial Revolution set the cultural stage for the "freedom wars" of the $20^{th}/21^{st}$ centuries and the ideological and theological challenges of the Modern Age.

After the Civil War America was rapidly becoming transformed morally, industrially, economically, ideologically, demographically, and socially. Yearning to be free and prosperous, America became a land filled with immigrants, who became displaced by their native land to start a new life in the New World. From the year 1879 to the onset of WW I, twenty five million immigrant workers were welcomed to America. These foreign workers took their place in the new ways of production, agriculture, transportation, communications, and manufacturing. Machines replaced hand-labor and many conventional tools. Power was the module that made goods cheaper and more available. Petroleum, coal, and steel led the way to this power conversion. Railroads, elevated trains, and trolleys built by heavy industrial products, electrical dynamos, telephone wire, lead pipes, copper tubing, and all sizes of motors were needed in this rapidly transforming economy. Yet with paradox, the result of these advanced, engineering technologies impacted the many forms of freedom and socio/ political rights fought for, died for, and enjoyed by colonists and frontiersmen slowly dissolved away, became appeased, and diminished in God's set-apart nation. The cost for industrial progress vying with human freedom came high. During the late 19th century America was undergoing a socio/economic "freedom calamity" that needed innovative management, unskilled labor, women, immigrants, and child workers.

Accordingly, within the political framework of America, many forms of spiritual and emotional bondage materialized plaguing the once "free and brave" who survived the blood shed for its basic liberties previously gained both in its Revolutionary Epoch (1776-1812) and Manifest Destiny/Civil War period (1844-1865). Once more, God's plan of a gift of freedom to humanity-at-large became spiritually compromised that led to a number of oppressive, socio/bondage consequences. Since the year 1865 a cultural war emerged addressing the threat to basic freedoms. Dehumanizing technology quickly was replacing the desire for freedom. Historically, this cultural war began to introduce the "bondage effects" brought about by both the impersonal, socio/detached aura of the Industrial Revolution and the poyential horrors of World War I. Granted, although not in a conventional military sense, but rest assuredly, the Industrial Revolution and its dismal, human consequences fully qualified as a major American War at the close of the 19th century. To be sure, the socio/destructive impact of the Industrial Revolution and its War of ideas spreading unChristian values, and inhumane technological progress, led directly to WWI two decades later that instigated 16 million human causalities. No longer did the lame, the last, the least, and the lost, receive Jesus' compassion or count for anything.

During the Industrial Revolution that began two decades after the American Civil War, Country folks and immigrants chose to relocate to the cities where unskilled jobs became plentiful. Yet instead, what was set into motion was an ill-advised anticipation of employment hopes that the promised migration to America cities would rescue them from economic poverty and social uncertainty.

Below the surface, there were many social and political counter-forces operating that threatened America's stability, causing cultural disintegration, and individual isolation. By the year 1889 thirty percent of the national populace lived in urban areas, mostly in Chicago, New York, Detroit, and Philadelphia. Even today these cities are notorious for their blight and crime. Even today in the dangerous slums of these large American cities, homes to rent or buy are very difficult to find. At first the prospects of sustained or rising economic growth seemed to be worth the wretched human cost. Even though, both rural and immigrant families had to share small, dingy, living quarters, abiding under unlivable circumstances. The Industrial Revolution, which had countless, unintentional consequences, brought about a chain of depressing conditions that included sullied working surroundings, child labor, employment of pregnant women, along with low wages at an appallingly rate of 20-cents per hour, paid across a minimal 60-hour workweek. After food, rent, light, heat, and clothing were financially allocated, the typical family budget was able to save a merger $30 a month. Furthermore, economic cycles, which unexpectedly shifted from prosperity to depression, resulted in mass unemployment, overproduction, collapsing prices, vanishing profits, unethical competition, and worker/investor panic. Trusts and monopolies mushroomed in the business sector, such as the "sugar trust" that controlled 95% of sugar production, causing restricted goods and supplies along with elevated prices. In the year 1890, Congress passed the Sherman Anti-Trust Act. Immigrants abounded; arriving from Italy, Poland, Greece, and Jewish Russia, who banded together in non-English speaking, ethnic ghettos, were willing to absorb these financial and employment ill-treatments. Ideologically, the Marxist Proletariat (poorer worker class) as compared to the Bourgeoisie (the rich, ruling class who controlled the means of production) earned ten times less money than the owners of industry. This glaring difference in standard of living gave rise to public protest, industrial unionism, the prospects of economic socialism, and godless, radical Marxism that infected and caused the ***Modern Age of Human Carnage (1930*-1945 AD.)** Still, on the hopeful side the American Federation of Labor (AFL), which was organized in 1886, devoted itself to the well-being of all of its workers. At that time, factories, mines, and mills lacked decent ventilation, minimal heating, clean sanitation, and an essential, healthy milieu. Worker safety was summarily disregarded by factory owners and their managers. The safety factor within manufacturing plants, mines, and mills were virtually ignored by owners, managers, and supervisors. Workers became emotionally demoralized by their unmerciful, inhumane exploitation. These working conditions in factories, mills, and mines were dismal at best, producing a worker populace subjugated under unmitigated, socio/economic bondage, devoid of fundamental freedoms and political rights. America was overflowing with moral degradation, unbridled prostitution, godlessness, and public drunkenness. By the early 20th century, over 25 thousand workers were killed on the job and 250, 000 injured with no compensation offered by the companies. During the early Industrial Revolution, the environmental abuses of the urban labor force became widely accepted as an acceptable phenomenon. How to control the destructive, economic forces of a young democracy became the primary issue and challenge during the 1890s. Operationally, the synchronizing and harmonizing of the needs of the urban working class in the Northeast with the farmers of the Midwest was the single-most, difficult political task yet to be achieved. In the late 19th century, even with the freedoms originally planned as God's gift to humanity, America the once Beautiful was no where to be found. Thus, an angry, rebellious mood swept across the nation's psyche calling for ideological reform that better focused on conventional religious, ethnic, and cultural values. Although the results of the Civil War shaped the mindset of generations of Americans, a new democracy with new values was demanding a national dialogue addressing the yet-unresolved concerns left behind by the Industrial Revolution, such as:

Unregulated Capitalism vs Communism;
Godless Atheism vs Judeo/Christianity;
Inalienable Freedoms vs the Bondage of Autocrats;
Sovereign States Rights vs Absolute Federalism;
Large vs Small Governments;
Overregulated Industry vs under regulated Commerce
Personal vs Dehumanizing Technology.

Over time, political, technological, and managerial reforms corrected much of the harmful, social consequences brought about by the Industrial Revolution. Gradually, economic transformations combined with God's natural law were needed to reintroduce personal freedoms and socio/economic enlightenment to the unregulated, laissez faire capitalism in-vogue. In academic and intellectual circles there was much speculation as to whether crops produced alone could support an expanding populace. Thomas Malthus opined that unchecked population growth, when increasing geometrically, inevitably will cause a famine because food growth and level of wages only increase arithmetically. Nevertheless, by the end of the 19th century food production did increase. Along with, slowly but surely, automatic spinning and weaving machines appeared to meet the clothing needs of a escalating populace. Further textile inventions came along that replaced hand-power, such as the cotton gin invented by Eli Whitney. To boot, new techniques for the extraction of coal and oil better helped produce iron and steel by increasing production, while civilizing the safety of workers, miners, women, and children. Ventilation was greatly improved in the mines to limit coal dust and carbon monoxide, along with the reforms needed to reduce the hazards of floods, cave-ins, and explosions.

To deal with the unexpected consequences of the Industrial Revolution the improvement and frequency of transportation systems became mandatory. Tediously, large groups of workers walking long distances from home to job became intolerable. Along with, for small businesses the shipment of goods, services, and material that also required greater efficiency and more frequent mobility. Hence, improvements of roads, canals, railroads, harbors, and steam-driven sea-vessels received high priority, Congressional legislation. Also demanded in the urban centers was an boost in available food supplies. Increased food production gave rise to an Agrarian Reform Movement that also increased the social standing of the farmer class. And so, Congress had to pass legislation that protected farmlands, while financially rewarding the more efficient farmers. Cheaper transportation and better communications assured the flow of ample supplies of foodstuffs to the industrial, urban centers. Ethnic foods flourished; poured in by ships across the Atlantic Ocean. In toto, the reversing of the austere, humanitarian crises that sapped the freedom rights of Americans during the early part of the Industrial Revolution took a series of technological reforms, mass production, imaginative re-mechanization of industry, competent, managerial advanced planning, material improvements, and innovative, business practices. All these improvements took place during the second half of the Industrial Revolution.

However not all "freedom advances" and socio/political rights acquired during the past American wars were salvaged by these socio/economic reforms of the late Industrial Revolution. Can God's freedom, human rights, and enlightened capitalism be made to coexist in a democracy? Will the evil presence of godless ideologies cropping up that preached the social merits of citizen bondage be tolerated? Will these counterrevolutionary, amoral philosophies continued to plague the Modern Age? However proposed by godless Marxism by the spin-offs of the Industrial Revolution, the attraction for new and newer technologies and the lure of the social values became the "unresolved evils" bequeath future generations. Ideologically in the first half of the 20th century, the Industrial Revolution of the late 19th century passed on two major, ideational evils: (a) a dehumanizing, yet profitable, technology gnawing at the soul of Man; and (b) in due time a godless Marxism conceived in the late 19th century that inflicted humanity with the wicked origins of Nazism, Communism, Fascism, Japanese militarism, and Islamic terrorism.

This was the worker/manager legacy left behind by Karl Marx, a godless archfiend springing out of the mindset of the Industrial Revolution during the late 19th and throughout the 20th/21st centuries.

Karl Marx, a 19th century atheist, misguided philosopher, extremist economist, and politically, a hardcore socialist, who was unconsciously terrified at the prospect of dying must be considered the principal, contributory originator of the socio/ economic evil and its autocratic mayhem that mete out a revulsion upon the lives of so many innocent men, women, and children in Euro/Asia during WWII and beyond. Without a doubt, within a gruesome context, Marx must be considered the utmost archfiend affecting the views and values of the modern day. Yet, what remains for humankind to think through via its scholarship and theology is the enigma of "why and how" did most of the world's population become sedated and seduced by the evil theories of Karl Marx? For the sake of the survival of the human race, the historical events left over from the social consequences of the Industrial Revolution can **neither** be tabled for future scholars to decipher and mulled-over **nor** be allowed to be swept under the proverbial rug of existential guilt. Why so? Simply because, as Sacred Scripture tells us, God will avenge the sinful nations and never forsake the innocent victims massacred by godless rulers. Surely, God will forgive individuals, but not evil nations. After confession and repentance, He will never forget to offer once-evil countries in Euro/Asia the opportunities to restore their spiritual integrity of righteousness, justice, freedom, and love.

Yet to be historically scripted by scholars that illustrates how the ideological venom of Karl Marx carried forth into the 21st century, what must be considered is the comparable political ideology between Marxism of the 19th century, as featured in the *Communist Manifesto,* and those political decisions made by the left-winged, Obama Administration during the years 2008-2016. Consider this parallelism. In the *Communist Manifesto::* (1) the impounding of landed property, along with the application of all rentals of land are to be assigned for public purposes; (2) the centralization of credit via a national bank that will be operating as an exclusive monopoly to be administered by federal bureaucrats; (3) all factories and apparatus of production are to be exclusively owned or controlled by the State, in accordance with a common plan; (4) the creation of industrial militia and laws to implement the notion of collective farming; (5) the abolition of geo/distinction between towns and counties, along with the redistribution of wealth and population; (6) free education and meals for all children in the public schools; (7) the history of mankind to be rescripted as a class struggle among class distinctions; (8) in all societies there will always be two opposing classes antagonistic to each other; mainly the Bourgeoisie, the ruling class, which owns and manages the means of production and the struggling working class, the Proletariat, which are the oppressed workers; and (9) that the expressions of religion is a myth and the opiate of the masses. If truth be told, Classical Marxism and current day godless Neo/Marxism, i.e. Liberalism, run parallel in both ideological substance and political style. Obama learned the politics of Neo/Marxism at home at Columbia University in New York City.

In the 21st century, the ghosts of 100-million innocent people, who were slaughtered by the godless leaderships of Euro/Asia, 60-years prior, will be demanding vengeance, along with a targeted reprisal aimed at individual reckoning. A sterilized dissertation by scholarly historians, who might try to rationalize and sweep-away the sins of the ***Modern Age of Human Carnage*** (1930-1945) with incomplete, deceitful paradigms, will not remove the millstone of guilt. As to what actually happened to the immoral, uncivilized character of the 20th century will neither abate God's wrath nor attenuate Man's existential guilt. Without any hesitation, these innocent souls will be avenged sooner, than later, either by the ideational and spiritual enlightenment of 21st century's Mankind or by the fury and wrath of an angry God, who cherishes freedom over bondage.

As a derivative of the Industrial Revolution, eventually leading to the *Modern Age of Human Carnage*, (1930-1945), the devastation and wreckage reeked upon Jews and Christians by the conventions of the godless nations of Western Europe, Asia, and the countries of the Mideast and Africa, especially by Russia and Germany, which also caused women and their children to became targeted for Marxist annihilation. Pretextually, ill-defined accusations and murders of innocent fathers, mothers, and their offspring were carried out by the psychopaths of Nazism, Communism, and ISIS. Women regularly were raped by both the Nazi secret police and the Red Army, before they were executed. The Lame, the Last, the Least, and the Lost had no safety net. In the smaller farm towns, Jewish and Christian homes were ransacked, producing unattended, homeless children looking for their parents as they were left to starve alone in the fields. Out of desperation, women had to resort to prostitution, then, became branded to be done away as moral undesirables. In the late1930s, over 10,000 adolescents and children were confined to the concentration camps as work-slaves. Few children under ten years of age ever survived. Work communes utilized close to 200,000 teens and younger as slaves. Capital punishment was applied indiscriminately to young, repeat offenders. State-declared, juvenile delinquents lived on the streets. Under the pretext of national stability, Molotov and Stalin, arch/Marxists, let loose indiscriminate terror upon guiltless families. Extracting confessions from these families became the terror MO employed by the secret police. Close to half a million of related, family members were arrested, 2/3 of which were executed. In the process of trumped-up investigations, fathers and mothers alike were tortured to death, then their children were taken away and sent either to government-sanctioned homes or to slave camps. The living conditions of women in concentration camps, who comprised 10% of the population, were sickening. To prevent rape and daily, sexual abuse by guards and other prisoners, women had to offer sexual favors to select powers-that-be. All this horror and terror is being replicated by 21st century Islam, Iran, and North Korea.

Marx polluted Stalin's political thinking. Pathologically paranoid, Stalin was a brutal Russian despot, who mistrusted his own military, officer corps. In the late 1930s, Stalin ordered the deaths of 1000s of his top commanders in both the army and navy. Their wives and children also were arrested and killed. In reaction, these events demoralized the Russian troops and as expected, had a noticeable, dismal effect on Russian, military morale and efficiency in their battles with the Nazis in the early 1940s. Add to these atrocities, sterilization laws were enacted that later targeted the "lost," the "least," "the lame," and the "last." With minimal, legal restraint, legal statutes were applied by genetic, health courts to execute the weak, the disabled, the socially undesirable, potential criminals, sex offenders, and the incurably sick. Against their wills, a half a million men and women were sterilized in Nazi Germany. Eugenics became the national craze. Moreover, so as to increase the incidence of births and larger families among Aryans-only, who agreed to be medically and culturally screened, Nazi eugenic programs offered interest-free loans and other perks to younger, German women. In the late 1930s, close to a million families took advantage of these Nazi, eugenic benefits. The godlessness left over by the dehumanizing mindset of the Industrial Revolution reached its evil apex.

Furthermore, ethnic cleansing, sometime referred to as racial hygiene, was a modus operandi used to support the Muslim, Communist and Nazi transformation of human nature and their societies. These transformations of human life-and-love were also a guiding theme from the Industrial Revolution of the 19th century to the Obama Administration of the 21st century. Both these Eras severely compromised freedom and human rights. Socio/political and human transformation became a sinister policy intended to achieve world domination by the godless nations of Europe. In Nazi Germany toward the end of WWII, this policy was amplified as the "final solution" of the Jewish race and Christianity.

Medical and political atrocities caused millions to be agonized, tortured, and left breathless in the gas chambers and later on beheaded by Muslims, whose Allah doesn't reflect the true nature of God. Cynically, in both the Soviet and Nazi domains even the young idealists and well-schooled residents, who adulated their despotic, godless leaders, endorsed the mass murder of Jews, Poles, Ukrainians, and the physically and emotionally infirmed. Mass murder was also applied to non-Germans and non-Jews. In the late 1930s, 100,000 selected foreigners from Afghanistan, Greece, Korea, China, Bulgaria, Finland, Iran, Iraq, Macedonia, Estonia, and Romania were beaten, targeted for arrest, and extermination. Out of the yet-unresolved godless mindset of the Industrial Revolution, the Marxist, worker/owner ideology, the escalating atheism, and dehumanizing spinoffs of technology produced the delusions of world domination through State-sponsored homicide via mass jailings. No national boundaries were set for their immoral limits. On Planet Erath few godly values, i.e. love, justice, goodness, and freedom, were safeguarded. In Russia, the Gulag in the late 1930s was comprised of over fifty, forced-work camps with two million slave laborers, similar to the Nigerian kidnappings of young schoolgirls. Without adequate food and warm clothing, prisoners were worked to death on railway and other public projects. Both in the Gulag and by African Islamic sadists, the supervisors and managers of slave-labor, who ran these camps, had strict quotas to fill, dispensing them with little humane treatment. In the early 1940's, the European landscape became dotted with 100s of concentration camps. Dachau, Sachsenhausen, Flossenburg, Mauthausen, Regensburg, Gross-Rosen, Mettelbau-Dora and

Neuengamine were the better known centers of slave labor, mostly stationed across Eastern Europe. These "camps of revulsion" and their terror activities were widely reported by the Media; accounts known and well-accepted by the common everyday, Jew-hating citizen across the Globe. With Divine conviction, God will never forget these victims. With His fury of Divine wrath and reprisal, 21st century Europe is fast becoming economically, culturally and genetically depleted; a Dark Continent drenched in the blood of innocence, now hardly morally viable, existing as an "inert museum" for gaping tourists hoping to partake in the past achievements of the Western World. In the same way, the Islamic World is rapidly geo/disintegrating into chaos.

What is emerging as the true fundamental causes of the German Holocaust, the Russian "terror eradications," Mao's butchery, the Japanese bloodbaths, along with the Italian, Spanish, Austrian, Estonian, Hungarian, and Romanian annihilations of the most vulnerable, helpless people, tribes, and communities, never can be explained away or justified with economic theory, socio/political conjecture, military superiority, the charisma of despots, or the pursuit of unnatural, philosophical theories targeted for a New World Order. Appearing as new scholarship, if truth be told, the underlying dynamics of this primordial lapse of human incivility have been two-fold: (1) *an historical ignorance* that would have annulled the Marxist thought of a classless society emerging out of the Industrial Revolution; and (2) *godlessness,* and its dependency upon the fanatic trust of human reasoning and mistrust of faith concerning God's gift of freedom.

These primary factors, i.e. human sin plus the lack of the full reliance on God, accounted for the basic metaphysics of human, evil existence. The denial of these two ABCs of life on Planet Earth, violated by Marxist theory and other ideological mindsets, bequeath to Mankind by the Industrial Revolution, created havoc in the 20ᵗʰ and 21ˢᵗ centuries.

The delusional hope to transform society and human nature with a classless society, devoid of religion and God, within the socio/political context of a highly centralized, despotic, bureaucratic government was erroneously fallacious. So, why did the world's social institutions, its literati, and formal academicians buy into these philosophical myths that defied the moral fiber of a created, intelligent design of Mankind? How did the writings of Karl Marx and the Koran become the "root conspirator" of these horrific proceedings that splattered the evolutionary history of humankind? Today, any discussion of the validity of shria law and Marxist "classless politics" and "socialist economics" seem to be incredibly flawed and irrelevant for future societies.

Yet across the nations of the world, the ideology of Mohammed, political Communism and Socialist economics have failed to deliver the freedom, human rights, and sustained prosperity sought by Mankind. Only the universal, individual-based liberties assured by democratic nations and the free-market principles of enlightened capitalism, as set within the promises of the message of Jesus, can ever become the viable dynamics of individual fulfillment, societal realization, and species survival. As Jesus tells us: "don't be anxious for anything;" "go and sin no more," "love your neighbor," and "come to Me for moral guidance,"

While otherwise, the message of Marxist reasoning, along with the caustic effects of inhuman technology sends-out a mirror-image, inverted interpretation of the Judeo/Christian belief. In spite of this inversion of truth, segments of the hard-left, Liberal politic, mainstream journalism, Liberation theologians, and academic figments of the imagination, directly continue to indirectly revere the writings of Karl Marx's evil theories. As yet in the 21st century, will the Neo/Marxism of secular Liberalism continue to be ingrained and not renounced by the Midterm election of 2016?

As seen, the consequences of the 2008 and 2012 Presidential elections, which voted in the most Liberal, Neo/Marxist candidate in American history, Barack Obama, the USA finds human nature itself in a steep decline; economically, politically, culturally, and morally. As leftover from the Industrial Revolution when workers vied with the owners of production, Neo/Marxists in modern-day history naively hoped to install the socio/political expectations for a transformed human nature and New World Order. Instead Americans chose the unfortunate aspirations of the Industrial Revolution, along with, Euro/Bolshevism, the Left-winged lunacy of big government, the acceptance of cultural depravity and its amorality and immorality of: (a) abortion; (b) legalized drug usage; (c) rampant divorce rates; (d) dysfunctional families; (e) gay adoptions, same-sex marriage, and homosexuality; (f) the unforgivingness of capricious lawsuits; (g) high urban crime; (h) decadent art and entertainment; and (i) the legal assaults against Judeo/Christianity beliefs. At the root of most of this decadence lies the acceptance of raising innocent children by single parents. Patently unAmerican, this presidential election of 2008 and 2012 has revealed that experience, accomplishment, character, self-reliance, and a moral society no longer matter to the American electorate. Voters for the Democratic Party have turned America over to the Chicago mob, Neo/Marxists, and the immoral murdering of a millions of innocent pre-babies through Federally-financed abortions. In some way, these evil events came out of the way of thinking of the Industrial Revolution and its attempts at socio/economic transformation of the American freedom-culture. Has the survival of the American ideal of God's gift of freedom and human rights crossed a point of no return? How God will deal with this American condition remains to be seen. No doubt, there is an unmistakable parallel between the principles cited in Marx's, *Communist Manifesto* during the late 19th century's, Industrial Revolution and the left-winged politics of the American 21st century. Not unlike Karl Marx, Obama and the secular progressives want to transform America and the Western World into an utopian, Socialist State.

To withstand the evils of Liberalism, only the Evangelical Christian Church of America, representing a variety of Separatist denominations, all of which rely upon the Holy Spirit for protection, strength, and guidance, is expanding across the Globe at an accelerated pace. Rest assuredly, an angry God, who already has selectively withdrawn His saving grace from Old World Christianity will demand from the spiritually stained, Euro/Asian nations a sweeping confession and repentance, or else a reckoning, to be subjected to the wrath of a Divine judgment. By now, South Korea, which can boast of Christian churches with memberships approaching 100,000, might become the Christian role-model fit for all Asian nations. Today, as a consequence of its godless, Marxist leanings, Europe and much of Asia finds itself out of touch with the true God. The status of Judeo/Christianity in 20th Century's Europe has become disconnected from the American Christian Separatism, i.e. Evangelical Christianity. As an example, in Belgium only 1% of the population claims to be Christian. In Germany, to attend a Roman Catholic mass on the Sabbath requires a federal tax. Dolefully, Europe today has been receiving its quasi/spiritual input from three sources of human, not Divine, religious kings, i.e. the Papacy, the Patriarch, and the Archbishop of Canterbury. This Old World commitment to "failed Christianity" signifies a denunciation of the "theologically convincing," character of the message of Jesus. Evangelical Americans instead are opting for and relying upon the Holy Spirit as its King and directly from God for spiritual guidance. As original Euro/Separatists, Evangelical Christians of the New World reject the established, religious authorities of the Old World. Clearly, at this juncture in the history of Judeo/Christianity, the established and conventional religions of the Euro/ Continent have not succeeded in inspiring the credibility and confidence of the souls of Western Mankind. Did Euro/ Christianity embrace evil because it became enthralled with the godless Age of Reason, the technological perks of the Industrial Revolution, and the writings of Karl Marx?

Steadily, in their efforts to transform America into a European-style socialism, Neo/Marxist voting patterns of the Democratic Party have been losing momentum during the years 2008 to 2012. The American President, Barak Obama, a stealth Neo/Marxist, who has a distinctly exclusive, radical, Liberal record as a Senator of Illinois, has advanced his ideology into a full-blown economic debacle. Ghostlike, similar to Mohammad of Islam, Obama's radicalism comes from his family upbringing that was dysfunctional. As a child, he was psychologically abandoned by both his father and mother. Obama's natural father fled to Kenya in Africa, while his Kansas mother followed her lover to Thailand. As a boy, Barack was left behind to be raised by his grandparents only to be tutored by hard-core Marxists. Similarly, Mohammad, an orphan, was raised and shifted among relatives. In reaction, after the national elections of 2010and 2014, a new generational cadre of Americans emerged, e.g. the Tea Party, that began to reverse Obama's Neo/Marxist conspiracy by voting-out the professional politicians of the Democratic House of Representatives and the Senate in 2014.

In America's 21st century, irrespective of the ill-advised, irresponsible funding of antiquated, failed, outdated, and obsolete, utopian tenets, the Obama Administration has been actively pursuing a number of full-blown Neo/Marxist policies, laws, executive regulations, and rules. By being reassured via his past style of Chicago corrupted politics, and irrespective of the will of the electorate, with unabashed arrogance, Obama keeps hoping to convert America from a hale democratic, free-market, prosperous, exceptional society into a failed, flopped, Socialist, European, style culture. In spite of the ill-advised, irresponsible funding of antiquated, failed, outdated, and obsolete, utopian tenets, the Obama Administration has been actively pursuing a number of full-blown, ultra-Liberal policies, laws, executive regulations, and rules. The polling will of the electorate and the dictates of the US Constitution were ignored with unabashed arrogance. Obama keeps hoping to transform America from a hale democratic, free-market, prosperous, exceptional society into a failed, Socialist, European-style culture. Was he motivated by Black revenge?

By politically pursing with disdain for the American ideal, Obama has been opting for: (1) a huge, centralized, bureaucratic government; (2) an unsustainable fiscal debt and deficit; (3) special union privileges, in support of the Marxist Proletariat view of society; (4) high taxation policies in conjunction with the redistribution of wealth benefiting the marginally productive classes; (5) the control of small and large business through unredeemable, stifling regulations, unproductive stimulus loans, along with an oppressive Tax Code; (6) the direct control of universal standards as Common Core with the mindless funding of the ever-worsening schools; (7) "liberation theology" as acquired from his Pastor Jeremiah Wright, who hates America, and loves the frivolous lawsuits that alleges "all are victims" by citing political correctness; (8) the single payer for healthcare to be administered at all ages, including "death panels" for seniors; (9) the support for any anti-American, anti-Christian, and pro-Muslim views; and (10) the military attenuation and impotency of America's international power. If Obama's ideals of Karl Marx are fulfilled by overlooking the consequences of the Godless, immoral events of the 20th century, when 100-million innocent men, women, and children were abruptly slaughtered, America as a freedom-transformational bastion will cease to exist.

How did the catastrophic socio/afflictions imposed upon humanity-at-large in the 20th century by Karl Marx's 19th century evil-suppositions come about? Conceived by the mindset of the 18th century, the Enlightenment, its Age of Reason, and the godless French Revolution, caused Mankind to succumb to Utopian musing by disregarding the bio/spiritual principles of God's Freedom Plan. Later-on after the dreadful slime of Marxism took hold and spread like a raging wildfire across the world, the forward thrust of civilization became deferred, slowly hanging and twisting in the wind. Historically, the deceived citizenry of many lands endorsed politically and amorally Karl Marx, who was an artifact of the Industrial Revolution and indisputably responsible for the atheistic ascendancy of power-mad leaders. Does Mankind really believe that God has forgiven and forgotten the socio/political wickedness of the mid-20th century without requiring a national confession and repentance across multi-generations? Has there been a common "causal linkage" to account for the madness of the past two centuries? Are the self-absorbed paradigms offered by misguided, Liberal scholars and academicians be enough to assuage the "Global sins" of the

20th century? Undeniably, there are in-common "underlying links" to the Euro/Asian carnage that occurred during the past seven decades that must be addressed theologically, then atoned and ultimately resolved, both intellectually and spiritually during the tenure of the 21st century. Unequivocally, this moral dilemma can only be solved with the democratic acceptance by any free people, who must spiritually desire, courageously choose, and act-upon either a god-centered or a godless society.

Freedom: Faith vs Reasoning?

No doubt the Industrial Revolution was a war; a war of the soul, whereby godless reasoning and dehumanizing technology became set against faith in God as the pathway to freedom, justice, and prosperity. Will the full dependence on Providence give us true liberty and human rights that we deeply yearn and long for? Or, will an individual's self-reliance of godless reasoning and inhumane technology be allowed to "permeate and infect" us across the cultural institutions of our socio/politics?

Irrespective of our great scientific, mathematical, literary, and aesthetic achievements, insightful, religious historians tell us that the Enlightenment Period, in its search for the fundamental truths of God's, Creation Plan, theologically was immature, rebellious, superficial, and shallow. Spiritually, this period of history can be distinguished by its naïve theology of doubt. Being driven by Faith, in lieu of Divine uncertainty, the "Founding Fathers" of America, censured this godless Euro/

Epoch and its devotion to seek truth solely within the light of human reasoning. Humbly otherwise, American leaders sought the guidance of Providence, i.e. the Holy Spirit, who indwells and cares for individuals and nations alike. To counter the theological darkness of those Euro/times, i.e. the Age of Reason, when organized, traditional religion became grimly earmarked by superstitions, bigotry, and fanaticism of the Roman Church, seemed to be socio/politically palatable to the common Euro/Man of the 18th century. Actually, religion itself was not the culprit, only the self-serving interpretations and corrupt practices by the power-mad Catholic clerics, who distorted and defiled the holy message of Jesus. Accordingly, the Enlightenment Era as being portrayed by noted, French philosophers of the 18th century became a time of unwarranted disrespect for the sinews of Divine tradition and its upright authorities. By overrating the merits of human reasoning, in lieu of spiritual logic, i.e. Faith, this Age of Reason chose to disregard the Divine Realm and the God of History's involvement in freedom socio/politics. In so doing, the Enlightenment Era proved to be unconvincing as a credible and enduring frame of human, spiritual reference. As a result of these fundamental, ideational/spiritual flaws blanketing an entire Era and soon thereafter the Industrial Revolution, the human cost in anguish, totaling out of these philosophical ego-trips of "reason only," resulted in 10s of millions of innocent lives taken needlessly by evil Euro/Asian leaders during the first half of the 20th century and beyond. Indeed, the theoretical "godless musings" of the 18th century must be held fully accountable for the socio/chaos of the early Industrial Revolution.

As a result of the bloodbath caused by the Age of Absolute Rule, the French agnosticism and intellectual doubting of the 18th century, and the atheism of the early 20th century, the 21st century finds the Post-Modern Age wavering indecisively at a theological, fork-in-the-road. Socio/politically, we now know that any godless commitment to "reason alone," by any Epoch or nation is bound to produce untold, human havoc, faltering as a community, and ultimately crash/failing. Without the Lord of History guiding human choices, nothing good happens. Just one hundred fifty years after the French and American Revolutions, somehow Karl Marx inherited these flawed delusions of "godless reasoning" and then applied them economically and politically to the inhumane, work environments and its consequences being generated by the technological mindset of the Industrial Revolution. While the indecisive scholars of the Age of Reason had to contend with the transitional dissonance between the new theology introduced by Luther's Reformation and the fading authorities of the monarchies and its clerics of the Roman Church, Karl Marx and his associates attempted to transform the basic socio/political/economic nature of human life with a godless, socialist model. Marx's bipolar ideologies of worker vs ownership proved to be contentious and political stumbling-blocks for the free nations of the Western Hemisphere. Hence due primarily to their denial of God's existence, jointly the philosophical extrapolations of Marxism and the Enlightenment ought to be judged by four ***major factors*** that led to incalculable, human butchery, misguidedly exploited by evil-possessed, godless leaders of 20th century's Euro/Asia.

Factor one, the *Age of Absolute Rule* by the Roman Church attempted to negate the Christian Reformation launched by Martin Luther. ***Factor two,*** the ***Age of Reason*** introduced theological doubt and spiritual confusion to the souls of the once-believers. ***Factor three***, the ***Communist Manifesto*** written by Marx and Engel attempted to formalized Man's socio/political and economic transformation. And, ***Factor four,*** the ***Age of Human Carnage*** of the mid-20th century that took the lives of a 100-million innocent men, women, and children. To avoid future mayhem and socio/political chaos, will the 21st century's philosophical theology of Man admit to the calamitous effects of these four factors? If so, looking back about 250-years ago, just prior to the French Revolution, God decided to begin revealing the dazzling components of His Freedom Plan. The laws of science, mathematics, biological evolution, political and economic liberties and their majesty were being discovered. For the human mind, the laws of science and mathematics, along with their aesthetics, began to account for a new and awesome reality, i.e. the Creation Plan. Conceptually, both deduction and induction began to form the logic and empiricism of these "philosophical times." In tandem, the notion of a Supreme Being or Providence was being rejected as the means of discovering the fuller truth. Nonetheless, out of the events and theories of the 18th century's French Epoch, we now know that a single human is but a speck in the Multiverse. God had to be the breathtaking Being whose love and mercy created both us and the elements of Outer Space through a time-process of transcendence. Yet, in the Western World of the 18th century, this celestial message was not righteously accepted. "Reason" became championed, in lieu of God's direct and indirect participation in both the Creation and Redemption Plans,. "Reason" was substituted for Faith in academic and scholarly discourse. Morality, as built into the human soul, became confused with cultural ethics. Eternity and the indestructibility of the soul were downplayed as superstitious, while the finality of the tenure of individual life on Planet Earth was featured as the ultimate fate. And so, these and other misguided theories gave birth to the Age of Reason, also referred to as the Enlightenment, along with, the Euro/Epoch that proposed the intellectual and cultural acceptance of godlessness during and after the Industrial Revolution. Ultimately, these dangerous musings produced the "evil of Marxism" that rationalized the mass murders, carnage, and torture of 100-million innocent men, women, and children. How could this have happened? How did the evolved, socio/bonding brain of humans produce such suffering, butchery, and bloodshed? Nonetheless, these souls of millions of innocent victims will not rest in peace. They deserve, demand, and will receive Divine reckoning for those nations deemed guilty, along with, a more plausible, scholarly account by historians and theologians.

Furthermore, by looking back over a span of two centuries, historians tell us that the godless, French Revolution seeking the nobility of universal freedoms evolved with the Enlightenment Period and the Age of Reason. This Euro/Revolution became instigated by a number of special circumstances, ideational curiosity, and flawed religious factors all coming together at once. Misguidedly, this complex Epoch chose and ideologically relied upon human reasoning as its sole, intellectual vehicle for truth-seeking. God and His guidance as the God of History became eradicated from the French, cultural consciousness. For a decade (1789-1799), passionate and radical changes in socio/political outlook marked the ambiance of the French culture. This citizenry, in common, demanded a greater share of French prosperity and representation in Church and governmental affairs; deja vu, not unlike the Muslim uprisings occurring in the Mideast in the 21st century. Then and upfront, emerged protests by a host of French intellectuals against the Absolute Rule of the Roman Church and their power-seeking, military allies in the monarchy. The bigotry and intolerance common to the attitudes of priests and princes were inconsolably begrudged. The special economic and socio/political privileges previously afforded the clergy and the Royal Court was bitterly resented by the French populace. Both Kings, Louis XV and XVI, who ruled during this tumultuous decade, failed to timely identify and address these grievances. Hence, a financial crises lasting years caused by incompetent and corrupt fiscal decisions, judicial abuses, and the high cost of war with England, in toto eventually ignited the legendary, French Revolution that toppled the Age of Absolute Rule.

Voltaire (1694-1778) led the philosophical charge, followed by Montesquieu (1689-1765), Rousseau (1712-1778), and Diderot (1713-1784). These French scholars and their counterparts in mathematic, art, science, economics, politics, and education, produced an ideational transformation, in tandem with a full-blown, secular Europe devoted exclusively to reasoning as the sole arbiter of truth. Belief in both God and organized religion were negatively and myopically linked to bigotry, superstition, intolerance, and dogmatic fanaticism. No doubt, this was the *Age of Doubt and Skepticism*. While Protestants and Catholics dueled as theological adversaries, the mainstream of the French populace reacted to this theological contest by drifting into full-blown atheism and hyper/rationalism. The true nature and message of Judeo/Christianity, especially in its unique belief in an incarnate, indwelling, personal God, was yet to arrive and was spiritually unappreciated right up to the Evangelical Christianity of the Pre-Modern Era. It took the migrating Separatists to the New World beginning with the Pilgrims at Plymouth Rock in the 17th century to forge an upgrade to Christian Thought, while delivering the final coup to Old World Christianity. In the 21st century, we are witnessing the soaring escalation of this Evangelical Movement in the New World, aka American Christianity, whereby its tele/evangelists reach a billion souls worldwide every Sunday with the spiritual/philosophical thoughts of Jesus. A message that insists upon loving the lame, the last, the least, and the morally lost. Although "faith," as the Divine gift of spiritual logic, was totally obliterated from the mindset of the Euro/French 18th and 19th centuries, the message of Jesus slowly but surely engulfed the "religious ignorance" of the past 250-years. By continuing to impact and guide the spiritual growth of humanity-at-large, these past Eras of philosophical suppositions confirmed the dynamics underlying significance of philosophers and their theological speculations as they might pertain to the righteousness or unrighteousness of the freedom socio/politics of the present and future. As innocent victims, the 100-million casualties of the mid 20th century proved the enormity of moral truth vs the immoral falsehoods of reasoning.

Over the millennia, philosophers, heretics, and schematics alike sought the truth with a number of intellectual/religious paradigms. With paradox, most all the philosophers across almost 3000-years of Western history struggled with the issue of God, His existence, His Creation, His socio/politics, and His intentions for individual life on Planet Earth. This philosophical thirst for cosmic search for universal truths began with the Greek poet Homer in the 6th century BC. All in all, the extrapolative conjectures of 2500-years by philosophers concerning knowledge, man's nature, the existence or not of God, eternity, morality, social ethics, the political role of the State and the workings of the cosmos, proved to be only rough approximations of the universal, scientific and metaphysical truths. The study of philosophy turned out to be no more than an incomplete theology. Yet as certainty, the spiritual philosophy proposed by the Moral Evolution of Western Man, as initiated by Moses, augmented by Paul, formalized by Augustine, and reformed by Martin Luther, told it all that needs to be told about the spiritual/ philosophical realm. Within this Judeo/Christian context, all the musings and speculations of 2500-years of philosophical theories ought to be considered null and void speculations, thereby tossed out to the junkyards of ideas gone by. *De facto*, it's all about Jesus, who is the only true philosopher/king, whose universal and infinite message, not the aimless babble of imperfect, intellectual conjecture, who represents the assurance that has been craved by the legion of philosophers of yore.

For the 21st century audience, the *Redemption Plan* of Jesus can put into plain words and perspective the individual search for truth, forgiveness, Divine intimacy, eternity, and one's fated destiny. The persona of God the Father, with His *Creation Plan,* shows us the righteous role of the socio/political domain, along with the pursuit of scientific knowledge that aperiodically is revealed to elucidate the transcendent workings of both the Multiverse and the Phylogenetic Order. These two Divine Plans, Creation and Redemption, contain all the philosophical truths that ought to lead to the indisputable clarity of ideas, principles, theology, and the encompassing theories needed for the future. If truth be told, philosophical inquiry for 2500-years has been floundering in a sea of non-sequiturs trying to find a comprehensive, indisputable, rationale for life on Planet Earth. Within the framework of God as the God of the Multiverse, the Lord of History, and His personal indwelling presence, lies all the truth about the existence of life on Planet Earth. The Industrial Revolution strayed disdainfully from God's gift of freedom.

Dating as far back to the Ancient Days, the study of philosophy that began in Greece at a costal port across the Aegean Sea set into motion the ideational evolution of a newly-evolved intellect. Here in Iona, philosophers and poets began their search for the certainty or uncertainty of reality. Homer was the first who sought out the cosmic panorama on Mount Olympus via the mythology of Greek gods of which their quasi-divine appeal was moral, righteous, with supernatural strength, and socially just. Beginning in the 6th-7th centuries AD, both Neo/Platonic and Aristotelian premises led the full course of Western philosophy, by way of an indirect, but profound, theological speculations, eventually leading us toward the formalization of Christian Thought. In the past, many other Greek scholars tagged along with these two giants of pure thought, including Socrates. They all were looking for, but coming short of, the universal understanding and the ultimate principles of reality. In Ancient Days, both religious and secular premises concerning God, morality, society, nature, and knowledge, proved to be haphazard, irreal, incomplete, and syllogistically flawed. Actually, Socrates left no scripts. His thoughts were conveyed and preserved by his students, such as Plato, who further extrapolated through his book, *The Republic* that explored the political ramifications of a righteous State. With political risk, the avant-garde theories of Socrates offended the cultural correctness of Ancient Greece. He at first was advised to go into exile, then was prosecuted and executed with a self-induced poison. Along with Plato, the influential Sophist philosophers of Ancient times, also were Aristotle's pupils. Their view of morality was anchored in culture, rather than in the Divinely built-in nature of Man. Sophists believed that morality was unnatural and hinged upon the community, not God. So too, their justice came out of the principle that "might is right," so pursuing a life of pleasure ought to be the ultimate goal of life. All in all, the Ancient Greek philosophers who had a continuing and profound influence on academia across the Ages fell short of the cognitive and spiritual integrity of Christian Thought.

In due course, the French *Age of Doubt, Skepticism, and Godlessness* led to the evils of the American Industrial Revolution, then Marxism of the 19th century, German Nazism, Russian Communism, China's Maoism, Japanese Militarism, and Euro/Fascism of the mid-20th century. All these ideologies were godless offshoots of Karl Marx's ideational venom. So too with satirical paradox, the once-noble American Liberalism of the 1960's AD disintegrated into the depraved vile of neo/Marxism of the 21st century. Somehow, across corner to corner of the Globe, East to West, and North to South the post-WWII values of political freedom, social liberty, and capitalism proliferated as the notion of universal human rights. These freedom values spread across all sorts of individual bio/variations, economic classes, and socio/political regions. However gradually, these gains of equality-for-all became annulled by the excesses of the dehumanizing technology of the post Civil War and the Liberal political establishment that controlled the Media, progressive Christian Churches, and the University. Eventually despoiled, America sank into a societal cult of pan-victimization, i.e. Neo/Marxism, aided by the intemperance of litigation by activist judges, who ruled that all are victims in some fashion and weren't responsible for one's choices or fate. This trend by Liberal Courts sent the "socio/political vitality" of America into a steep decline and negatively accelerating vortice. As proof-positive of this supposition, in the national election of 2008 AD the American electorate chose Barack Obama,

Harry Reid, and Nancy Pelosi, all Neo/Marxists, to lead and govern America. Our democratic society traditionally devoted to socio/political, religious, and economic freedoms, by way of the risks posed by self-reliance freely chosen by citizens, no longer dominated our national way of thinking. The assurance of guaranteed entitlements replaced the dignity of freedom. With little doubt, what followed the anguish and horrifying plight of the 100-million victims of the mid-20th century by the godless Marxist philosophy of the 19th century was the ever-decomposing, Liberal values of the *late*-20th century. Also with little doubt, the philosophical fidelity by the academic communities that naively pursued truth devoid of a mystical understanding, grace, and guidance by God severely impeded the ideational and spiritual progress of Mankind.

By injecting the heinous, Marxist philosophy of the 19th century that trailed lockstep after the godless values of the French Revolution and the Industrial Revolution, later became the Liberal socio/politics of modern times. It ought to be concluded by ingenuous scholars that the atheist aura of these various Ages of Reason and inhumane technology had to be the principal "evil root causes" that set the stage for the Euro/Asian mayhem of the mid-20th century. Hitler, Lenin, Stalin, Mussolini, Mao, Tojo, along with the leaders of Spain, Romania, Austria, Hungary, Estonia, and the Imans were all unbelievers of the true Divine Nature. These leaders and their sanctioning citizenry relied upon the toxic socio/politics of irrational hate to govern their nations. Fore sure, they will be held spiritually accountable by an angry, avenging God.

Yet with the wisdom, generosity, and love of God, sprouting now as a giant leap forward in the ideational progress of Mankind, the current-day literati became Divinely permitted to explore the philosophical, scientific, aesthetic, and mathematical aspects of the Creation Plan. Accordingly, during the past two centuries the emerging fields of physics, biological evolution, astronomy, mathematics, chemistry, philosophical cosmology, art forms, medicine, neuroscience, and the budding technologies of engineering came about. These were amazing intellectual feats formed an up-and-coming Modern Era of untold enlightenment; a truly astonishing Epoch that self-importantly and disdainfully still refused to acknowledge the role of the Divine handprint in history. This *Age of Godless Reasoning* gave us new astronomical insights into the mysteries of the cosmos. New, were the theoretical concepts revealed by physicists. New, engineering technologies to enhance our daily lives. And, the new mathematics to better explain the working of our Multiverse. New, medical chemistry, physiology, and neuroscience to prevent, diagnose, and treat our maladies. New, bio/evolutionary insights into our origins. New, expressions of art, as visual aesthetics, music, architecture, literature, ballet, fashion, and cuisine. In spite of these wondrous leaps in understanding due to their surprise disclosures by God, the legacy of this enlightenment continued to hinge itself to the bitter fruits of godlessness. Both atheism and Islam indirectly contributed to the human carnage of WWI, WWII the Wars of Terror. Religion, or lack of, became ravaged by the irrational views that avowed: all value systems are comparable and the belief in Divine revelation and miracles was intolerably superstitious. This spiritual Rebellion of the Modern Era led to religious anarchy and Papal denunciation by the once-common Catholic believer, who became seduced by the spiritual naïveté of initial French scholarship. To the worldly, Man and his brainpower was the prime focus of belief, while his awareness of and dependency on an indwelling, personal God was not taken into account. Thus, what took place was a general disregard for morals and lack of concern for the universal forces of evil. Thoughts of duty, religion, and/or moral principles were considered culturally passé and moronic. Meism, egotism, and intellectual arrogance, both during the Age of Reason, the Industrial Revolution, and within modern-day academia, mainstream Media, and Liberal, religious denominations became widespread and in-vogue. With the passage of time, Mankind slowly discovered that the 18th century philosophers, who infiltrated the thoughts and morals of Mankind, had corrupted everything of importance and value in Western civilization.

So, who were these dramatis personae, who refused to acknowledge the brilliance of God's, revealed Creation Plan? Or, refused to concede to the spiritual notion of dependency and submission to an indwelling God? Or, to the ingrained reality of the Moral Order? Or, to the eternal perks of salvation freely given as Divine guidance, protection, unconditional love, and providence, as provided by the Holy Spirit? Or, fail to offer praise and gratitude on the Sabbath? Was this Period of history the originator of the violent French Revolution, or vice versa, or was this Era simply a caricature of a ideo/spiritual mockery, a derision and denial of time-honored, deep-rooted values? Did the view of faith vs reason become the opening volley, an Epochal aperture, for the early-20th and 21st centuries' extremism, fanaticism, and human carnage? Or, simply a pseudo/religious heresy hoping to dampen the theological luster of the 16th century Reformation of Christianity? Or, was these Ages of Reason primarily blinded by the prospects of freedom, both individually and socio/politically? In any case, by the limiting of human life to the confines of Planet Earth, the course of "freedom history" leading to the 21st century has proven that any godless movement could only cheapened Man's life, love, and morality. According to noted-philosopher Georg Hegel (1770-1831), a counter-Enlightenment figure, this unreasonable, constricted view that supposed that Man was independent of God, self-contained, self-ruling, and contingent solely upon his experiences on Planet Earth was evil exemplified. By omitting religion as a major component of truth, the consequences leading to the Industrial Revolution fell woefully short of the transcendent dynamics of human evolution and denied itself of the respect of a more plausible macro-theory of yore. Rightly so, in 1789 AD, the French Revolution defended the Natural Rights of Man by abolishing the monarchy, beheading the king and queen and despoiling the Roman Church by expropriating its property. Hence, while the violence of warfare continued to sprawl into the French, civilian sector, it took the imposing and august leadership of Napoleon Bonaparte to end the social unrest by working-out a compromised accord between the Papacy and the new rulers of France. Although the French "Rights of Man" of 1793 AD did influence the aspirations of the American Founding Fathers, whereby henceforth and forevermore liberty, safety, and private property were cherished as inalienable rights. In tandem, the anti-religious tyranny of the French Age of Reason did not, nor could not expunge the theology of the Lutheran Reformation. Good theology will always trump bad philosophy. Thus religiously the spanning the 18th through the mid-20th centuries will forever be socio/politically known and disparaged for its codes of atheism, amorality, agnosticism, secular humanism, neo/Marxism, religious skepticism, and its indirect contribution to vast human carnage.

In conclusion, in addition to godless Marxism, *a primary root cause* of the menacing convoluted rise of Nazism, along with the twisted ideologies of Communism, Fascism, Militarism, Socialism, Islamic terror, and modern-day Liberalism, aka Neo/Marxism, the deist notions of the Age of Reason during the 18th century also ought to qualify as a *primary root cause* of the horrific mass-murders of 100,000,000 victims of the socio/political wars occurring during the 20th century. In French philosophy, it was Voltaire (1694-1778), who was one of the foremost, respected scholars of those times, who with intellectual passion doubted with skepticism the indwelling, ever-presence of a personal, incarnate God, i.e. Deism, while fully relying upon "reason" to comprehend and solve the socio/political disputes affecting 18th century' Euro/Mankind. Voltaire's works formalized the seething, anti-Papal tide that resulted out of many years of religious wars in Europe. In a nutshell, Voltaire vehemently opposed any clerical intrusion on civil matters instead he resorted to the views of the Greek and Roman scholars of yore to spew contempt for the corruption, idolatries, and heresies of Roman Christianity. Voltaire, unlike the Lutheran theology of the 16th century, which included the personal, indwelling, dependent relationship between a believing soul and a loving God, failed or refused to recognize the definitive and unique beliefs of Judeo/Christianity. During his scholarly days, Voltaire became a deist and rationalized an impersonal view of the Creator's scientific and mathematical laws by scripting: "if God did not exist, it would be necessary to invent Him." As an alternative to reformed Christianity, Voltaire's naïve theology of deism concluded that an impersonal God created the Universe and Mankind, then, abandoned them to care for themselves rationally. Socio//politically, Deists view all religions as spiritually comparable and basically anchored to universal freedoms and equality. Picking up on this theme, later-on in the 19th century, Marx would expand on this powerless theology by avowing and stating that: "religion is the opiate of the masses." Thus, the rebellious, philosophical continuity of three centuries of quasi-spiritual and anti- religious, pseudo/intellectual sentiments eventually led to an up-and-coming ideology of godlessness that reached its zenith with the ghastly wars of the 20th-21st centuries. The philosophical rejection of an ever-present, personal, indwelling Deity and the rise of the "cult of reason," both in pursuit of universal freedoms and rights, came about out of the corruption and the spiritual bondage of unbelievers in support of the Global ambitions of a declining, Roman Catholic Empire. Ranging from the religious emancipation by Martin Luther up to the doubt-filled deism of the Enlightenment, a series of Ages up to the upcoming inhumanity of the Industrial Revolution, the *Age of Secular Socialism,* along with the hate-filled postulates of Karl Marx, caused human havoc throughout the 20ᵗʰ century.

In sum, who would deny that the deist philosophers of the French Enlightenment, i.e. Voltaire, Kant, and Montesquieu, along with those of England, i.e. John Locke and Adam Smith, inadvertently contributed to the God-free, rational empiricism of the Modern Age, along with the carnage, mass-murders, and torture of 100-million innocent men, women, and children by the godless leaderships of Euro/Asia? Or, who would deny that the search for universal freedoms driving the French Revolution originally was based upon reason devoid of the grace and guidance of God. Otherwise, the leaders of the American Revolution recognized, praised, and humbly relied upon Divine Providence in their quest for religious, political, and economic freedoms.

In the end, the ideational/spiritual message needed for the 21ˢᵗ century becomes clearer: ***"without God nothing good comes about."*** Although throughout the millennia, a plethora of philosophers have been known to wonder and muse pointlessly and often aimlessly about Jesus' message that has been shown to have the universality and certainty craved and sought out by 2500-years of philosophical probing. Jesus is the only true, philosopher/king that explains the reasons for life on Planet Earth. As the history of philosophy unfolded throughout the Ages, Eras, and Epochs, the critical thinking of the Scientific Revolution, bolstered by the descriptive mathematics of Descartes and the calculus of Isaac Newton et. al, carried forth heretical remnants of the Age of Reason well into the godless, mid-20th century. In reaction to this theological skepticism and doubt, in the 21st century: (1) God and Church is being reinstated via the fastest growing denominations encompassing Evangelism; (2) nature vs nurture, as the Divine engines of human behavior--via the biotechnology of the DNA--has become socio/spiritually credible and fully in-vogue; (3) built-in religious morality is replacing the pseudo ethics of today's socio/politics; (4) Globalism and the liberating love of God, along with the great ideas of the Western World, are steadily being valued by both the developing and under/developed nations in Asia and Africa; and (5) universal human rights and freedom, as bequeath by God and scripted in the Declaration of the American Independence, along with civil liberties for all, and economic parity, bar none--stand in defiance to the Age of Absolute Rule of kings, clerics and the philosophical atheism of the Ages of Reason. Hopefully, this tortuous sequence of historical events and their evolving ideas will better explain and begin to soothe the anguish of the 100-million deaths of innocent men, women, and children occurring during the segments of the 20th and 21st centuries.

PART II

Freedom in the Modern World

CHAPTER 6

The Rise of the Sadistic, Barbarism of the Evil German Empire

World War I

Again God's ***Gift of Freedom***, specifically planned for His set-apart America by way of democratic/Evangelical institutions, was placed in urgent peril by malicious, foreign aggression. In the late 19th century following the Industrial Revolution, Prussian Germany decided it was its destiny to rule the nations of the world with utopian delusions and military might. As early as 1871, Chancellor Bismarck created a German Empire to impose Prussian supremacy upon the European continent. Militarily after the Franco/Prussian defeat of France, the settling of scores by the French could not be possible. Both the powerful Austrian/Hungarian kingdom and Russia joined together in defense of the German utopian cause. Just five years later Bismarck formed a Triple Alliance to include Italy. By the year 1890, Germany's total dominance on the European continent became absolute. These events set the stage for a worldwide war with the clandestine intention of imposing international bondage upon smaller nations in lieu of God's gift of universal freedom. As a counterbalance to Germany's power, Russia switched sides joining Great Britain and France to form a military alliance dividing Europe into two armed camps, i.e. the Central Powers and the Allies. This time it became total war, Global war, known as World War I. Prior to the onset of WW I in the year 1914 all these nations were economically prosperous filled with manufactured goods, markets to sell, strong budgets, and were fiscally sound. Within this hyper/nationalistic aura there was little thought of European peace.

What lid the fuse to the European war was a number of coconspirators who planned the assassination of the heir to the Austrian/Hungarian throne, Archduke Francis Ferdinand. On June 28th, 1914, both he and his wife were brutally murdered. Without delay, Germany was prepared to honor its diplomatic relationship with Austria and risk a large-scale European war. So too, Germany followed with a declaration of war against Russia and France. When Germany tactically attacked Belgium, Great Britain declared war against the Central Powers. Now all the powerful nations of Europe were at war, known as World War I. Ultimately, the British war cost 35 trillion dollars with a million dead and wounded. Conceptually scholars tell us that World War I can be understood in three phases. From 1914-1916, the Euro/Allies controlled the seas while the Euro/landmass was ruled by the Central Powers. In 1917, America entered the war which changed the balance of power during the Russian

Revolution, on March 1917. After there was food riots in St. Petersburg and the toppling of the czars, Russia had to desert the European war that caused Germany to transfer its Eastern troops to fight in the Western front. Lastly the third period of WW I was marked by a number of failed German offensives, finally the Argonne. The Kaiser, Germany's Supreme War Commander, sought his safety under the protection of Army and Navy. Temporarily, he hid in Berlin then fled to Holland as a life-ending, final exile. A 14-point Armistice was proposed and signed on the eleventh day on the eleventh month on the eleventh hour in the year 1918. As history has shown, there is a strategic difference between an Armistice and an Unconditional Surrender. This incomplete concord helped give rise to World War II almost a quarter of a century later Dividing German territories became the spoils for the victors. Russia got Constantinople; France, Alsace/Lorraine; Italy, Trieste; and Great Britain, a number of German colonies. Likewise South Africa, New Zealand, and Australia were given German territories in South Africa, Samoa, and New Guinea. And Japan took over the German Islands in the Pacific Ocean that were originally taken from a weak and helpless China. In addition to the 14-point treaty of the Armistice, five additional treaties were scripted designed to totally emasculated Germany. These treaties include the famed Treaty of Versailles, along with separate treaties with Austria, Bulgaria, Hungary, and Turkey. All the military assets of the German Army and Navy were confiscated, leaving once-proud Germany as an agrarian, second-rate nation. The Global evil ambitions of the defeated German Empire were thwarted and unfulfilled. Preserved and protected were freedom of the seas, the free flow of commerce, and for the smaller nations, freedom of self-determination.

During WW I, directly and/or indirectly, most of the nations on Planet Earth became involved either in battle or diplomatically. The human and economic price-tag generated by a dehumanized military technology was enormous and staggering. An arrogant, German Genome that preached racial superiority, affixed to the godless disregard for human suffering, instigated by a "total Global war" proved that freedom is never free. God's gift of social and individual liberty came about only with untold anguish and torment especially for the lame, the last; the least, and the lost of us that were deemed expendable.

The ultimate consequences of a pointless, 4-year Global war, which was instigated by the genetic sadism of the German Genome, negatively transformed much of the world map and its human-based cultures. France was left economically and culturally feeble. So too, the international, martial power of the once British Empire became severely diminished and curtailed, both in manpower and with an enormous financial debt. Culturally, most all vestiges of feudalism and their monarchies became replaced with the new security and the freedoms found in nationalism. Otherwise, America thrived, flourished, and prospered, rising to be the most powerful, military nation in the world.

In preparation for the possibility of upcoming wars and the training of an officer corps, just prior to WW I the USA became engaged in minor skirmishes and then major fighting with the all-powerful Spanish Empire that sought the riches of helpless nations. These American experiences with various Empires across the Globe provided America with much of the military know-how needed for a Global war, like WWI. The same might be said for the Wars of Manifest Destiny that produced an experienced officer cadre needed for the American Civil War. Or, the French and Indian War of the early 18th century and the valiant, fearless, and heroic leaderships it produced for the Revolutionary War. Throughout America's war-history God always prepared His set-apart nation with able-commanders and ample resources needed in support of His gift of freedom.

America's military prowess in the Modern Era began in the year 1895 by invoking its Monroe Doctrine when it kept vigilance across the Western Hemisphere. The British were warned not to coerce Venezuela over its border with Guiana where much gold was mined. This Anglo/Venezuela quarrel over gold stretched-out across a century. In the next year Spain, not unlike the British, sought control over Cuba's large sugar plantations, an industry worth in excess of fifty million dollars. Again America sympathized with the freedoms and rights of smaller nations, stepping-in under the authority of the Monroe Doctrine to intercede for Cuba, which has been suffering from a year long uprising by its rebels who were victims of wide-spread, Spanish carnage. Madrid approved of this Cuban bloodshed by forcing the insurgents and their families into concentration camps where women, children, and the elderly died of starvation and disease. In due course, by recalling the sadistic Spanish General Weyler back to Madrid, a new policy of conciliation was forced upon Spain by the threat of American intervention. Cuban insurgents under the protection of the USA simply sought their independence from Spain in the year 1898. Swiftly retaliating, Spain, by sinking an American battleship, the Maine, in the Havana harbor that took the lives of 252 American officers and men brought about the Spanish/American War declared by Congress in defense of Cuban freedom and in reaction to the sinking of the Warship, the Maine. President McKinley commissioned the financing of 125,000 volunteers to fill the ranks of the army and ordered the blockade of all Cuban ports. Battle-hardened, the Spanish forces in Cuba had 89,000 soldiers and sailors ready to do battle with the Yankee. As the war fever swept across the American/Cuban landscape gave President McKinley all the political capital needed to deal with the anti-war politics-in-vogue.

Prior to WW I, the Spanish/American War was fought on two fronts, the South Atlantic Region, consisting of Cuba and Puerto Rico, and in the Pacific, in the Philippines. Tactically, in the Southeast, the blocking of the harbor leading to Santiago caused some Americans to became captured, then rescued by the American Marines at Guantanamo Bay. The Under Secretary of the Navy, Theodore Roosevelt, who inspired Americans to sign up to join the fight for Cuba's freedom from Spain, tactically chose San Juan Hill to do battle. Overlooking Santiago, Cuba at its San Juan Hill was the strategic heights that protected this major city. Roosevelt's Rough Riders, along with Lieutenant John J. Pershing's 10th Cavalry, took

1000 casualties to capture the high ground at San Juan Hill. Unprotected with a now-demolished Spanish fleet it took just two weeks for the Spanish General Jose Toral to surrender his full garrison at Santiago; a city surrounded and outgunned, doomed to certain defeat. All the while the Cuban populace cheered the American liberators. Both malaria and yellow fever devastated the soldiers of both Armies.

Also prior to WW I, on the Pacific front Commodore Dewey sailing out of Hong Kong wiped out the Spanish Armada that was idly anchored in Manila Bay. By acquiring its first possession in the Pacific, Guam, an American Captain convinced the 60-man Spanish garrison based at Guam to surrender and cede to the USA. Furthermore, after long years of Spanish abuse of the natives, the American forces proceeded to seize Manila, the capital of the Philippines. Promptly, at the French Foreign Ministry President McKinley signed an accord of surrender with Spain ending the Spanish/American War, a near-bloodless encounter that lost more men to malaria and yellow fever, than from gunfire. Inadvertently by way of an assassinated William McKinley and his successor Theodore Roosevelt, this Pacific War against a powerful Spanish military was also preparing an impressive, American Officer Corps fit for the upcoming WW I with the overbearing German Empire.

However at the turn of the century promising a list of new forms of liberty, it was the God-sent, set-apart Woodrow Wilson, who led America and its "freedom cause" into WW I; a calamitous event that left Old Europe diminished as a cultural and economic rubble. Again as in the past wars in American history, God's gift of freedom became a principle motive for the shedding of righteous bloodshed. As early as the year 1912, Woodrow Wilson was elected with an overwhelming count by the Electoral College to the American Presidency. At his inauguration in the national capital, 5000 suffragettes marched and tested Wilson's oratory by demanding the right to vote. On Pennsylvania Avenue, female Quakers were represented, along the notable Susan B. Anthony and the penetrating oratory of Cady Stanton. Consequently, nine States gave women the right to vote. Regarding human rights and their universal freedoms, Wilson opposed any bondage imposed by big and autocratic Empires. On November 24, 1913, Wilson refused economic aid or diplomatic approval for Mexico's dictator, President Huerta. He fully supported the rebels in their fight for Mexican freedom. Success after success, Pamcho Villa and Zabata led the rebel cause for Mexico's liberty. With his US Navy and Marines Wilson contributed to Dictator Huerta's defeat at the dawn of the European War on July 15th, 1914. In this regard, Wilson declared a neutral America in European affairs. Why so?

Woodrow Wilson (1856-1924) felt he was God-sent to defend the Divine gift of freedom. During these years, Americans believed in the free market and honored God's moral code rather than a government devised by man's reasoning. Wilson was always a deeply religious man coming from an Scots/Irish heritage. He was a strict Calvinist, a Virginian. His close family was widely read, always in teaching, and as Calvinists, righteously rebellious. Woodrow knew his history and admired both Jefferson and Hamilton.

Early in his life he acquired the conviction that his spiritual destiny was to lead in great historical events. He was known to utter: "life is meaningless without religious certainty, the direction of God, and personal goodness." Wilson had all the attributes needed for an American President. He was tolerant, persuasive, professionally driven, and dedicated to the truth. He taught at Ivy League Universities. but preferred writing. It has been said the Woodrow Wilson conceived the subject of politics with his writings; ***Congressional Government (1885), The State (1889),*** a five-part history of the American people (1908), and ***Constitutional Government in the USA (1908).*** While teaching at Princeton University, a college devoted to the training of Presbyterian ministers, Wilson became its first lay President.

But it was WW I (1914-1918) and the events that followed that distinguished Woodrow Wilson. This Global conflict was an horrific War that shaped the menacing character of the 20th century. As a peaceable man, Wilson offered to mediate among the members of the Central Powers and the Euro/Allies. Yet, without any hope for peace events that took place acquired a life of their own. Events that included; the murder of the Archduke of Austria, the provocation of Serbia, Russia's support of Serbia, the French support of Russia, the German strategy of a two-front war against France and Russia, and the entrance of Britain to rescue Belgium from the Germans. Again without American involvement, Woodrow Wilson offered to reconcile the approaching European suicidal disaster. Yet, it was the German U-boat that turned Americans against the Central powers. Without warning on May 7th, 1915 a

German submarine sunk a unarmed, non-combative British passenger ship, the Lusitania, killing 1200 passengers, 128 of them Americans. The Lusitania that was the largest passenger ship in the world exposed the true barbarism of the Teutonic DNA/character as an internationally criminal.

The Germans continued their atrocities by sinking a number of American cargo ships and leaving the scene causing the American crews to freeze to death in a frigid Atlantic Ocean or drown. U-boat commanders were ordered to sink all merchant ships without warning that approached the British coast. Germany did not fear the USA with its fleet of 120 submarines they hoped to bring Britain to its knees. Reacting, England had to place mines across the full length of the English Channel. Next, the American Congress passed the ROTC officer program in its land-grant colleges, the National Defense Act, Armed Ships Bill to protect the merchant fleet, along with The Navy Act authorizing 10 new battleships, 6 battle cruisers, 10 light cruisers, fifty destroyers, and 67 submarines to confront the German threat. In tandem to these war preparations American intelligence intercepted a German communiqué that urged Mexico to enter the war against America by offering them all the Mexican land in the Southwest, including Texas that were lost during America's Wars of Manifest Destiny. Politically, the growing concerns of German U-boat warfare and the loss of American, unarmed merchant ships along with, Germany's offer of the return of Mexican land convinced the once-pacifist Woodrow Wilson, who now held the moral high ground, to ask Congress to issue a Declaration of War against Germany. What's more, Germany's order to saboteurs to blow up American military establishments further supported Wilson's strategy. Prophetically, six months prior to the sinking of the Lusitania, Congress proclaimed the creation of the Coast Guard, which mission was to guard the American Coastlines and to halt, search, and keep in custody all smugglers and saboteurs. Also prophetically, Congress expanded and doubled the army from 100,000 to 200,000 in preparation for possible war in Europe.

On April 29th, 1918, the final year of the war, Germany in desperation launched its Spring offensive toward the Marne River. Unexpectedly its army utilizing trench warfare, heavy artillery, and mustard gas ran headlong into the AEF with its 325,000 troops. Together, the French and British counterattacked and slowed the German offensive to a crawl. The American doughboys of the First Division and the Fifth Marines took many casualties, fought bravely and defeated the German Seventh Army on June 4th, 1918. Three weeks later, a brigade of 2nd Division American Marines, cleared Belleau Woods of Germans after 20 days of fierce fighting and the loss of 5200 causalities. Although Canadians, French, and Australians fought well, the American Marines distinguished themselves in all battles. To end WW I, it took over a million Americans available in Pershing's army that had to include Colonel Billy's airforce that flew intelligence missions over German lines, strafing German trenches, and engaging German aircraft. Since only 109 noncombat, American aircraft reached the front, American pilots had to fly the available 4800 French combat aircraft. At this stage of the war, the German loss of 600,000+ men proved devastating to its future, national existence.

In the midst of national pride and patriotism, America officially entered the "Great War" on April 6th, 1917 motivated to save democracy, its human rights, and hard-earned, socio/political freedoms. It was to be the war to end all wars, but as history has shown, it was no more than a preamble to an even greater war just two decades later, i.e. WW II. In WW I, a military draft had to be put in place ordering all males from 21 to 30 years of age to register with their local draft boards. Ten million men became available for duty. In France the American Expeditionary Force (AEF), under Black Jack Pershing began the American offence. With the American entry, WW I ended within a year and a half on November 11th, 1918. At once President Wilson proposed a 14-point Armistice protecting God's gift of freedom. It read:

1. No secret diplomacy. Freedom requires political transparency;
2. Freedom of the seas;
3. Freedom of international commerce;
7. Full Belgium sovereignty;
8. Return of Alsace-Lorraine to France;
9. Redrawing of Italian boundaries with equity;
10. Freedom for all nationalities in Austria/Hungry;
11. Restoration of the Balkan and Serbian nations;
12. Sovereignty for the Turks in the Ottoman Empire;
13. An independent Poland;
14. Creation of the League of Nations to assure freedoms.

President Wilson called this Armistice Agreement: "the moral equivalent in the war for liberty." Yet the cost of this pointless war proved staggering. In toto, the Allies assembled 42 million men of which five million were killed and 21 million wounded. Many Americans died in battle, from wounds, to exposure to deadly gas, and disease. In turn, Germany and Austria/Hungary activated 23 million men losing four million. Economically, it has been estimated that thirty trillion dollars were consumed by the Allies, with 32 billion contributed by America. Worldwide, an entire generation of young men was wiped out.

How could this have happened? How could the most enlightened, open-minded, forward-thinking nations of the Euro/Western World allow themselves to be devastated and overwhelmed economically and culturally fighting a Global war of little consequence? How could the Caucasoid of Europe who led the ideational evolution of Mankind choose to fight a war of Global attrition? Only America survived and temporarily benefitted from the freedom challenges of WW I; that is, for the next decade or so with its Roaring 20's until the Great Depression unexpectedly struck in the early 1930's. Obviously, the justification for WWI must lie elsewhere, away from economic theories, military suppositions, and/ or socio/political presumptions of scholarly and ideational history. What the 21st century intellectuals must consider is the "genetic vision" with its advanced biotechnology to better account for the causes of pointless wars. With WW I as a starting point, what might be failing the survival, bonding, and political Genomes?

As an ethnic factor, 20th century Germany, which incited two World Wars that caused the death of 10's of millions of innocence, seems to have possessed and expressed the brackish, backwash, dark-side remnants of the Cro/Viking DNA/database. All the while their "national cousins," i.e. the German pioneer, who chose to venture to the New World as the first Americans, became partners in the development of the North American society, especially during the Revolutionary Wars and Westward Movement. The "Euro/German squatters," in lieu of the New World "German explorers," became the Kaiser and Nazi collaborators of Germany and the purveyors of stark socio/evil. As a glaring eugenic contrast by the portrayal of their mirror-image DNA/profiles whether German, French, Irish, English, or Scandinavian, the émigrés to the New World when compared to the Euro/Continental populace or the 16th century AD European, pointed to distinctive, bio/cultural and bio/political differences. Indeed, Old Europeans and New World inhabitants became DNA/severed as separate bio/breeds. Old Europe has become "genetically depleted," and an "immorally impoverished" Continent of yore—no more and no less than a Museum of the Western World. As a result, in the 21st century the beautiful Christian Cathedrals of Western Europe have been abandoned on the Sabbath.

Consider this eugenic sequence. Vikings, the alleged descendants of the Cro Magnon, have been known to plunder, extort, raid, slave-trade, form tight and efficient settlements, and covet their neighbor's resources. Not unlike: the exploitive adventurisms of the British Empire which "colonial sun" almost never set; nor the Spanish Empire of the

19th century, nor the conquests of the French, Napoleonic Era; nor the expansionism of America's "manifest destiny" that gobbled-up Indian lands with an inspired trek to west of the Mississippi River. Add to this Global pattern of Vikingesque expansionism add the Teutonic tribes who accounted for: (a) the fall of Rome; (b) Euro/militarism;(c) the colonialism of many European nations which opium-trade decimated the moral underpinnings of China's economy in the 19th century, (d) the British/Portuguese conquests of India for centuries, and even, (e) the horrific, Viking-esque extremisms spawned by the Kaiser and the Nazi/Communist human experiments during the 20th century. Interestingly as historic "mirror-images" to these Caucasian conquests, most of the Black, Brown, Yellow, and Aboriginal races of Planet Earth *were hardly ever* prone to invade or explore the remote lands of their neighbors. Bio/historically these nonassertive races/ethnics of Mankind ought to be genetically classified as "human prey" rather than "conquering predators." As DNA/hypotheses, one wonders: oughtn't these well-documented, bio/territorial styles of Caucasoid vs non-Caucasoid people be examined scientifically as significant, bio/historic accounts? *De facto*, as been militarily scripted for millennia and by virtue of national, economic policy, only the White-race societies have embarked and trod upon the paths of "continental colonialism" and/or Global imperialism; or as in the 20th century, technologically sought the reaches of Outer Space as their national destiny. Undoubtedly as future, DNA/inquiries will unfurl: the cross-cultural interactions of predator nations vs preyed-upon nations will be titillating the scientific curiosities of both the bio/historian and bio/anthropologist. Step-by-step by pointing us toward the inheritable secrets of bio/tribalisms such as been conducted in academic milieus, those nations that have been involved both in proactive exploration as well as its negative reflections as in war and territorial aggression, should be leading us to the ideational merits of the "genetic vision." As a potential backlash, this new model of bio/ behavior will continue to haunt and erode the doubts of liberal professors, liberal Media. liberal clerics, and polititions who have been deluding, dominating, and defiling the cultural proceedings of the American mainstream. In time, these left-winged scholars and practitioners will acquiesce, cede, and give-up their flawed dictates and lead us to a new philosophy of bio/anthropological science. Deductively logicians will be mulling: *"...chronologically and genetically: how did the Cro Magnon Mutant beget the Viking, who begot the Northern Europeans, who led humanity into destructive wars, and who also begot the demographic ingredients of Americana?* And its corollary: are there DNA/correlates between the bio/territorial patterns of societies and their socio/political inclinations? Along with asking: have the bio/ social, democratic impulses of Western Man been energized by exceptional DNA/impulses? As well as lamentably, have these same, but combined DNA/impulses of territoriality also energized the aberrant Teutonic, who as a Northern/ German Viking derivative may have evolved as an anomalous prototype of this same genetic line?

Arriving as pioneers to the New World prior to the 18th/19th centuries, the Viking bio/paradigm, i.e. the English, French, German, and Irish, in parallel with their progenitors, the Danes,

Swedes, and Norwegians, seemed to have initiated the skeletal shaping of the social and political forces driving the American character seeking liberty and human rights. Nonetheless as been noted, a "national contour" of free government is never enough. Historians remind us: "...before WW I the United States was still a minor world-power and industrial fledgling." If so, it should now seem obvious that in potential it took the inoculation of other bio/factors to make America--American. What actualized the USA had to be a number of demographic events which included: (a) the humanizing/ideational inputs of the Greco/Roman tradition: (b) the Christian ethos: (c) the modern-day hordes of Mediterranean immigrants; along with (d) the intellectual traditions of the Jewish refugees. Both the Ancient and Classical Worlds, bordering the coastlines of the inspirational landscaping of the Mediterranean Sea, seemed to have been the missing DNA/pieces needed to complement and supplement the Neo-Viking lands. In the United States this gathering of Mediterranean tribes fleshed-out the 20th century character of the New World; a hypothesis awaiting a fuller, bio/technological justification.

What America of the 21st century must politically digest is the notion that the genetic seed of its Caucasian people accounted for both WW I and the embryonic roots and subsequent structure of its extraordinary democracy. Eugenically other than Euro and Asian Caucasians, scientists have strongly suggested that in addition to Black/Brown/Yellow/Aboriginal races, "archetypical White Americans" have become the 5th racial category on Planet Earth. This DNA silhouette of the *Genome of America* has marked the beginning of a new level of humanity. In part, this is why most of the nations of the world envy our wealth, resent our power, think highly of us, fear our military, and dream with hope for our freedom lifestyles. Immigration has always flowed toward America, never away from it. Are Americans unconsiously perceived by most societies as a separate subspecies of Humankind? Or just like the adventuresome, often brutal and savage, incursions by the Northmen, mostly Continental Norwegians, who brought "new blood" to the top-coastline of Europe, British Isles, and then to the New World, have the later, Caucasian immigrations to America prior to and during the 18th/19th centuries, fashioned and formed a "new genetic," i.e. the dawn of a Global citizen? By following a timeline, ranging from the 15th-century, Renaissance voyages to the incursion into Outer Space in the 1960s AD, freedom-living, freedom-marketing, universal human rights, social justice for all, civil liberties bar-none, and the economic equal/opportunity for those who dare apply have been the profound "genetic statements" of Woodrow Wilson and the Caucasian émigré of the New World Order. Did this same neo/society alsdo create a neo/prototype of the HomoSapien? After which as it might pertain to today's American, Globalized, cultural diversity, politicians must begin to debate: *are all other Black&Brown races and Asian ethnics been and will continue to be, "genetic visitors," "genetic strangers" and/or more precisely "DNA/guests," of the USA?.* In a nutshell, America is loved, hated, coveted, and unique because of its eugenic socio/political transcendence, not unlike the Cro Magnon vs the Neanderthal. For as a matter of bio/historic fact, after millenia of "creative cerebrals" illuminating Humankind by the Ancient/Greco and Mediterranean Man merging with the bio/adaptive socio/ character of the Euro/Nordic, eventually what ensued were the proverbial, thirteen, original colonies of the New World- -the fetal democracy of the USA. Looking ahead, *in* potential during the 21ˢᵗ century, which might become the sun-up of a New Era of cerebral enlightenment, we can foresee that the effects of the DNA/feats of the Anglo/Mediterranean upon the American government will serve as thetterritorial prototype to be eventually emulated by most all the nations of the Globe.

It's already happening!

In a nutshell, at first and for millennia, the Viking communities of Northern Europe-Proper, which would include Scandinavia, along with the British Isles, the lands bordering the uppermost region of this same Continents, most probably were genetically derived out of the many generations of inbreeding by the roving, remarkable, Cro Magnon mutant. On or about 60,000 years ago, this new DNA/profile of human life suddenly blossomed and gelled via chromosomal "mutational abruptness" that played-out on the Earth's stage. Heretofore according to anthropological speculation, physical, psychological, political, economic, and sociological attributes that never existed before actualized within a neo/hominid prototype. This was a DNA/phenomenon which signaled the birth of Man fit for the Space-Age. By virtue of the scholarship of Scandinavian prehistory, we know that the Cro Magnon in the Northland was alive thousands of years prior to the birth of Jesus. These studies have suggested that some semblance of an elevated level of potential civilization existed as far back as the Paleolithic, Neolithic, and Bronze Ages. Yet the actual links between the Cro Magnon and its progeny, the Scandinavian, remain unknown; most likely it was a DNA/relationship that came about via the mercurial, mutational laws of the shifting biochemistry of the Natural Order. Conceivably, what ensued was a precipitous metamorphosis of body, bonding, and psyche looming out of the basic dynamics of the Human Genome. By extrapolation both from the past and present, these survival surges of evolution can be postulated as consistent with the conventional, socio/political comportment of the Swedes, Norse, Danes, and Prussian Germans; along with, most of those who resided in the northernmost sectors of France-Proper and all of the British isles. These peoples reflected the psycho/social, genetic attributes of the orthodox Viking stock, hence ought to be considered as a societal composition, pre-formed as a "genetic nation." As an evolutionary forcefield, Mother Nature is a continuing lifeforce, always gravitating toward greater survival, greater health, and greater, meaningful fulfillment. As it DNA/happened, as part of this Euro/Northern DNA/ society the British became the pick-of-the-litter, the elite of the Viking Genome. Those who dwelled in the cities and townships on the rim of the English Channel seemed to have acquired the best of the bio/heritage from their Cro Magnon progenitor. As Western history has already scripted, out of Viking incursions, the British, Irish, Scots, and the Welsh became the major players to the socio/political, American DNA/puzzle. Then again as has been past-noted in biological research and as part of her charm, Mother Nature always likes to baffle us by including exceptions to her cosmic rules. The general canons of her evolutionary conduct always has been confounded by the special-case scenario. As an example of these specialized eugenic laws operating for human speciation, the Basque people, who also are Caucasians and who geo/ straddle France and Spain, somehow seemed to have become "genetically encased" and sequestered apart from the typical, Viking Genome; sort of a genetic mutation arising out of, or perhaps incised from, the bio/social mainline of the Nothmen. In this day of terrorist instability, this subtribe of the Northern Caucasoid, the Basque community, continues to fiercely protect her borders and cultural identity, her unique language, and her ultraconservative, religious practices. Somehow mostly as bio/political dynamics, these ethnic safeguards must be corresponding to the territorial elements of their Genome. Indeed from this eugenic digression what must be rationally concluded is that the DNA/thrust of our "commune drives" are deeply ingrained. What the Basque experience suggests: with the many instances of seemingly irrational, social clashes, among nations, ethnics, races, and religions that sate the daily Media, the causes and motivations behind these acts of violence serving as rationalizations in the preservation of borders and ways&means, ought to be studied as Global genetics. As further evidence of this dynamic phenomenon of racial/ethnic splintering and containment, the DNA studies by high-tech linguists, who were seeking an explanation for the uniqueness of the Basque language have inadvertently discovered and confirmed that these Caucasoid people carry genetic markers that are distinguishable apart from the mainstream, Northern Euro/Caucasian. The modus operandi used by these linguistic studies included hair samples taken from Basque teenagers.

Beyond question, as their conclusive, eugenic expression revealed, the Basque ought to be considered an hermetically-sealed subspecies of the Viking heritage.

In support of the principle of human-speciation and as genetic evidence of the Norse influence on WW I and the modern world via the British/Irish/Scot/Welsh subGenomes, scientists have determined that in the north of England 60% of the populations within their communities "reproductively echo" the genetic roots of Norway. In particular, what was DNA/ascertained was that in these regions, as well as in the northern coastline of Europe, a high incidence of Norwegian, genetic bone-disease was present. This medical evidence included modern-day notables, such as President Ronald Reagan and Prime Minister Margaret Thatcher. Moreover, there is a great deal of archeological evidence linking these Norse incursions during the 8th-11th centuries to the demographics of Iceland, Greenland, Scotland, Ireland, England, and Wales. During their Viking raids, it was the practice of invaders to kill the males and mate with their most beautiful females. Ergo; a strewing of sperm set in motion a eugenic libretto, which when viewed from a bio/historically perspective confirms that the Vikings and their derivative heirs should be deemed a uniform "genetic empire." As a matter of DNA/fact, the international bio/politics of the 2oth and 21st centuries will aver that artificially drawn borders don't necessarily define a nation; most probably, it's the DNA/composition across boundaries that constitute a valid society.

However as the "world politic" of the early 20th century has shown: it takes more than the talented, socio/political grit of a Viking personality to originate and execute the dynamics of a free-society; one which also is committed to a free marketplace. The sinew-ed skeleton of a Viking society needs to be embellished and complemented with the DNA/flesh of a notable, creative, and congruous "ideational people." Somehow for the miracle of political freedom to have transpired, it required a fuller fruition of imaginative, cerebral attributes and scholarly traditions of a "genetic people" who find themselves DNA/compatible with the basic, Viking socio/paradigm. Mutationally unexpectedly, the brilliance of an ingenious people did emerge-out and immigrate from the Mediterranean Region, so as to psycho/ideationally merge with the socio/politics of Viking/America. In time, this neo/Global, racial composition molded out of this DNA/partnership. No doubt, as the future annals of reinterpreted, American bio/history will be scripting: *the Nordic pioneer became a necessary, but not a sufficient, ingredient in the fashioning of the American, racial character.* In order to have completed this amazing socio/amalgam of democratic freedom, it also took the inoculation of "Classical Thought," as provided by the grit of the 20th century immigrant who fled the oppressions of Southern and Eastern Europe. Prior to WWI and the horde of Euro/immigrants, historians concurred that America was but a minor, world power. It later flowered with the integration of the Viking/Mediterranean gene-bases. Where do these territorial DNA/mysteries lie? As singular units of human tissue, how are they nestled within the dynamics of 40,000+ genes per human cell?

In partnership, this derived composite of Viking/ Mediterranean Genomes seems to possess the chromosomal markers which would have accounted for the political handprint of the United States. Although often affectionately referred to as America the Beautiful by the insightful sentimentalism of poets, there must also have been an underlying, Divine reading to America's, economic/political marvel. Already proven beyond the relativisms of cynics and beyond all the mathematics of probable events, this land of the brave and the free has been launched with a commitment to a godly DNA/vogue of governing by citizen injunction. This mandate included: (a) individualized, political liberty; (b) freedom in the marketplace; (c) a safety net for the downtrodden; (d) especially for Modern Asia and SubSaharan Africa; a packet of Western ideas sharing with these nations the axioms of high-mathematics, high-science, high-technology, the economics of capitalism, central banking and the insights of modern, socio/behavioral sciences. Although the theorems of participative government don't seem to apply to Muslim nations and their lack of emancipation of females and minorities, with little doubt, our democratic edifice by way of its Viking/Mediterranean building-blocks as judicated by US Constitutional precedencies, has been constructed thanks to the basic "bio/social personality" of a mutant subspecies, the Viking. Soon to be DNA/disclosed by bio/technologists and identified by bio/historians as the original, American Genomal Archetype, most likely, the targeted, exuberant energy of this joint, racial/ethnic persona, the Viking/Mediterranean, has been, and is, what the sinews of democracy is, and has been, and should be, all about.

Yet, for the imaginations of the non-skeptical, non-cynical scholar, a 21st century reading of the early formation of the United States could be broadened by a formal consideration of the extrapolated roots of the "venturesome bio/traits" of the Cro Magnon mutant. Chronologically from the very onset of this Early Man, a time period spanning 75,000 years up to the 21st century, this new hominoid became the archetype of Global Man. Anecdotally, the inhabitants of Washington Island in Wisconsin who have imaged a notable, genetic succession from the Cro to the Viking to the Skandia ought to be selected as part of this line of scientific inquiry. By traveling to this Wisconsin community, what becomes apparent within their tiny port-of-entry are the six flags flying in a row from Iceland, Sweden, Norway, Denmark, Finland, and the USA. Surely, this sequestered island-community must have been the remnants of a relatively pure, Viking community. And surely as a reflection of the original, Norse survival ways&means, this community must be mirroring the Cro-to-Skandia DNA/trail; such as, utilizing ice-breaking seacrafts during their harsh, winter months to shop for basic supplies on the mainland of Wisconsin. Truly as this anecdote implies, within the fullness of time and via the prisms of the future, bio/social speculations, the bio/political accounts of the New World will be evaluated by future scholars as a government created by the compassionate DNA/adventurism of the Caucasoid people of Europe-Proper. For sure, humanoid scientists will be writing that a "suddenly new" bio/political configuration of the Homo Sapien ought to be studied, adopted, embraced, and extrapolated more so out of robust, bio/historical theories, than out of flaccid, socio/cultural speculations. Then by referencing with academic analyses, it might be written that at his "bio/chemical onset," the Cro Magnon and his eugenic derivatives grew six-feet tall, were socially aggressive, pale-pinked skinned, with less body-hair, highly mobile, intellectually self-reflective, and curious as a nervous cat trapped in room filled with moving, rocking chairs. Wouldn't this DNA-profile also be describing the prototype of the modern, Euro/Northern Caucasoid or the American pioneer? Or, the 21st century, Space traveler? Or, the Caucasian neo/citizen?

At their onset, in order to survive the earliest of Ages, the he/she Cro had to deal with the perils posed by: (a) a mercurial geology; (b) a hungry, zoological array of predators; along with, (c) the competing phenotypes of the Homo Sapien, whether subhuman primate and/or Earlier forms of Man. In addition to the climatic peaks and vales of humidity, varying landscape heights, and vacillating heat&cold, what became the physiological and behavioral challenges for the Cro Magnon were both his/hers metabolic and immune systems that also had to evolove. Subsequently, these uncertain, precarious, and perilous conditions were adaptively passed down to the Viking Genome, via the DNA/compilation of the special attributes needed for individual and group survival--not excluding an uncommonly adeptness for the socio/politics of freedom-living. Via these geo/behavioral acclamations, the Cro Magnon had to outlive his/hers daily skirmishes with other human predators-on-hand, mainly the Neanderthal. As a consequence, the surviving Cro, by fine-tuning his food-gathering skills, which accommodated his mating rituals, was able to establish territorial protections and the cultivation of intertribal relationships. Thus, this lineage of preViking lifestyle widened, broadened and reached-out to expand his/hers spheres of influence across Planet Earth by way of Scandinavia, Northern Europe, the British Isles, and ultimately to the Caucasian pioneer of the New World. While eugenically the mating potencies' of this DNA/ pedigree waxed and waned, yet reproductively multiplied, thereby allowing the Cro Magnon to evolve into the Euro/ Viking, and later into the American archetype. Much later, politically in the 18th century AD, this particular bloodline of Early Man eventually became transformed as a Jeffersonian archetype, who successfully abided in a modern democracy and its freemarket. Ultimately during the past millennium, specifically from the Medieval to the Modern Day, a pedigree of Euro/Northern Man became maligned as an invading barbarian, when in fact, he was the idea transporter and conveyor who was responsible for the political demeanors noted in today's, liberty-loving societies and the Global Agora. Looking back through the prisms of speculatively reliable scholarship, the survival traits of this remarkable "New Man," a Caucasoid, can be subsumed by the traces of both the prehistory and subsequent history of Scandinavia.

Even prior to the 10th century, the Viking proved to be a direct kin to the Anglo/American. He/She was to be enterprising, socially aggressive, fearlessly explorative via their shipbuilding skills, ideationally inquisitive, not unlike the 20th century German who in WW I displayed a brutal savagery toward bordering neighbors as much so as his ancestor, the

Cro Magnon, who also had to behave accordingly in order to establish and maintain a survival foothold for its very subspecies life. Ultimately during the past millennium, and as noted in the layer histories of the Modern and Space Ages, a pedigree of Euro/Northern Man who has been characterized as an invading barbarian, in fact was the "idea shipper" who was directly responsible for the "great ideas." Granted not all genetic expressions have been spiritually upright, socially constructive, and ennobling to the ongoing evolution of the Homo Sapien.   It is especially worthy to note that Christian artifacts appeared in the Viking World as early as the 7th century. Likewise, their monetary systems which took the form of silver when artifacts such as sliver and coinage have been discovered as of Viking origin. It also seemed that the roots of both the moral evolution of Western Man and the rise of capitalism appeared early in the historic interchanges between the North and South of Euro/Proper. Furthermore scholars tell us that the belligerent life-and-love styles of the traditional Viking mysteriously disappeared on or about the 10th century AD. Actually there was no mystery. What happened was that the Viking conqueror decided to settle-down to agrarian and fishing modes of living on the British Isles and along the northern, European coastline. Concurrently in Viking history, their longboat excursions to the frigid New-World were discontinued and abandoned as potential sources for fertlile farmlands. Spiritually the mythological heroes of the Northmen gave way as Christian saints; not unlike, the Greco/Roman gods, who also became Christianized by Papal Bull. As the irrefutable history of Christianity in their continual search for reality, truth, and goodness, part of the history of Catholic sainthood might be comprehended as a "reform upgrade" of both the Viking heroes and the Greco/Roman gods. All in all, while at first it took the bio/social sinews of the Viking Genome to construct a stable, self-reliant, well-managed, and dominant nation, only its partnership with a cerebrally self/reflective and morally compassionate people, who were inspired by the genius of the aesthetic surroundings of the Sea of Rome, did a truly free-society and free marketplace emerge for all of humanity to partake.

In a capsule, only by acknowledging two distinct constructs: (a) the *"idea factor"* of a liberty-craving society, as separate from, (b) the *"socio/personality factor"* capable of framing a sturdy, stable, and secure society, might scholars be able to DNA/formulate the principles of a new school of thought, called the "genetic vision" of bio/history. *De facto*, piecemeal via Divinely revealed ideas, all of history's events in some way have been bio/spiritually driven. In potential, genes have had an influence on both body and soul. Surely in themselves, these paired genomal profiles, i.e. Viking/Mediterranean, were necessary, but not fully sufficient, conditions needed to create from scratch the miracle of a compassionate, America the Beautiful. We now know that what was also needed for democratic living is an "ongoing vision" which doesn't exclude the genetic processes, as modulated and expressed in both our wars and day-by-day, political interactions.

Already as breakthrough knowledge, it has become technically possible to identify a Caucasian gene harbored in any biracial, Black/American, or the Norse genes in England's northernmost provinces, or even the descendants of the Biblical Aaron in Africa. Interestingly, sperm-banks cropping-up in the Orient are marketing the availability of Caucasian, male donors for Asian women. India too is involved in a form of economic eugenics. They are offering dual citizenship to 20 million Indian business and professional men and women who have been abiding in distant lands. Their leadership expects that this enactment of Global, joint citizenship will be impacting their economy like a "GI Bill" did for Post-WWII America. India, which has been "preyed-upon" for centuries, needs help turning around their P&L from "red" to "black." One wonders if this Ancient land would fair better economically if they set up "British sperm banks" by inoculating predatory genes into all their communities. In India it has become common lore that mixed-race Anglo/Indians are more successfully assertive in sports and commerce. Irrespective of their huge population-base to draw from, every four years India fails to be adequately represented in the World Olympics. Why so? For over a century, India has experienced a "national brain drain" which has sapped and shipped its brightest and bravest across the world communities. What is "genetically left" is the bottom of their Genome—hence irrevocable poverty.

Is this a genetic statement? One ought to ask: across Planet Earth will these irradiating trends of the "genetic vision" become the political ways&means of the future? Or ponder, accordingly in genotypic, chronological sequence, will it be eugenically affirmed that the Nordic DNA will become the bio/dominant and sought-after bloodline of the Globe? Or, as if bred by a "genetic Abraham," have the Scandinavian; Dane, Swede, and Norse alike, acquired the "unique and able" bio/ adaptations out of the bio/behavioral legends of the amazing, Cro Magnon mutant? Indeed as Early Man, the Cro was a surprise; a mutational addendum to the human race. He/ She was biped, pale-skinned; 6-foot tall, mobile, intelligent, aggressive, and fiercely tribal--while possessing a physiology which yielded an estimated "longevity and health" of six decades or more. Surely the studies of the Viking ancestor by historians, via their numismatics and archeology should become basic to all industrial/political, eugenic movements or to marginal nations; whether these findings apply or not for the "genetic enhancement" of India, China, or Africa. For centuries upon centuries, history has shown that these three mega-lands have been preyed upon by the West; notably China and Africa during the 19th century and India for hundreds of years. To boot, add to this supposition, the ongoing pradations by the Causacoid of the aboriginals, i.e. Amerindians, Central Americans, Pacific Islanders, and the Northern regions of the Western Hemisphere. Why should we lack the knowledge about the bio/history of wars on Planet Earth?

Verily, the incursive voyages of the Viking have demonstrated that their "capitalistic appetite" for the goods&services of others resulted in the establishment of the early, predatory trade-routes across the North Sea, the Atlantic Ocean, up&down the Russian rivers, and up&across the prevailing waterways; mainly the Baltic and Black Seas.

Weren't these deportments liken-to those of the 17th-18th century Americans who pressed on toward the Westward Movement and who assertively sought the natural resources of the New World which allegedly belonged to "racial others?" As recorded from the 8th through the 11th centuries, the ***Cro/ Magnonitized Nordmenn*** possessed a barbarous drive to excel and accrue, ostensibly comparable to the British, French, Germans in WW I, and Americans who later were engaged in their own lusts for the lands of more-indigenous members of the human race. In concert during different periods of history, the New-World pioneers were comparably DNA/loyal to their OldWorld counterparts. They were covetous, double-dealering, inhumane and violent; while at the same time modulated by the dictates of their Judeo/ Christian Code; generous, liberty loving, and benevolent. In truth, humanity functions as two-sides of the same coin; good&evil, predator&prey, and benevolent&exploitive. Both the American colonist of the 2nd millennium AD (whether German, British, French, Skandia, or Irish) and the Viking of the first millennium AD (whether Dane, Norse, or Swede), searched-out spacious acreage for their offspring, open meadows for their flocks, and a freedom-loving society which sated their latent, unquenchable thirsts for emancipation. Accordingly out of this genetic pool, a cutting-edge of survival adaptation emerged for America and its marketplace. At first, with piracy, then, with the annexation of lands, and finally, with the open-trade practices which we seek and cherish today. Verily as the future bio/historic truth is bound to reveal, the offspring of Americana and the offspring of the Cro Magnon were attuned by genetic yoke; linked by Genomes which have been bio/politically endowed with parallel DNA/structures. Although separated by thousands of years of psycho/social bonding, these Caucasian bio/cultures, past and present, will be verified and linked by the bio/technologies of the 21st century. Clearly it would be difficult to deny that the bio/economics of the Viking Genome became the root source for today's capitalism. What we know: that at the very onset of their social consciousness the eco/politics of the Viking centered about a 3-tiered, caste society organized by those who ruled, as separate from those who were free; and apart from those who were denied full liberty. Yet, it would be inaccurate to assume that the very bottom of their social barrel was maintained by an institution of blatant slavery. In part, even this bottom-rung of their society consisted of relatively-free men. Periodically and with political compassion, enough time was allotted to their quasi-slaves to buy and sell, along with time to marry, and to seek-out some of the perks available to any other fully free citizen.

Out of the blue and at the end of the 10th century the Viking as a roving predator vanished. Instead, he became domesticated, formed stable communities, and via the process of social sublimation gave up much of his barbarous behaviors. He became quasi-civilized. He even became Christianized, helped along by the spiritual vigor of the virgin legend of Santa Lucia. Eventually, the Danelaw and its Scandinavian, judicious customs became part of English Law, which in turn ultimately crested and was conveyed in court practices and precedencies of the New World. Likewise, Skandia languages became much of the English, 500,000+ word vocabulary which Americans use today. In the Global Agora of the 21st century, this lexicon, i.e. English, has become the most powerful language ever conceived by the mind of human life. English usage is capable of describing the realities that encompass us better than any other devised means of communication. Granted as scripted, while the original ideas of democracy emanated from Mediterranean sources, nonetheless the language of British/America must be indirectly attributed to the Viking Genome. Both politically and economically, freedom-living when viewed genetically as ideas + language+DNA/personality, may become self-evident to the future generations of bio/lingual scholarship. In addition to their writing and speech, today's Americans from the Northern and Central Great Plains still retain their DNA/traces of Viking traditions and mythology. For example, on Washington Island, Wisconsin, you can sail into their port by ferry and notice the Skandia theme by the 6-flags flown daily in their harbor; Icelandic, Danish, Swedish, Norwegian, Finish, and the Stars&Stripes. Plain-to-see by bio/culture, both the original Americans and original Euro/Northmen are DNA/related.

Culturally during its early timeline, the shrouded, socio/political theme in Scandinavia Proper was to court freedom living--just like now in America. Although fierce rivals, the cultural connections among the English, Scots, Welsh, French, Germans, and Irish were, and continue to be, deeply-felt. Equally intense in style and substance, the DNA/linkages of these people were unmistakably committed to the whispers of early-American democracy and its free marketplace. Although both were challenged by the German Empire during WW I, in common, the notion of the right of "capitalistic possession," i.e. personal property, of land and livestock were the stated desires and unstated drive-states of these pink-skinned, Teutonic types. At the very onset, the primordial seeds of capitalism were based upon agriculture; fishing, hunting, buying, selling, or if need be, baron robbing, divesting and annexing land and natural resources. These were some of the ominous issues drivingWW I. These also were the roots that set the stage for British colonialism, the American, Western Movement in the 19th century, the Global wars of the 20th century, and served as a 21st century prototype for the trading of stocks and bonds on the Global Marketplace. Independently, along with the DNA/deployment of Viking inheritance across much of the civilized world, the Mediterranean Genome broached the "great idea" of the democratic society. In the fullness of time, this radical construct was eventually offered to the Ancient World, first by Pericles, Aristotle, Socrates, and Cicero. They were our Classical luminaries. Later on from this Greco/Roman Era, a dichotomy of sentiments, pitting national stability vs individual liberty, aka as the Machiavellian arena seeking the persona of a Viking-esque society. Indeed in the 18th century, America became one of these derived, Euro/Northern nations. Yet it was "Spanish politics" that named America after Americus Vespucci, a 15th century ocean explorer. It became a common nomenclature which described the USA as America by way of this Italian, personal pronoun, which later indirectly echoed the visions of Locke's concept of the "social contract." Occurring in parallel, the theories of Montesquieu; Rousseau; Jefferson and Kant cascaded and disclosed a fuller, social consciousness of Mankind. Now set-in-stone as politically institutionalized, these democratic phenomena which time have come can never be reversed, repealed, or rescinded. As these events and ideas must have sounded as unprecedented, neo/political ideas, it would have seemed freakish, cultist, and threatening to upend the power-bases of the entrenched monarchies. Be that as it may, these radical, freedom notions took root by irradiating into various formats including: the defense of freedom; the social origin of liberty; the natural rights of Man; along with the peaceful absorption of cultural pluralism based upon the force of law and individual merit--not violence or privilege. Combined with the wisdom-of-the-ages, these revolutionary constructs provided both workable theories and a unique, socio/ political personality, as noted by the only ways&means of America the Beautiful. Within the fullness of Viking-induced freedom-living, the democratic cores of both the Ancient and Classical Worlds, which were further embellished by a post-Renaissance Europe, became amplified as new "judicial thought," especially tailored for the Anglo/American socio/ psyche. The evil German Empire of WW I never could have upended this human desire for universal liberty.

In the light of a New Era, a ***Bio/Behavioral Age***, we ought to be inquiring: was it fortuity or fate that America became and blossomed-out from the throng of Southern and Eastern European immigrants who just happened to land on the 20th century's shores of an already structured, Neo/Viking World? Indeed, prior to the mass infusion of Euro/immigrant genes, occurring from the late-19th thru early-20th centuries, America

Proper already became "piecemeal inhabited" by the various Euro/ethnics; (a) English-types, (b)Germans, (c) French, and (d) Scandinavians. Then again liken to a human tidal-wave a second batch of émigrés drifted ashore on makeshift freighter-vessels. Via an impending, British-induced economic genocide, en masse these were the potato-famished, Catholic Irish who sailed into the American harbors during the early-to-mid 19th century so as to escape their hunger fate. The 1928 book *"Gangs of New York"* helped describe this exodus from potato-starvation to the hopes of prosperity and freedom. Prior, it has been estimated that one-million of the Irish in Ireland died of starvation. With hindsight and historic wisdom, these arrivals from the land of Erie filled the American groundwork as "genetic mortar." These people held in-common the grit of a Viking heritage, emanating out of the enduring DNA of the amazing Cro Magnon. Then beginning in the late/19th century, just 400-years after the Plymouth Rock landings, a complementary Genome sailed and docked in the USA from the same Old-World. These were the immigrants from the South and East of Europe; Italians, Jews, Poles, Russians, Greeks, Mideasterners, and sundry Slovaks; most of whom registered their incorrectly spelled names through Ellis Island from the years 1890 well-through the 1920s. Racially, most were Caucasian. At that time, America ranked on the world scene as a minor-power, minor-culture. and minor-economy. Brick by brick, these neo/immigrants composed the footings of what a democratic society ought to be and look like. While as an operational structure, early American history placed the French, English, Irish, and Germans as the bio/progenitors of the American politic, along with, the purer inoculation of the Danish, Swedish and Norse bloodlines. These Caucasians were the original pioneer/settlers, who formed the pre-American imagery and bio/politically bonded together as a consolidated genotype--called the American Race. Hence, a new socio/political principle was introduced: *any phenotypic behaviors of nations as imaged within the raw bio/personalities of a democratic citizenry, can only beget from like genotypes.* As logic dictates, America couldn't have been formed by chance happenstance. In itself, the Northern Euro/personality could not have produced a final draft of a free society and free marketplace. America's personage was created by a joint, eugenic-venture programmed by the musings of chromosomes, which had to be Divinely predestined and pre-imaged within the genetic contours of the Viking/Mediterranean Genome.

In the fullness of time dating back to the Tigris and Euphrates Era, we can expect that within the scholarly communities of Western nations this bio/political proposition, i.e. America, will eventually become accepted as unquestionable, bio/scientific lore. Our understanding of history as "nurture" will cede to the bio/history of "nature." By spiritual predestination, the pink-skinned and olive-skinned peoples were those "bio/socially poised" to operationalize the tenets of democratic politics. They also were enticed by the self-seeking prospects of prosperity as lured by the bio/axioms of capitalism. Or, by both the freedoms of politics and freedoms in the marketplace. Was it a fluke of chance happenstance that these same 19th/20th century, Caucasian immigrants adapted to pioneer, American life--*in just one generation*? While to date, all to many Blacks, Asians, Amerindians, and Hispanics haven't, and DNA/can't, seem to "get it democratically right." This premise must Include the Oriental/Americans who have been struggling to DNA/appreciate the full significance of freedom, as they continue to isolate themselves in neo/ Asian ghettos within the safety of their communities. Even at the cusp of a closing, booming millennium, America's, nonCaucasian subsocieties continue to wrestle with the identification, absorption, and assimilation issues needed for New World living. As contrasted with the pioneer Caucasoid, Euro/immigrant parents, whether Irish, Italians, Jews, or Poles never contended with the basic task of socio/political identification, absorption, and assimilation. These 19th-early 20th century émigrés rapidly fit into the American mandate *in just one generation*--all this transpiring mostly within a short period of time between the years 1870 through 1920 AD. Biohistorians can't ignore or deny this glaring contrast. Although working side-by-side in the workplace, all to many within the conventional, minority subpopulations continue to gravitate toward the demagogic lures of their leaderships, who promise greater social dependency, more political exploitation, and the myopic futilities of cultural alienation. *Regrettably, due to the territorial dynamics of genetic forces, both the conventional and recent minorities aren't, and may never be, fully American.*

Thus decade-after-decade, as the 10-year Census revealed: we still find the American Indians reservation-bound and secluding themselves and their offspring from the Yankee world. Why so? They, along with the Barrio Hispanics, who still cling to their Spanish tongue more as cultural protection, cultural protest, and/or as cultural expression. In their politics, the Latino has been falling-short of communing with the American society-at-large. So too might be said of urban Blacks, who still squander the goodwill efforts of tax-based programs, which are compassionately designed to include them into a full-freedom mode. Thus, what ought to be inferred in defense of the peerless, self-reliant, Viking/Mediterrean, DNA/persona who engendered the dawning of America: should the taxpayer be willing to daringly ask, why do most Afro/Americans who abide in the inner-cities express so little appreciation for the "democratic advantages" inherent in the voting booth since these inalienable, civil rights would truly set them freer from social tyranny? Emotionally, are they still living on the cotton plantation? Sociobiologically, might it be said that by failing to exploit the perks of freemarket capitalism, perchance unconsciously the Afro/American, innercity community prefers the modern visages of slavery as wards of the Federal Government. Surely, the economic tenets of America would lace their dinner tables with horns of plenty, while setting them freer from the chains of "big brotherhood" Oddly, even after 400-years of susceptibility to democracy's ways freedom politics and the free market haven't become an integral part of the bio/social, traditions of the Black ghetto. Might the basal issue operating be differential racial genetics?

No doubt, the dismal dynamics of WW I can't be explained with socio/political rationalizations, nor with economic pretext, nor with evil, godless leadership, nor with psych/socialobabble. The suicidal, cultural destruction of Euro/nations after WW I can only be explained with genetic models. Europe's Caucasian societies that led the way of humanity's ideational evolution instead chose the path of self-devastation in a war that could have been easily diplomatically reconciled. Instead the German Empire, not unlike the British Empire and the Spanish Empire, desired world domination and the bondage of preyed-upon societies that were weaker and smaller. So with much bloodshed and dissipated treasure, God's gift of freedom and individual human rights again triumphed, with American involvement and Woodrow Wilson's spiritual commitment to freedom and universal human rights.

CHAPTER 7

The Godless Emergence of Global Socio/Political Bondage
World War II

Thusfar, the American wars upholding God's gift of freedom have not been as noteworthy and momentous as World War II; a war that lasted from 1939 to 1945 AD. Scholars have described these ghastly 7-years as the *Modern Age of Human* **Carnage** that caused the massacre of the lame, the last, the least of us, and those spiritually lost. In excess of 100 million of these innocent men, women, and children were slaughtered during these 6-years. This was a Global War that featured the cosmic evil of socio/political bondage. The goodness of universal, Divine freedoms and individual human rights that are needed to bring-about the very survival of the human race were now in grave jeopardy. God had to intervene.

This total war pointed toward the dire consequences of the godless collisions of atheist rulers throughout Europe and Asia contending with God's set-apart nation, America. These half-a-dozen years generated a negative vortice to the essential cause of freedom. If truth be told, God was thinking ahead. That is, since the proverbial year 1776 AD, with a series of American wars and their "spiritually justified" bloodshed of freedom combatants, God created: (1) a Revolutionary Period; (2) the *horizontal* expansion of the American territory, from the Atlantic to the Pacific, out of the national zeal calling for the Wars of Manifest Destiny; and (3) the *vertical* elimination of the Mason/Dixon line of the Confederacy by Lincoln's preservation of the Union. Thus prior to the 20th century and in preparation for the two World Wars, a full-bodied nation readied for combat became Divinely created that was protected by two oceans. Although surrounded by godless and powerful evil nations, only America was strategically capable of defeating and overcoming the worldwide malice that was gripping the very soul of humanity and the very existence of Planet Earth. Global evil could never assure the continuation of the Organic Realm. All in all, in opposition to the bestiality now professed by most all of the nations of Western Europe and Asia that were wickedly committed to the ideology that "its all about reasoning" and the successful predation of vulnerable people and nations via their socio/political bondage, in lieu of religious faith, universal freedoms, and human rights, it becomes understandable that God's wrath and intercession formed a Divine handprint that guided the battles, the commanders, and the proceedings of WW II.

The Historical Background Preceding the Campaigns of World War II

Since the defeat and surrender of the German Empire in WW I and for about 15-years later during the mid-20th century the Euro/Caucasian again found himself in total war battling the barbarian Axis Empire; called World War II. During this period of history, it has been intellectually scripted as **The Modern Age of Human Carnage** when for evil and godless ideological justification millions of innocent men, women, and children were slaughtered and massacred. The lame, the last of us, the least of us, along with those lost-to-be among us were considered socio/politically expendable, subject to annihilation. Yet, Jesus taught the converse. Today spiritually depleted, most of Western Europeans consider themselves living in a post-Christian Era. In Belgium and the Netherlands only 1% of the population consider themselves as worshipping Christians. In Germany, one would be taxed by the government if you choose to attend the Catholic Church to honor the Sabbath. In Italy and the Vatican a fuming God has withdrawn His Grace from the Roman Catholic Church. The august cathedrals built throughout Europe-Proper are virtually empty on Sunday morning. Spanning the years 1939 to 1945 "godless reasoning" in lieu of "Divine faith" ruled the Caucasian World throughout Western Europe and Asia. A Planet devoted to evil could never survive in the vast, God-created Multiverse. Not unlike WW I, goodness vs ruthless evil became a spiritual theatre of warfare. For Epochs, this theme clashing good vs evil has been iterated in many ways in literature, visual arts, drama, dance, sculpture and blood-soaked warfare. Yet, God's gift of freedom in opposition to human-generated bondage neither can be tabled nor ignored by Mankind. If need be, for God the shedding of rivers of blood by war combatants must be permitted as a Divine deterrent as noted in all of America's wars. Biblically, Israel then America has been chosen as set-apart nations with the aid of God's armies to bring about a number of individual freedoms and human rights to Planet Earth. During WW II, most all the nations of Western Europe and Asia were led by godless rulers who worshipped the evils of reasoning in lieu of righteous faith. WW II promised to become an existential confrontation for the very soul and survival of the human race.

Indeed, it was the "Marxist Aura" and its consequences following WWI that proved to be devastating to the safety and health of the conventional families and communities of Europe and Asia Proper. In many ways these socio/damaging, Marxist outcomes took the form of: (a) a multinational, budgetary commitment to a socio/military model; (b) the demeaning of democratic and capitalistic freedoms; (c) major obstructions to private industrial viability; (d) A growing intolerance toward cultural differences; (e) widespread food scarcity used as political weapons; (f) the breakdown of international law, honor, and integrity; and (g) the socio/ acceptance of unjustifiable violence directed against those most vulnerable. Particularly victimized following WW I were the Jews, God's chosen people. In the year 1917 came the Russian Revolution. Hundreds of thousands of innocent Jews were slaughtered during this godless Civil War. Also during this historic period, Russian deaths approached one million, with a half a million more wounded. After WW I, German losses ranged between two and three million, with five million wounded. Every German family experienced at least a loss of a loved one and/or a lifetime of medical disability. This was the direct and indirect legacy spawned by the evil tenets proposed by Karl Marx.

Almost immediately after the Russian Revolution in 1917 AD, any formal, outward, spiritual expression quickly became the focus of governmental animosity. For Karl Marx, organized religion was imparted to the Euro/masses as no more than an addiction that soothed the psyche of the populace-at-large. Marx believed that true progress comes out of societal chaos, not from an engaging, god-centered, individual adjustment to unpredictable circumstances, as proposed in a Christian democracy. So too, in the early and mid 20th century the Eastern Christian Church in Russia, administered spiritually by a "King Patriarch," became an impotent, abysmal failure. This once-viable, Christian Church fell woefully short of conveying the compassionate, peaceful message of Jesus and His care for the lame, the last, the least, and the spiritually lost. What ruled was Karl Marx's socio/politics of hatred toward frailty, infirmity, and defenselessness; outright rejected was compassion, empathy, and the tolerances proposed by Jesus' message and ministry. Hence, without a socio/spiritual force to counteract the godlessness and wickedness of Russian Communism and the future of German Nazism and their ideological acceptance by the deluded, Russian and German citizens, triggered a Malthusian evil threat to surface and fuel the "spiritual impotence" of both the Orthodox, and Lutheran Christian Churches. It might be said that compassionate Christianity in early and mid 20th century's Europe stopped breathing, while the wickedness of Communism and Nazism prevailed, all due primarily to the bipolar, philosophical differences posed by Marx vs Jesus.

The first major stage of the appalling, godless, socio/politics of the 20th century was echoed in World War I. This 4-year conflict helped set the tempo, first, for the rise of Fascism in Italy, militarism in Japan, followed by anti/Marxist Nazism in Germany, and Pro/Marxist Communism in Russia and China. This First World War was the opening volley to the involvement of the near-entirety of Planet Earth, included the developed, developing, and undeveloped nations of the Globe. By the end in the year 1918 AD, well over 75 million people were involved of which close to 40-milllion were killed in battle, wounded, or neuro/disabled by gassing, famine, and/or infectious diseases. When compared to many of the wars of yore, historians tell us that this first Global conflict was both unnecessary and meaningless to the ideational and spiritual progress of Humankind. Now, it seems apparent that the underlying and initial cause that fueled two Global clashes was the genetic immorality imbedded within the German Genome.

Following WW I, and by way of the widening influence of Marxism, the ill-omened statistics of wars, genocides, famines, show trials, disease, rapes, torture, and massacres caused by the godless, Euro/Asian socio/politics were staggering and spiritually irresolvable. The needless victims and deaths of over a hundred million, innocent people occurred during this cataclysmic 45-year period of the 20th century. Surely, their ghosts would require the intercession of Divine wrath, then consolation, and His vengeance. As pivotal events, occurring before and since 1918 AD, the Argonne defeat, German surrender, and the Treaty of Versailles that was signed by all parties, gnawed at the distressed ego of the Euro/Germanic pride. Rapidly Europe began sinking into an abyss of national self/doubt.

The "Marxist Aura" and its dire consequences following WWI proved to be devastating to the safety and health of the conventional families and communities of Europe and Asia Proper. These socio/damaging outcomes took the form of: (a) a full multinational, budgetary commitment to the rise of the military/industrial class; (b) the humiliation by victorious democratic and capitalistic liberties; (c) the destruction of private-sector businesses; (d) a belligerent intolerance of cultural/religious differences; (e) a widespread food scarcity exploited as political weapons; (f) the collapse of international, law, honor and integrity; and (g) the socio/acceptance of unjustifiable violence against the lame, the last, the least of us, and those spiritually lost. Especially affected before, during and following WW I were the Jews, God's chosen people.

Further degrading human civility by the newly established, Russian autocrats a directive ordering the separation of Church and State was expeditiously passed, not unlike the law passed in Paris in the 19th century. A contiguous, philosophical link emerged out of the Age of Reason, the Enlightenment, the godless French Revolution, and Marxist Communism of the 20th century. Simply stated, without God's grace, the course of history was bound to deteriorate, not fruitfully evolve. As specks set in the Multiverse, nations, not unlike individuals, cannot spiritually achieve their destiny without a submission to the Divine Will. And so, this pretxual Soviet verdict of separation of Church and State led to the removal of all religious symbols from public view, along with, the illicit misappropriation of religiously owned properties, its art, and sacred valuables. Communist Russia also decreed the jailing of the Orthodox clergy as political enemies, the closing of Christian educational centers, and by means of terror, launched a resolute crusade designed to remove all outward, religious expressions. Today Communist North Korea is behaving the same.

It was the League of Militant Atheists that led the charge against Eastern Christianity. Under their militancy, churches and monasteries across the Russo/landscape were razed, bolted shut, and/or converted into concentration camps. This anti-religious mayhem spread to include the destruction of the famed 17th century cathedral, the Church of the Blessed Virgin and the Cathedral of Christ the Redeemer. Out of many thousands of churches open prior to the Russian Revolution only a few hundred survived to the onset of WW II. Moreover, as relics dating back to historic times, art valuables were confiscated, collected, and sold to fund the excesses of the new Russian regime. In toto, with show trials, torture, and executions, over 10,000 priests, monks, and nuns were massacred by Russian brutes. Without any respect for religious decorum, over a short period of three years the revered Patriarch of the Eastern Church was intimidated, periodically held in detention, and repeatedly threatened by officials, causing his untimely death. All this and more became the fulfillment of the new, citizen-accepted, socio/political model of Russian society in the 20th century. Thus, Russia devolved into a spiritual wilderness.

In order to fathom the enormity of social hate expressed prior to and during WW II, what must be considered are the economic exploitation of the weaker subpopulaces and the mass killings of innocence by both the Nazi and Communist Overlords. These atrocities backfired to created a Global psycho/political backlash among the free nations. This angst mounted and gripped the world's few remaining Western democracies. Yet Marxist aspirations grew ever more arrogantly and spread among the godless, psychopathic leaderships of Italy, Spain, Austria, Estonia, Hungary, Romania, Germany, Russia, Japan, and later, Mao's China. For a while it seemed that the human race was becoming irreversibly possessed by evil and about to become an extinct species on Planet Earth. As historic fact, Karl Marx, an archfiend destined to be marooned in the Outer Darkness surrounded by weeping and gnawing of teeth, forever, was able to briefly produce an epidemic "spiritual plague" across most of the world.

Along with the spreading of evil ideologies across the German and Russian landscapes, the military technologies bequeath by World War I and its newly conceived machines of death became the springboard and the rationalizations brought into play to justify the diligence of Marxist terror 10-years later. Throughout history the immoral, impersonal misapplication of the use of the new technologies in war always has been a Global dilemma. As example, the Japanese techno/militarism that developed a half a century prior to WW II immorally conducted sneak assaults and the pillaging of China's, fragile economies along the its coastal cities.

Embolded by these military conquests of helpless Chinese peasants, Japanese war crimes during WW II became commonplace, including: (1) the rape of Nanking, where 600,000 vulnerable Chinese were bombed-dead, in order to assert Japanese, military dominance over civilians; (2) the kidnapping of 1oo,000 young women from North Korea to be exploited as "sex slaves" for their military troops; (3) the cruelty of the Bataan March of American and British POWs; and (4) the retaliatory execution of 250,000 Chinese for assisting the American pilots after the famed, Doolittle raids on Tokyo. The merciless, godless, Japanese leadership led by Tojo was as horrendous as that of the Euro/Asian dictators. For over 200-years, the Japanese military establishment was committed to crimes against humanity. Indeed, the Global hate of the 19th-20th centuries needed God's attention.

Consequently, most, once-civilized nations drifted into a ***Dark Age of Human Carnage.*** Totaling in excess of 100-million deaths, the innocent "victim stats" generated by the godlessness and its immorality of Marxist philosophy were staggering. Even prior to WW II, during the "unnecessary"

Great War of 1914 AD, thirty-five million soldiers and civilians alike became casualties and fatalities; either physically wounded, or diseased, including those gassed to became neuro/emotionally disabled for life. Later-on beginning in 1917AD, many 1000s of Russian civilians needlessly died of starvation and infectious diseases from the inhumane, political treatment by sadistic Communist overlords. Rest assuredly; God's wrath has not forsaken the victims of the past century, nor easily forgave the consequences of the immoral pronouncements by the leaders of Nazism, Fascism, Communism, and Militarism of the early 20th century. These tyrannical rulers were motivated by evil decrees. They carried out godless sadistic pleasures that resulted in a worldwide: (a) erosion of individual freedoms and democracy; (b) chaos in the industrial and agricultural centers; (c) decline of capitalistic credit and wealth; (d) rampant, social violence, coups, and assassinations across the full breath of defenseless communities; (e) food scarcity leading to famines; and (f) breakdown of family stability and international civility. This comes about when reason subjugates faith.

During this social/political catastrophe, the Jewish community became especially earmarked and targeted for hate-mongering and annihilation across Europe Proper. Yet, with Divine power and guidance, the Jews, who have been and still are God's, chosen people fated to carry out the Moral Evolution of Western Man, were able to sustain the brunt of these terror shocks during the past 3000-years. With Divine vengeance and human justice, the Lord will not ignore the Jewish plight today. Operationally, the philosophical and administrative roots to this ghastly bedlam germinated out of the 19th century writings of Karl Marx, a Jew by birth, who renounced his family's religious legacy and for a moment became a "culturally correct" Christian. Marx, coupled with the Fascist paradigm supplemented by Mussolini's, anti-Papal Italy during 1920-1945 AD, both provided the socio/political framework to Russian Communism, German Nazism, Euro/Fascism, and the Maoism of China. In common, the immorality of "godlessness" was the principal driving force to the Euro/Asian atrocities of the past, two centuries. Therefore although innocent, the living offspring of Europeans are suffering deep, unconscious, personal guilt from the horrid proceedings caused by their parents and grandparents. Without an authentic multi-national sorrow, a voice crying in the desert calling for forgiveness and repentance, today's Germans, Italians, Russians, Chinese, and other secular Euro/Asian socialists nations run the risk of being marooned in the Outer Darkness, surrounded by weeping and gnashing of teeth, forever. The screams, shrieks, and screeches of those souls put to death by Hitler, Mussolini, Lenin, Stalin, Mao, and Tojo, continue to resonant rage out of their eternal abyss. To ease their collective psychic from the denial of genocidal blame, Europeans ought to quit rationalizing their guilt away by trying to sweep their sins under the rug by claiming to be in a Post-Christian Era. Ugh!

Will Europe-Proper, which has rejected Christianity, become engulfed and enslaved by the Moslem world? Devoid of political freedoms, will China's denial of basic liberties, not unlike happened in the USSR, result in her composite nation to geo/disintegrate? Moreover, psycho/spiritually, will Japan continue to fear with a "national phobia" their next nuclear holocaust? Yet anchored in spiritual bondage, will Russia continue to put up with its widespread addictions to drugs, alcohol, and an abridged longevity for its average citizen? And, will Germany from its past, egregious sinfulness suffer from a gnawing ache of guilt and psycho/dissonance? Historically yet-unresolved and imagined beyond any rational and civilized standard, the accrued statistics of the "Euro/Asian holocaust" of 100-million human souls in the early-mid 20th century remain stunning and unsettling to the individual, moral sensorium. Never in the course of 1000-years has there been such a collaborative, wanton politic of terror inflicted on humanity. These horrific facts now set-in-stone can't be denied, rationalized, or sanitized by a composite, contrived portrayal of them by "emotionally disengaged" politicians, secular scholars, and/or naïve academicians. God's wrath will have the last word and demand that these events that represent individual torments ought to be reported and studied as spiritual horrors of yore—destined to be Divinely avenged. Will the biblical prophesies of the end of Planet Earth as scripted in Revelation soon be fulfilled? Only Jesus, who remains the antidote for the disease of evil, can forgive and forget the moral revulsions of the 20th century. Only Jesus can protect, provide, guide, unconditionally love, and offer a Divine sense of internal, individual peace to the souls of 20th century Euro/Asia.

God's Military Plan for World War II

In the context of these dire, Global circumstances when evil reigned among nations and was about to consume life on Planet Earth, it became most reasonable to take note that God had to intercede to save humanity from extinction. Simply stated only goodness, justice, and the freedom to love can assure the continuation of human, physical and spiritual life. In the Multiverse, evil is consistent with human extinction and the destruction of Planet Earth. Evil sets into motion a negative vortex heading us to the abyss. As in the past since the proverbial 1776 AD when God selected America as His chosen nation to advance the cause of God's gift of freedom has war and bloodshed become so inevitable and unavoidable. Hence, a Divine plan for WW II had to be set into motion.

It all began with Hitler's takeover of Czechoslovakia in the Spring of 1939 to gratify German demands lingering unresolved from its defeat and surrender in WW I. Fascist Dictator Franco of Spain, who had a sizeable army, became bolstered by German and Italian warplanes and troops. Just a few months later Hitler launched a sadistic and unprovoked attack against Poland, later the Netherlands and Norway. England and France had an mutual aid treaty with Poland and declared war against Germany. War in Europe began while the USA and Belgium declared their neutrality, Russia failed to honor its treaties causing Italy and German/Americans leaned pro-German. France fell and the British retreated to Dunkirk abandoning their arms, military supplies, artillery, and tanks on the French beaches. Germany now-embolded concentrated on the strategic defeat of England first by destroying the Royal Air Force, then by bombing the English cities, and finally by invading the English homeland. However, It never happened. The British pilots flying Spitfires and Hurricanes out-maneuvered the German Luftwaffe and saved England from defeat. Winston Churchill's inspirational diplomacy, along with the Americans industrial might, supplied England with warships and military equipment to offset the growing fleet of U-boat attacks. Democracy and God's gift of freedom were now at stake. Scripted in Roosevelt's fireside chats to the nation God's four freedoms were highlighted as: (1) freedom of speech and expression; (2) freedom of religion; (3) freedom from want; and (4) freedom from fear. Six months later still in 1940 as a monument to freedom, Mount Rushmore in South Dakota depicting four American presidents was commissioned and constructed. God's universal human rights drifted to the forefront and were forever etched in the American consciousness, not unlike the fervor of the mid-19th century during the American Wars of Manifest Destiny. On March 27th, 1941, to defeat the Axis, President Roosevelt signed the Lend-lease Act pledging America's wealth, bounty, and industrial might to the Allies. Fearing America's economic power, in reaction Germany began to sink American ships with its U-boat fleet. Early as May 27th, 1941, the American freighter Robert Moore was sunk by the German submarine U-69. This incident convinced President Roosevelt that "freedom of the seas" was in peril and Global conquest was the ultimate goal of the Axis. Calling for a national emergency, Roosevelt addressed the Congress and described the incident as the German aboarding of the freighter, the ordering of the American crews in lifeboats, and then torpedoing the American freighter. From May to November 1941, German wolf packs continued killing merchant seamen by sinking American cargo ships headed for British and French harbors. Outraged by the American destroyer Reuben James sailing from Ireland took a torpedo broadside killing all its officers, Congress approved of arming of all merchant ships.

Meanwhile in the Pacific, Japan was acting militarily belligerent and adventurerous. President Roosevelt noting this aggression ordered an embargo of oil and rice and the freezing of Japanese assets. As Japan became encircled by four nations, it countered with the appointment of General Tojo to replace their Cabinet as the war Minister. On December 7th, 1941, a Sunday morning, Japan launched a surprise attack on the American Pacific fleet based at Pearl Harbor, Hawaii. Thousands of American soldiers, sailors, and airmen were killed by Japanese dive bombers, fighter and torpedo planes attacking American warships in port. Four days later America declared war against Japan and in just eleven days after the Pearl Harbor sneak attack, Winston Churchill, the British Prime Minister, met with America commanders to draw up a strategic plan to counter German and Japanese aggression. Thus, the beginning of World War II. At once Japan invaded Thailand, Wake Island, Guam, Hong Kong, and the Philippines. On May 6th, 1942, after 27 days of fierce fighting in Corregidor, the American General Wainwright surrendered his 2700-man command to the Japanese. Due to their suicidal aggression, the Japanese losses were five times greater than the Americans. Stationed in Burma the

American "Flying Tigers" and the Royal Air Force aided the Allies response by shooting down a number of Japanese fighter planes without any losses. In the Philippines, two noteworthy battles took place. General Douglas MacArthur, who took command of the Allies, knew that he had to fight an overwhelming Japanese army, however the war took an unexpected turn when the merciless Bataan March of captured Americans and Allies resulted in thousands of corpses by beheading, bayoneting, shootings, starvation, dysentery, and exhaustion. The Bataan March received Global attention that inspired the "American Cause." Throughout World War II and for many decades prior, "Crimes against Humanity" became the imprimatur of the Japanese rules of engagement causing fear against the Japanese/American citizens abiding in the USA. Consequently under the authority of the War Relocation Authority, the families of Japanese/Americans were ordered to become interned in concentration camps located in Western states for the duration of the war. As proof of their patriotism, ten thousand Japanese/American males volunteered to be come part of the American Army to fight in combat zones in Europe.

God's participation in the battle tactics of WW II occurred at the very onset. Just four months after Pearl Harbor sneak strike, on April of 1942, Colonel James Doolittle a B-25 bomber pilot, organized a surprise attack on Tokyo, Osaka, and two other Japanese cities. These raids undermined the complacency of the Japanese commanders who assured their populace that American aircraft could never reach their homeland. After this surprising bombing raid launched from aircraft carriers, sixteen American B-25 bombers that flew directly to China and were rescued by Chinese peasants who hated the Japanese for their past atrocities. Consistent with their history of "crimes against humanity," Tojo retaliated by executing thousands of Chinese peasants who allegedly aided the American flight crews. This Divinely conceived attack on the Japanese homeland proved to be a great morale booster for America and a troubling national concern for Japan. Strategically, sea battles close to the Japanese homeland continued to increase. In the Coral Sea a series of encounters erupted over a number of days across a large expanse of ocean. Both Japan and America fought valiantly and lost aircraft carriers. The American carrier, the Yorktown that survived the battle of the Coral Sea was able to rescue almost 200 sailors from the Lexington.

The turning point to this war in the Pacific was the Battle of Midway, a major sea encounter of great consequences. As in the past American wars during decisive battles God's faithfulness and involvement became noticeably manifest and pronounced. Again, the issues of evil, universal human rights, and the gift of freedom would not be Divinely conceded or ignored. Hence in WW II the Battle of Midway became such pivotal event. At Midway on June 6th, 1942, the Japanese sea forces proved to be indisputably superior, yet suffered a humiliating defeat. They lost four aircraft carriers, a large cruiser, and over 300 fighter aircraft. With their sizeable fleet consisting of over 200 ships, including carriers, destroyers, two dozen submarines, and cruisers, Japanese commanders expected to pull off an another Pearl Harbor. Like their sneak strike in Hawaii, the Japanese attacked Midway Island with substantial force. With faulty tactics and Asian smugness, their initial ill-conceived battle plan was to invade a key island, at Midway, instead, Americans commanders wee humble and astonishingly exceptional. Admiral Nimitz, who used surprise as a tactic with three aircraft carriers, no battleships, and 200 or so aircraft to take on the Japanese Armada stepped in to cloud Admiral Yamamoto's military vision. With the element of surprise like bolts from the blue, the American torpedo planes from the American Enterprise bravely diving vertically from 20,000 feet was able to sink three Japanese carrier and their fighter planes *in just one hour*. The remainder of the Pacific war of WW II consisted of a series of Allied island victories; at Iwo Gima, the Solomons, Guadalcanal, and Okinawa, followed by atomic bombs dropped as God's wrath on Hiroshima and Nagasaki. Japan's evil heritage that rationalized away their unending "crimes against humanity" by way of the theological delusions of their "cultural religion," Shinto, invoked God's fury via two nuclear holocausts. Surely God's guidance in WW II had to be in play with His selection of set-apart commanders who were granted the needed military/spiritual enlightenment.

No doubt, the unanticipated victory at Midway Island, which began to turn around the Pacific War in favor of the Allies, had understandable biblical implications. If truth be told, all the American "freedom wars" since the proverbial 1776 AD had spiritually-selected commanders by God, along with the military resources needed during key battles like the Battle of Midway. God would not hesitate to intervene to defeat the gains of evil or to preserve His Gift of Freedom via universal human rights. To believers, the analogy between biblical leaders and American commanders is conspicuous. Such as: (1) George Washington's performance was akin to *Moses* in the Battle of Valley Forge and his crossing of the Delaware River to defeat the Hessians; (2) Commander Perry's heroics at Lake Erie proved to be a decisive victory that protected the freedom of the seas in the War of 1812. It was a *Gideon* victory of a small American navy defeating the British sizeable fleet of man-of-wars; (3) the Wars of Manifest Destiny during the mid-19th century that featured President Polk and *Joshua trek to Canaan*; (4) Abraham Lincoln who was a *King David* who won battle after battle to free the slaves and preserve the Union; (5) Woodrow Wilson's spiritual wisdom in WW I easily might be compared to *King Solomon; (6)* General Patton who read the Bible daily amd drew his strength and guidance from God and His prophet *Daniel;.* along with, *(7) Dwight D. Eisenhower,* who was baptized just prior to the invasion at Normandy on June 6th, 1944 and who won both WWII and the Korean War. He was a biblical figure defeating Global evil. In toto, God's interventions protected goodness from Global evil, along with His gift of freedom and universal human liberties. These biblical analogies came in two forms: (a) the selection of God-fearing commanders who became a replica of OT leaders; and (b) a spiritual/military enlightenment via the Holy Spirit during decisive battles. As a matter of spiritual fact, God's participation could be witnessed in every American war since 1776 A.D. His gift of freedom to humanity-at-large would not be forsaken.

World War II that consisted of two fronts; the Pacific and the European, with five strategic battle stages; North Africa, Sicily, Italy, France, and Germany, along with its surprise victories at Midway and a number of key islands, prevented America's loss in either theatre of operation that would have meant the triumph of Global evil and end of Planet Earth and discontinuance of human evolution. Goodness, freedom, and universal human rights in lieu of worldwide human bondage became the existential, Divine themes in WW II. Operationally, the war for Europe's soul began in North Africa. The now-defeated France by the Nazis produced a land divided, North and South, Vichy and French Patriots to the south. The Vichy was froth with German collaborators. At first the invasion of Casablanca in North Africa encountered minor French opposition, although over 600 Americans were killed by the Vichy shore batteries. The battleship Massachusetts, two cruisers, and four destroyers were battered until the Vichy shore guns were silenced. At this *Phase I* of the European front it was the God-selected, General George Patton who commanded and landed the American Army in Algeria. After days of fierce fighting the French surrendered and the famed, highly mechanized, Rommel's Afrika Korps was neutralized by both Patton's Army and the British inspired heroics at both Kasserine Pass and across North Africa. Promptly, the German Army was reassigned to Sicily, the beginning of *Phase II* in WW II.

In Casablanca, Morocco, President Roosevelt of the USA and Prime Minister Churchill of Great Britain met to map out the Allies response to *Phase II,* known as the Sicily campaign. Both agreed that nothing but a full unconditional surrender would be accepted from the Axis. Philosophically, these two leaders understood that the evil ideologies they were encountering included Global conquest and universal human bondage. Again and again in history freedom and human rights for all were endangered. Operationally, both leaders agreed that *Phase II* should start with the invasion of Sicily. On July 10th, 1943, on the southern end of Sicily, the Allies amassed an Armada consisting of 3000 ships and military equipment. A half a million Allied soldiers were disembarked at this location. They faced 350,000 Germans and Italians. The next day, July 11th, the Germans counterattacked, but were repelled by the British 8th Army and the American 3rd Army. Seizing the initiative and without delay, the Allies moved northward toward Messina. Throughout the history of the Western World, Sicily has been the most conquered piece of real estate to be used as a jumping-off point to the European Continent. Since the Germans never intended to fight the Allies on this Island they promptly repositioned their troops on the Italian mainland, in Calabria. The flaccid Italian Army had immigrant families and brothers living in America and did not want to kill American soldiers of Italian descent. En masse, they began to defect and surrender to the Allies. *Phase III* of WW II began by invading with amphibious forces both at Anzio and Salerno, beaches just south of Naples; then fighting a hard-fought ground war on their way to Rome. Daily, in anticipation of an Allies ground attack on Germany, the American Air Force began a campaign of daylight, saturation bombing of German factories that manufactured military equipment. In turn, German defensive ack-ack rockets were utilized to abate the effective impact of the B-17 bomber fleet. Destroying the Luftwaffe became a secondary mission for the Allies. Simultaneously, both the American Air Force that committed 600 bombers and the RAF that conducted air raids over Berlin, the heart of the Reich, flooded with raging bombings of every German city, not unlike the nuclear bombings of Hiroshima and Nagasaki. The total destruction of Germany echoed God's wrath and fury.

Phase III, the Italian Campaign that took over a 1000 German prisoners, moved swiftly northward to liberate Rome from Nazi control. The Germans, who fought tenaciously, used the high ground as a lookout at Monte Casino, a Catholic Abbey. While the American Fifth Army attacked north, the British Eight Army protected the flank on the Adriatic Corridor. *Phase* III of WW II quickly came to an end and *Phase IV*, the invasion of France, via D-Day, came into strategic play. It was D-Day on June 6th, 1944 that was planned to liberate France on the way to the annihilation of Nazi Germany's illusionary "Atlantic Wall." Under the command of Divinely set-apart General Dwight D. Eisenhower, who became baptized as a Christian just before the Normandy attack, 150,000 Allied men and military equipment landed on the French coast. Prior to the main amphibious landing, American paratroopers from both the 82nd and 101st airborne dropped behind the landing zones both to attack and confuse the Germans. As designed and inspired by the Holy Spirit, D-Day became a surprise, secret attack by the Allies. In addition to the 150,000 man landing, three million followed carried by 10,000 ships. The German high command could not ascertain the Allies tactics when the Americans landed at Omaha and Utah beaches, the Canadians at Juno, and the British at Gold. In time, the Allies secured the beaches with considerable heroics and casualties. Moving inland swiftly, General Patton, a bible-thumping commander, and his 3rd Army along with the 6th Army group created a wedge, splitting the Germans defenses with its Operation Anvil. The French Underground with its 25,000 patriots, along with the Free French forces under General de Gaulle, aided the Allies with valuable information about German positions. In due course, Paris and France were liberated. Yet in Belgium, the Nazis regrouped and counterattacked to prevent the Allies from entering Germany by creating a Bulge in the American lines by reorganizing two elite Panzer divisions that attacked when the weather turned bad to avoid Allied air strikes. The American 101st Airborne became surrounded at Bastogne, but God stepped in to improve the weather conditions that allowed Allied aircraft to reverse the military outlook and causing the Germans to fail to take this key Belgium city. Now headed speedily into Germany, Patton's 3rd Army and Omar Bradley's 1st Army completed the final conquest of Germany and ***Phase V*** of WW II. On May 7th, 1945, VE Day, the Nazi Reich was totally destroyed, Hitler was dead, and the German leadership agreed to sign an unconditional surrender. Thus ending WW II in Europe. Four month later, Japan also surrendered on VJ Day.

Following WW II the world's people and God's wrath demanded justice from the crimes against humanity committed by both the Nazis and Japanese. On October 16th, a year after VE and VJ days in Nuremberg, Germany nine of Hitler's closest Nazis leaders were hanged. In the defense, they all claimed that they were just following orders. This argument was rejected on moral grounds which should always supersede any and all military orders. This legal standard became known as the Nuremberg Principle. In essence, the test for "crimes against humanity" included acts so wicked, so morally overwhelming, so heinous, that civilization could never survive its acceptance. Later, on December 23rd, 1948 following their convictions as war criminals, seven Japanese leaders, including two prime ministers, Tojo and Hirota, were hanged. Not unlike the Nazi leaders who shouted "Heil Hitler" at their hangings, showing no remorse. So too, the Japanese showed no remorse at their hangings, shouting "Banzaii." Diplomatically, General MacArthur approved of these convictions, but failed to convict the Japanese commanders of the Bataan Death March.

Seemingly as individual spiritual faith would discern, the wrath of God became attenuated and appeased with the atomic bombings of Hiroshima and Nagasaki and the Allied infernos created by the bombing of every German city. Again in history, God's gift of freedom and universal human rights threatened by the evils emitted by the "Empires of the day" that lusted for Global bondage was overpowered by Divine intervention. Throughout the Epochs, both God's set-apart leaders and commanders, along with the "battle guidance" provided by the Holy Spirit, assured the ultimate defeat of despots and tyrannical rulers of yore. Undoubtedly as Jesus taught us in Mathew 8:12, most of these evil heads of state have been marooned in the Outer Darkness surrounded by weeping and gnashing of teeth, forever.

CHAPTER 8

The Evil Expansion of Communism: USSR and China

The Korean War

President Dwight D. Eisenhower, who won WW II with military brilliance and his Christian baptism just prior to the Normandy invasion, also abruptly ended the Korean War within weeks after he authorized the shipment of tactical nuclear weapons to Korea in the Spring of 1953. All combat ceased in the Korean War on July 27th, 1953. Verily, Eisenhower must rank in stature with George Washington, who prayed on his knees in the snow before each winter battle, Thomas Jefferson, the Father of religious freedom, Abraham Lincoln, who regularly evoked God's justice for all, Ulysses S, Grant, whose spiritual courage in battle shortened the Civil War and helped save the Union, James Madison, who intensely studied Scripture for two years and became the Father of the US Constitution, John Adams, the only Founding Father who never owned slaves and who facilitated the Revolutionary War against Mother England, the Indian fighter, Andrew Jackson, who preserved the Union, and James Polk, of the Wars of Manifest Destiny. He was, deeply religious. Historically, Eisenhower ranks in magnitude with these past American Presidents.

With the defeat of the Axis in World War II in August of 1945 AD, the once-Allies, especially Russia and China, began to redefine the identity and boundaries of vulnerable nations about to be gobbled-up, exploited, and annexed. Prior these defenseless countries were ravaged by the Nazis and Imperial Japan. The geo/ transformation of Euro/Asia marked the onset of both the Korean and Cold Wars set treacherously in an unpredictable Nuclear Age. Without further ado, on August 17th, 1945, Russia convinced and politically seduced the ailing American President, FDR, to agree to divide Korea at the 38th parallel, whereby Russia would have power over the northern half and the American military the southern half. Yet unbeknown, this agreement set the stage five years later for the Korean War to erupt. Again in history the cause of freedom for all nations, large or small, was imperiled with the rise of the godless, Communist Empires in the West and Asia. Stealthily the Marxist ideology imposed political bondage via an overblown military upon many nations of the Globe. God's gift of freedom and universal human rights-for-all once more was about to be spiritually tested by evil Empires, i.e. USSR and China. This trial evoked a Divine wrath and involvement in both the Korean Conflict and two decades later in the Cold War. Always thinking ahead, God's wisdom planned a righteous, prosperous, free, vibrant democracy governed by

South Korea put side by side to an evil, darkened, starving, totalitarian nation, called North Korea. God's decision to take part in both the tactics and strategy in the Korean War came to pass when FDR's severe illness, his liberal ideology, and ensuing paranoia distorted his political judgment that began to favor Stalin, who soon died wretchedly as a crazed schizophrenic in June, 1953, while removing his support and respect for Winston Churchill. God, who knew the satanic heart of Stalin, who recently murdered 35 million of his own people, instigated a sudden and massive brain-stroke and death upon Franklin Delano Roosevelt, thereby allowing the elevation of the conservative Vice President, Harry S. Truman, to the office of the American presidency.

With little formal education, yet extensively read in history, Harry Truman turned out to be one of the greatest presidents in the international history of America. A man of the Midwest, the State of Missouri, Truman was a deeply biblically religious and politically honest public servant; profoundly committed both to justice-for-all and right over wrong. Truman was raised with traditional, Victorian, American values, with hope and confidence in the American future. Missouri, a prairie State that glanced westward for its identity became America's 24th State, enacted in 1821 as part of the Missouri Compromise. One of its two megacities, Kansa City, Missouri, then and now, has been a bureaucratic nightmare, corrupt to its core. Yet due to his strong Christian background Truman was able to resist the debasing temptations of public life. For three decades Colonel Truman served America in WW I as an artillery commander and at the end of WW II as

President of the USA. What American and British fighter aircraft and heavy bombers did to Nazi Germany in WWII; likewise, Truman approved the Pacific strategy of bombing Japanese cities with incendiary devices that set the stage for the horrific, nuclear attacks on Hiroshima and Nagasaki that killed close to 299.000 Japanese. Ironically Nagasaki was a Christian Japanese city. Yet, Truman felt no compunction or regrets at his approval as Commander-in-Chief of these quasi-genocidic, nuclear episodes for he was protecting the million lives of the American soldier from the proposed invasion of the Japanese homeland. The basic strategy in the Pacific War was to leapfrog across island to island until the battle victories of Imo Gima and Okinawa took the American bombers within range of the Japanese homeland. With overwhelming airpower, amphibious landings, superior fire power, plus nuclear attacks, America brought Japan to its knees and an unconditional surrender on the battleship USS Missouri. History will show that both FDR and Harry Truman ended WW II, that left the world at the mercy of the godless, evil Empires of Russia and China, leading indirectly to the Korean War on June, 1950.

Now President Truman, whose politics was nothing like his predecessor FDR, was neither duped by Stalin, who murdered 35,000,000 of his citizens, nor by the godless Marxist ideology that held that everything can be explained with economic theory, not spiritual principles.

Truman knew that Communism in any form was morally bankrupt. Truman also knew that Stalin was totally untrustworthy and that America was facing two Empires that sought Global bondage, not freedom or universal rights. The great Generals of WW II, i.e. Eisenhower, Marshall, Ridgeway, Walker, and Bradley, all hesitated to confront the 192 Russian divisions based in Europe. Accordingly, Stalin continued to snatch-up the nations of Eastern Europe and install Communist Rule. In March of 1947 Winston Churchill, whose wife was an American, delivered his famous "Iron Curtain" speech in Fulton, Missouri. Accordingly, due to this Soviet, military expansionism, a complex system of American bases had to be set up across the world in support of America's strategy of containment. In 1952 in Thule, Greenland with its minus 50 degree weather, a secret bomber base was constructed to prevent a northern attack by Russia. All the while in Asia, another corrupt power was threatening God's cause of freedom and universal human rights. It was China-Proper.

During the pre-years of WW II, President Roosevelt again showed his flawed international, liberal judgment by backing a corrupt leader, Chiang Kai-shek, who commanded the Chinese Nationalist Army. From the near end of WW II to the year 1949, first Roosevelt and then Truman provided Chiang with two billion dollars of loans and military equipment, much of which became stolen by Chiang and his corrupt officer corps. However, not unlike Russia's Marxist Revolution, a counter force was rapidly forming with the tactics of a inspired, peasant leader Mao-Tse Tung, also a godless Marxist, who appealed to and organized a formidable, peasant militia. The defeated retreat of the Nationalist Chinese

Army to the island of Formosa led to a second Communist Empire that renounced God's gift of freedom for all Asian nations, whether large or small. In concert, both Russia and China planned to pursue a godless Global domination by conquest. Mao declared the rise of a new nation, the People's Republic of China, a nation of 500 million people naively and desperately devoted to Marxist principles.

For the very survival of Planet Earth, God's answer to the events of Post WW II and the coercion of Global human bondage was the Korean War. Both Communist Russia in the Western World and Marxist China in Asia opposed freedom and universal human rights. They were the evil Empires of the Modern Age. When Communist North Korea invaded democratic South Korea it positioned Russia and China to dare oppose America's 500 tactical nuclear weapons and hundreds of fighter/bombers capable of delivering these atomic missiles. In Korea, on June 25th, 1950 the invasion by the North to the South below the agreed 38th parallel took place. Within a few months, General MacArthur, a hero of WW II was appointed commander of the now-assembled United Nations forces. He quickly began to plan a sneak invasion at Inchon Bay hoping to sever and conquer the North Korean Army and relieve the Chinese pressure at Pusan Harbor. While Chiang and the bits and pieces of his Nationalist Chinese Army took sanctuary on the island of Taiwan, Truman recognized the implications of the Russian and Chinese scheme to enslave the Planet. Without delay, Truman pledged a full economic, naval, and air power to both Taiwan and South Korea in their survival struggle with North Korea and Mao. At that point in history, the North Korean army had 90,000 men and a fleet of Russian tanks facing South Korea's ill-trained army of 40,000 without any anti-tank guns. Three months later, an amphibious landing was launched at Inchon Bay, led by the First Marine Division and the Army's Seventh Infantry Division. MacArthur's surprise invasion with 200 ships and aircraft was able to cut the North Korean Army in half putting them in full retreat. The UN forces relieved the pressure at Pusan while moving eastward to free Seoul, the capital of South Korea. Within two weeks, Seoul was liberated with the help of the ROK's 17th Division. The battle for Seoul was intense. A month later, moving Northward, American and UN forces captured the capital of North Korea, Pyongyang. On December 5th, 1950, unexpectedly the Chinese entered the Korean War with the full approval of Russia, confirming the Communist conspiracy of Global conquest. God's gift of freedom and human rights for all was again placed in jeopardy. The military advance by the UN forces was brought to a halt at the Yalu River, the border of North Korea and the Peoples Republic of China. Suddenly, a sizeable military intervention by Chinese forces caused both the American Eight Army and ROK units to take heavy causalities. A formal retreat was ordered by the high command to defensive positions south of the 38th Parallel. Truman, fully aware of the Global Communist intentions, declared a national, economic and military emergency and reaffirmed the enormity of preserving freedom and justice. By regrouping its units and tactics in the Springtime, the American offensive was again underway. Seoul, the capital of South Korea, was recaptured from both the Chinese and

North Koreans. General Ridgeway assembled nine UN divisions and launched a massive artillery and infantry attack, along with the famed 25th Division. As a result, both the Chinese and North Koreans withdrew. General MacArthur wanted to bomb the Chinese bases north of the Yalu by using his nuclear arsenal, while Truman opted for a more limited war. In view of these command differences, MacArthur was replaced with General Ridgeway as commander. The talk of a truce began to take shape.

In 1952, Truman decided not to run for the Presidency leaving the candidacy to General Dwight D. Eisenhower who pledged to go to Korea and end the war. Under the protection of the 82nd airborne and selected Airforce units, now-President, Eisenhower flew on a secret mission to face down the staled truce talks and said: "this war is over or I will nuke you." IKE had at his disposal hundreds of tactical nuclear weapons, some were shipped to Korea in the Spring of 1953. Just a few weeks later on July 27th, 1953 all combat fighting ceased as Eisenhower abruptly ended the Korean War with an Armistice proposed and signed by both parties.

****

Originally, the Korean War was to be a limited border skirmish; a post-WW II lingering symptom of an approaching Global evil about to happen by two giant Empires, the USSR and the People's Republic of China. Actually, the Korean War was about God's gift of democratic freedom vs the autocratic subjugation of human life and the suppression and exploitation of smaller and more vulnerable nations. God wanted humanity to see the difference between good and evil by way of freedom vs socio/political slavery. In essence, the Korean War was about the eradication of the lame, the last of us, the least of us, and those that are spiritually lost. Jesus loved these helpless people. The Korean War was about godless reasoning vs the freedom of religion. The Korean War was about the evil, godless ideology of Karl Marx and Vladimir Lenin, as socio/politically executed by two tyrannical archfiends, Joseph Stalin and Mao-Tse Tung. The Korean War became a continuation of the WW II massacre of 100 million innocent men, women, and children; a Era known in history as the ***Modern Age of Human Carnage***. The Korean War was about capitalism vs socialism as economic choices. In reaction, the roots of the amoral, evil socio/politics of Russian and Chinese Marxism of the 20th century brought about God's wrath and fury leading to His intervention in both the Korean battles and His selection of set-apart leadership during the War. Americans had great Generals that accounted for the short, 3-year duration of the Korean War. General Eisenhower, by threatening to use nuclear weapons, ended the fighting with his astonishing credibility as a WW II hero. Likewise, MacArthur devised a surprise amphibious landing in secret at Inchon Bay that cut the North Korean Army in half. Generals Bradley, Walker, and Ridgeway displayed great leadership in the retreat and counteroffensives during the thorny years of the Korean War. No doubt these commanders were set-apart by Divine fiat.

To grasp the perils to God's gift of freedom by World Communism as professed by 20th century's Soviet and Asian Marxism, it becomes imperative to scrutinize their futile ideological assumptions and their consequential effects on modern-day human life. In both the 20th and 21st centuries, the socio/politics of *Secular Socialism,* i.e. *godless Liberalism,* commonly practiced in the Northeast and Western states of America can best be described as *Neo/Marxist.* In common, all three ideological expressions of celebrated Marxism, Russian Communism, Chinese Maoism, and modern-day liberalism, offer the same personal and social subjugation message by adhering to the ill-advised, reckless, socio/political tenets of Karl Marx. His ideas constitute a spiritual plague to modern life by threatening the very well-being of Planet Earth. As in the past, American Wars of liberation, God's wrath, His fury, and His tactical participation in battles would not allow these aberrant beliefs of human bondage to succeed.

This was the legacy left by Karl Marx.

Karl Marx, a 19th century atheist, misguided philosopher, ill-advised economist, and politically, a hardcore communist was unconsciously terrified at the prospect of dying. He must be considered the principal, contributory originator of the socio/political evil and its mayhem that inflicted a "revolting revulsion" upon the lives of so many men, women, and children in Euro/Asia during the 20th century. Within this gruesome context, Marx must be considered the utmost archfiend of the modern day. Yet, what remains for humankind to think through via its scholarship and theology is the enigma of why and how did most of the world's population become sedated and seduced by the evil theories of Karl Marx? For the sake of the survival of the human race, these horrid, historical events can neither be tabled for future historians to decipher and mull over nor be allowed to be swept under the proverbial rug of existential guilt. Why so? Simply because, God will never forsake the millions of innocent victims of Russia and China. Surely, God will forgive individuals, but not evil Empires that threaten His gift of freedom. However, God will never forget to offer once-evil communities the opportunities to restore their spiritual integrity of righteousness, justice, freedom, and love. Yet-unrepented, most Europeans consider themselves living in a Post- Christian Era. They are in a desperate need of a voice crying in the wilderness calling for forgiveness and repentance.

What is emerging as the true fundamental causes of the Nazi Holocaust, Russian "terror eradications," Mao's butchery, and/or the Japanese bloodbaths, is reason vs faith. Along with, the Italian, Spanish, Austrian, Estonian, Hungarian, and Romanian that caused the annihilations of the most vulnerable, helpless people, tribes, and communities. These modern-day sins can never can be explained away or justified with economic theory, socio/political conjecture, military superiority, the charisma of despots, or the pursuit of unnatural, philosophical theories targeted for a New World Order. Emerging as new scholarship, the underlying dynamics of these primordial lapses of human incivility have been two-fold: (1) *socio/ignorance* that would hope to endorse the Marxist delusion of a classless society; and (2) *godlessness,* and its dependency upon the fanatic trust of human reasoning and mistrust of Faith. Both these primary factors would account for the metaphysics of human existence. They have been grossly misperceived by Marxist theory in their attempts to create a transformed humanity, comprised of a classless society, devoid of religion and God, all within the socio/political context of a highly centralized, despotic, bureaucratic government. Why did the world's literati and academicians buy into these philosophical myths that defy the moral fiber of a created, intelligent design of Mankind? How did the writings of Karl Marx become the "root conspirator" of these horrific Modern Day proceedings that splattered and impeded the evolutionary history of humankind? Today, any discussion of the validity of Marxist "class-free politics" and "socialist economics" already have proven to be flawed and irrelevant for the future of modern societies. Across the nations of the world, both political Communism and Socialist economics have failed to deliver the freedom, prosperity, and universal human rights craved by conventional Mankind. Only individual-based liberties assured by democratic nations and the free-market principles of an enlightened capitalism, as firmly set within the promises of the message of Jesus, can become the dynamics of individual fulfillment, societal realization and the survival of the human species. As Jesus tells us: "don't be anxious or fearful for anything;" "go and sin no more" and "come to Me for moral guidance," while otherwise, the message of Marxism sends-out a mirror-image, inverted interpretation of the Judeo/Christian belief. In spite of this inversion of truth, segments of the hard-left, Liberal politic, mainstream journalism, Liberation theologians, and hate-America academic communities, indirectly continue to revere the writings of Karl Marx's delusional theories. As yet in the 21st century, the Neo/Marxist facade of godless Liberalism continues to be promoted and ingrained within American culture.

In the 21st century the ghosts of 100-million innocent people, who were slaughtered by the godless leaderships of Euro/Asia will demand a retributional accounting, along with a targeted, national vengeance aimed at individual reckoning. A sterilized dissertation by scholarly historians, who try to rationalize-away with incomplete paradigms as to what really happened to the immoral, uncivilized character of 21st century's Homo Sapien, will not remove the millstone of guilt. God's wrath and vengeance will neither be attenuated nor appeased. Without any protracted hesitation, the innocent souls murdered by the cult Communism will be avenged sooner, than later, either by the ideational and spiritual enlightenment of 21st century Man or by the fury and wrath of an angry and just God.

The atrocities that occurred during this *Modern Age of Human Carnage*, in addition to the devastation and wreckage of both the structural and operational sinews of the male-dominated sectors of Russian and Chinese communities, blameless women and their children became targeted for annihilation. The "nebulous crimes" of these frightened mothers were motivated by their protection of their families from the dystopias of both Maoism and Communism. Regularly, women were raped by both the secret police and the Red Army, then executed. Their homes were ransacked, producing unattended, homeless children looking for their parents, as they were left to starve alone in the farmfields. In Russia, out of desperation women had to resort to prostitution, then, became branded to be done away with as moral undesirables. In the late1950s, over 10,000 adolescents and children were confined to concentration camps as workslaves. Few children under ten years of age survived. Work communes utilized close to 200,000 teens and younger as slaves. Capital punishment was applied indiscriminately to young, repeat offenders by psychopathic guards. Many State-declared, juvenile delinquents lived in the streets. Under the pretext of national stability, Molotov and Stalin let loose indiscriminate terror upon guiltless families. Extracting confessions from these families became the terror MO employed by the secret police. Close to half a million related, family members were arrested, 2/3 of which were executed. In the process of trumped-up investigations, fathers and mothers alike were tortured to death, then their children were taken away and sent either to government-sanctioned homes or to slave camps. The living conditions of women in concentration camps, who comprised 10% of the population, were appalling and sickening. To prevent rape and daily, sexual abuse by guards and other prisoners, women had to offer sexual favors to select powers-that-be. This was the horrendous makeup of Russia and China of the 20th century. This was why God commissioned the Korean War.

After the Russian Revolution, Stalin became paranoid about the loyalty of his military, officer corps. He ordered the deaths of 1000s of his top commanders in both the army and navy. Their wives were raped and children arrested and murdered. These events demoralized the Russian troops and as expected, had a noticeable, dismal effect on military morale and efficiency in their future battles with the Nazis in the early 1940s. Add to these atrocities, unChristian, sterilization laws were enacted that imposed upon the "spiritually lost," the "least of us," the "lame," and the "socially last." Without legal restraint statutes were applied by genetic, health courts to execute the weak, the disabled, the socially undesirable, potential criminals, sex offenders, and the incurable sick. Against their wills, a half a million men and women were sterilized in Russia. Eugenics became the national vogue. Moreover, so as to increase the incidence of births larger families that agreed to be medically and culturally screened were offered lucrative eugenic programs and social perks especially to younger, Russian women. In the late 1930s, close to a million families took advantage of these eugenic rewards.

Ethnic cleansing, sometime referred to as racial hygiene, was a modus operandi used to further back the Communist and Chinese transformations of human society. This was a sinister policy intended to achieve genetic domination across the godless nations of Europe and Asia. In Russia at the end of WWII, eugenic policies were extended aimed at the "final solution" of the Jewish race. Medical and political atrocities caused millions to be enslaved, agonized, tortured, and left starved. Cynically, in the Soviet domains even the young idealists and well-schooled residents, who adulated their despotic, godless leaders, endorsed the mass murder of

Jews, Poles, Ukrainians, and the vulnerable infirmed. Mass murder was also applied to non-Germans and non-Jews. All in all, 100,000 foreigners from Afghanistan, Greece, Korea, China, Bulgaria, Finland, Iran, Iraq, Macedonia, Estonia, and Romania were randomly beaten, targeted for arrest, and exterminated. The dystopic Marxist and their delusions of world domination through mass-jailing and State-sponsored homicide knew neither national boundaries nor moral limits. In Russia, the Gulag in the late 1930s was comprised of over fifty, forced-work camps with two million slave laborers. Without adequate food and warm clothing, prisoners were worked to death on railway projects. Gulag sadists, supervisors and managers of slave-labor, who managed these camps, had strict quotas to fulfill and dispensed little humane treatment.

Eventually, the Russian landscape became dotted with concentration camps and were the better known as centers of slave labor, mostly stationed across Eastern Europe and China. These "camps of revulsion" and their terror activities were hardly reported by the Russian Media. Yet these accounts were known and well-accepted by the common, Jew-hating, Russian citizen. With Divine conviction, God will never forget these victims. With His force of Divine reprisal, 21st century Europe and China became economically, culturally and genetically depleted; Dark Continents barely morally viable, now unfilled as "inert museums" exploiting gaping tourists hoping to partake in the past achievements of yore.

Within this historical context the Korean War can be understood as a Divine work of freedom and justice. Indeed history has no time restraint. Future scholarship will be addressing the past, via the present, while speculating about the future. In some fashion, the results of the Korean War is highly relevant for the 21st century. Flying over Korea in the darkness of night what strikes one is the gloom of North Korea *as contrasted to* the dazzling lights across the full length and width of South Korea. Without religion, North Korea lies in the Kingdom of Darkness while South Korea with its freedom of religion, capitalism, and universal political liberties lies in the Kingdom of Light. Is this airborne, visual contrast a parable depicting goodness vs evil that God had in mind for the world to see?

As current-day evidence of lingering Marxist thoughts, the consequences of the 2008 and 2012 Presidential elections voted in the most Liberal, i.e. Neo/Marxist, candidate in American history, Barack Obama. Step by step, the USA found itself in a steep decline; economically, politically, culturally, and morally. Neo/Marxists in modern-day politics, mostly members of the Democratic Party, naively claiming to transform American society by installing Euro/Bolshevism expectations for a New World Order, chose instead the failed socialism of a Left-winged lunacy of government, along with the acceptance of cultural depravity, and its amorality and immorality of: (a) abortion; (b) legalized drug usage; (c) rampant divorce rates; (d) dysfunctional families; (e) same-sex marriage and gay adoptions; (f) the unforgivingness of capricious lawsuits; (g) high urban crime; (h) decadent art and entertainment; and (i) the malicious attacks of police and anti-Judeo/Christian beliefs. At the root of most of this decadence lies the acceptance of raising precious children by single parents. Patently unAmerican, these presidential elections of 2008 and 2012 have revealed that experience, accomplishment, character, self-reliance, and a moral society no longer matter to the American electorate. Voters for the Democratic Party have turned America over to the Chicago mob, stanch Neo/Marxists, and during the next 8-years the immoral murdering of millions of innocent pre-babies through Federally-financed abortions. Are we experiencing a continuance of the gruesome socio/politics of mid-20th century's Euro/Asia? Has the survival of the American ideal already crossed a point of no return? How will God deal with this American spiritual condition yet-remains to be seen.

Logic tells us, there is an unmistakable parallel between the principles cited in Marx's, *Communist Manifesto* of the 19th century and the left-winged politics of the American 21st century. With paradox, in their efforts to transform America into a European-style socialism, Neo/Marxist voting patterns of the Democratic Party have been losing political momentum during the years 2012 to 2016. The American President, Baraka Obama, a stealth Neo/Marxist, who has a distinctly exclusive, radical, Liberal voting record as a Senator of Illinois, has been advancing his ideology into a full-blown socio/economic debacle. Not unlike Karl Marx and modern-day Russia and China, Obama wants to transform America and the Western World into an utopian, Socialist State. Obama's radicalism stems from his family upbringing that was pathologically dysfunctional. As a child he was "psychologically abandoned" by both father and mother. Obama's natural father fled to

Kenya, Africa, while his Kansas mother followed her lover to Thailand. As a boy, Barack was left behind to be raised by his grandparents to be tutored by hard-core Marxists. In reaction to America's downturn, beginning with the national election of 2010, a new generational cadre of Americans emerged, e.g. the Tea Party, that began to reverse Obama's Neo/Marxist conspiracy by voting-out many professional politicians of the Democratic House of Representatives.

Compared to America's democratic tradition of freedom and universal human rights, the godless ideology of neo/Marxism is patentedly unAmerican and unChristian. It fails to draw upon the hidden, spiritual wisdom, self-reliance, creativity, and strength originally built into the individual soul by God. In both style and substance, Liberalism, a euphemism for economic Socialism, i.e. Neo/Marxism, is mostly an amorally irreligious philosophical mode of governing. Liberalism has become a euphemism for social evil. It has little to do with the US Constitutional directive of separation of Church and State. In Socialist politics we see operating: (1) atheism, with its idolatrous worship of the created, not the Creator; (2) the flagrant abuse of the intent of the 1st Amendment; (3) reliance solely upon the limitations of human reasoning; and (4) its lack of trust in the voting judgments of the common citizen. Today, both Russia and China adhere to these Marxist principles. If truth be told, both the Western and Asian Worlds are devoid of Divine insights for both 20th century's Communists and 21st century's Liberals. Their misguided premises and operational beliefs of undemocratic societies have been distressing.

Indeed, as the Age of Reason of the 18th century has verified that the philosophical loyalty to "bad, bloated, and big" governments, when combined with the worldly reverence for the components and dynamics of the Multiverse, instead of the Creator of these marvels, is patently inconsistent with the traditional views of democratic living and God's Will for freedom.

In sum, Marxism of any form will leave anyone with a cynical and jaded view of reality and its psycho/spiritual consequences. Reasoning alone, devoid of a spiritual perspective, no matter how affixed to deduction, induction, sequential reasoning, language, and the arts will never yield a clear, fuller picture of the existential, ID questions of who, what, when, why, how, and where. As administered by a swollen, incompetent bureaucracy, both Liberal and Communist politics have been known to advance pan-victimization by the force of law, while instead, conservative/democratic politics insist upon an undersized, self-reliant, and unobtrusive government, as limited by the constraints of the State sovereignty clause of the10[th] Amendment. In both theory and practice, proponents of Secular Socialism are in denial concerning the philosophical constraints of the Divine Creation Plan. These Liberals tend to be socio/politically naïve, hence, psycho/spiritually attracted to those with evil personalities, regressed as unresolved adolescence. Paradoxically, the Liberal, Socialist, or Marxist derives its godless, political views out of the extraordinary events of the 18-19th centuries. The French Revolution, the European Enlightenment, the Age of Reason, the Age of Absolute Rule, and the Industrial Revolution, all Eras peaking with the socio/ toxic writings and social theories of Karl Marx, Lenin, and Stalin; despots who disseminated the misguided tenets of Communist Socialism.

In the 19th-20th centuries and with different, socio/political modalities, this warped, hate-filled, elitist philosophy endorsed the supremacy of raw power and reason, in lieu of faith, freedom, and universal human rights. During the course of 300-years, these radical leaders had the immoral support of most of their constituencies and chose to exclude God in their socio/politics. Instead, these same Euro/Eras have proven that Socialism is economically unenlightened and socio/spiritually destructive. In just one century, the USSR and People's Republic of China brought about carnage, bloodbaths, and mass murders across Euro/Asia with a bedlam of human suffering caused by two archfiends, Stalin and Mao Tse Tung. This Global, human slaughter totaling 100-million+ was consistent with the Socialist ideal of bureaucratic superiority and its denial and rationing of universal human freedoms. Along with, the limiting of civil liberty for all and the restriction of equal opportunity for economic parity. As democratic derivatives of these narrow-minded, errant, socio/ political views, the godless Liberals in American politics also believe in human bondage via big government, high taxes, redistribution of wealth, intellectual elitism, the supercilious misreading of 1st Amendment rights, and its corollary, contempt for the free choices by the common citizen. Mostly, Liberal judges in both State and Federal Courts have been appointed to rule as "activist judges," who interpret laws and the US Constitution according to their ideological whims. Yet, democratic living by its theory, tradition, and laws was intended by the Founding Fathers to be God-fearing, anti-Socialist, anti-Liberalism, and surely anti-Marxist.

   In truth, God is the Lord of History. If so, then: (1) a spiritual quality of humility begins to engulf a maturing soul that tells it: "you are but a brief speck in the Multiverse" in need of a personal God to protect, provide, guide, love, and make available the Divine resources for your life destiny; (2) with certainty that this immeasurable Multiverse had to be conceived, created, and is being maintained by the laws of science and mathematics; concluding, (3) that these laws of nature must have had a Lawgiver, i.e. an awesome God. A God is the God of the Multiverse, a God of History, and a personal indwelling God. By devising two spiritual plans for Planet Earth, Creation and Redemption, God is expressing His nature and intentions of conveying love, righteousness, freedom, and justice, set in a context of individual liberties, universal human rights, and Divine beauty. Thus, it becomes imperative that both our individual lives and socio/politics ought to reflect the clauses of God's plans of intelligence design and personal deliverance. Yet, whether one is a 21st century Liberal, Secular Socialist or Neo/Marxist, in unison what is being denied by these reason-only, pseudo-educated, non-believing crowd lie the created Divine dynamics of evolution. This transcendence includes our morphology, physiology, neuro/psychology, economics, technology, socio/politics, and theological insights/ Emanating out of the brilliance of a Master Inventor, God's launching of a far-reaching, *Creation*

Plan, was imaginative and based on science and mathematics. Also planned was the Creation Plan fit for the components and dynamics of Outer Space and Planet Earth. In tandem, a *Redemption Plan* was Divinely conceived to deal with the human responses to goodness vs evil, justice vs unfairness, freedom vs bondage, and love vs hate—all operating within the context of language and the arts. Universal liberties, whether expressed religiously, through the arts, socio/politically, technologically, or ideationally are fundamental to existential life and to the majesty of the entire Multiverse.

For the truth-seeking scholar and theologian, the asking of soul-piercing questions must always precede believable answers. Divine resolutions to the moral mayhem of the 20th century only can be resolved out of truth, forgiveness, and repentance and not self-serving spin, twisted logic, or ideological pretense. So one might ask, what might be put forward as the new ideas in the 21st century? *How* did reason get to triumph over faith during the past 300-years? *Why* did the cultured, civilized citizenry of Europe champion the hate-filled messages of their deranged dictators? *Where* and *when* did the philosophies, touted by the *Age of Reason*, alongside the *Age of Unlimited Rule* begin and spread across Europe? *What* were the antecedent conditions that led to the acceptance of anti-Semitism by most of the Global populace that helped establish an areligious, societal ambiance? *Who* were key players that produced this downward vortice to the human, spiritual journey? *Why* did organized Euro/Christianity, led by the Pope, the Patriarch, and the Archbishop of England, fail to impede the repulsive horrors being committed by the leaders of Euro/Asia?

In 21st century America, godlessness in socio/politics, journalism, Liberal churches, academia, and the entertainment industry has embraced left-winged politics and neo/Marxism. As a consequence of the 2008 and 2012 Presidential elections: (a) pan-victimization; (b) big centralized government; (c) high taxes to redistribute wealth; (d) political/sexual corruption; (e) 1st Amendment hyperboles; and (f) the Socialist Presidency of a hardcore, Marxist sympathizer, Barack Obama, will be challenging the American voter in the upcoming 2016 Presidential election. Americans, which find themselves in a steep, cultural decline--economically, politically, culturally, and morally, were once the last and only hope for a dying world. Why has the electorate chosen: (a) the socialism of a stealth neo/Bolshevist Commander-in-Chief,; (b) the Left-winged lunacy of a Liberal society; (c) the unconstitutional distortions of the 1st Amendment; (d) the acceptance of cultural depravity; and (e) the amorality and immorality of abortion, legalized drug usage, rampant divorce, single-parent families, teen pregnancy, the unforgivingness of capricious and frivolous lawsuits, soaring urban crime, decadent art and entertainment, and the ungodliness of anti-Judeo/Christian n beliefs. At the root of most of this depravity lies the unnatural acceptance of raising precious children by single or gay parents. Why has the Presidential election of 2008 and 2012 revealed that experience, accomplishment, character, and a moral society no longer matter to the American electorate? Voters for the Democratic Party have turned America over to the Chicago mob and to the abortive murdering of millions of pre-babies. Has an enveloping, moral decay placed America at a spiritual point of no return? Will the 2016 Presidential and Congressional elections be able to reverse this Malthusian trend? Does Mankind really believe that God has forgiven and forgotten the socio/political suffering and wickedness of the 20th century, without requiring a national repentance across multi-generations? Has there been a common "causal linkage" to account for the socio/political madness of the past two centuries? Will the self-absorbed paradigms offered by misguided, Liberal scholars and academicians be enough to assuage the "Global sins" of the Modern Era? Undeniably, there are in-common "underlying links" to the Euro/Asian carnage that occurred during the past nine decades that must be addressed convincingly, then atoned, and ultimately resolved, both intellectually and spiritually during the tenure of the 21st century. Unequivocally, these moral dilemmas can only be solved with the democratic acceptance by any free people, who spiritually desire, courageously choose, and act-upon either a godless or god-centered society.

Although innocent, the living offspring of Europeans are suffering deep, unconscious, personal guilt from the horrid proceedings caused by their parents and grandparents. Without a voice crying in the wilderness and an authentic national repentance, today's Russians, Chinese, and other secular Euro/Asian socialists run the risk of being marooned in the Outer Darkness, surrounded by weeping and gnashing of teeth, forever. The screams, shrieks, and screeches of those souls put to death after WW II by Lenin, Stalin, and Mao, continue to resonant rage out of their eternal abyss. To ease their collective psychic from the denial of genocidal blame, Europeans and Asians alike ought to quit rationalizing away their existential guilt by claiming to be in a Post-Christian Era. Ugh! Will Europe-Proper and Russia, which have rejected Christianity, become engulfed and enslaved devoid of political freedoms? Will China's denial of basic liberties, not unlike happened in the USSR, result in her now-composite nation to geo/disintegrate? Shackled to spiritual bondage, will Russia continue to suffer from an abridged longevity for its average citizen and widespread addictions to drugs and alcohol? Historically as yet-unresolved and beyond any rational and civilized imagination, will the accruing, statistics of the "Euro/Asian holocaust" of 100-million human souls in the 20th century remain stunning and unsettling to the individual, moral sensorium? Never in the course of 1000-years has there been such a collaborative, wanton politic of terror. These are horrific facts that can't be denied, swept under the proverbial rug, rationalized-away, or sanitized by a composite, contrived portrayal of them by "emotionally disengaged" politicians, secular scholars, and/or naïve academicians. God will have the last word and demand that these horrid events represent individual torments that ought to be reported and studied as individualized disgust of yore—destined to be Divinely avenged. Will the biblical prophesies of the end of Planet Earth, as scripted in Revelation, soon be fulfilled? Only Jesus, who is the antidote for the disease of evil, can forgive and forget the moral revulsion of the 20th century. Only Jesus can protect, provide, guide, unconditionally love, and offer a

Divine sense of internal, individual peace to the souls of 20th century's Euro/Asia.

Within this historical context, the Korean War seemed to be a limited border skirmish; a post-WW II lingering symptom of an approaching Global evil about to take place by two giant Empires, the USSR and the People's Republic of China. In actuality, the Korean War was about God's gift of democratic freedom vs the autocratic subjugation of human life and the suppressive exploitation of smaller and more vulnerable nations. The Korean War was about the Communist eradication of the lame, the last of us, the socially least, and those that are spiritually lost. Jesus loves these helpless people. The Korean War was about godless reasoning vs the freedom of religion. The Korean War was about the evil, godless ideology of Karl Marx and Vladimir Lenin, as realized by two tyrannical archfiends, Joseph Stalin and Mao-Tse Tung. The Korean War became a continuation of the WW II's massacre of 100 million innocent men, women, and children; a Era known in history as the ***Modern Age of Human Carnage***. Who would deny that the Korean War was about capitalism vs socialism as economic choices? In reaction, the roots of the amoral, evil socio/politics of Russian and Chinese Marxism of the 20th century brought about God's wrath and fury leading to His intervention in both the key battles and His selection of set-apart leadership during the Korean War. Americans had great Generals that accounted for the short, 3-year duration of the Korean War. Generals Eisenhower ended the fighting with his astonishing credibility as a WW II hero. Likewise, General MacArthur devised a surprise amphibious landing in secret at Inchon Bay that cut the North Korean Army in half. Generals Bradley, Walker, and Ridgeway displayed great tactical leadership in the retreat and counteroffensives during the thorny years of the Korean War.

In defense of God's gift of freedom, the Korean War proved to be a Global religious event with a newly-baptized President, Dwight D, Eisenhower, scripting the final chapter. After a secret mission to Korea in December of 1952 following his election. In the Spring of 1953, Eisenhower shipped a battery of tactical nuclear weapons to Korea, while notifying the Chinese by way of the Indian Embassy of his nuclear intentions. Abruptly a few weeks later, the Korean War ended. God's objective was to demonstrate to the world the difference between the socio/politics and economy of a desolate and austere North Korea, wallowing irreligiously within its *Kingdom of Darkness* and the individual freedoms, flourishing prosperity, and thriving Christianity enjoyed by South Koreans obtainable in its *Kingdom of Light*. At our salvation, Jesus plucked us out of the Kingdom of Darkness and placed us within the Kingdom of Light. Throughout the 1950's and after the Korean War, Dwight D. Eisenhower as President transformed America's culture by highlighting and merging religious faith with politics and commerce. He introduced prayers to the Inaugural affair, combined with a National Prayer breakfast. During his administration, "God" was added to the Pledge of Allegiance, along with "In God we Trust" as America's first endorsed motto. Along with, the religious and political institutions, which adopted the conventional adage in their daily proceedings "One Nation under God." As a result, church membership on the Sabbath rose to 70% throughout the American citizenry. Regular Bible-reading, the Holy Spirit, and the counsel of Billy Graham provided Eisenhower with the needed spiritual strength and wisdom.

After the Korean War came to an unexpected and sudden conclusion thanks to Eisenhower decision to "nuke" the enemy, Americans entered a period of spiritual reawakening. Billy Graham was convinced that Dwight D. Eisenhower, irrespective of his current politics and the economics in-vogue, was the right President to lead the moral future of America. At that time, Eisenhower was uncommitted to any religious denomination, but was convinced by Graham that voters would welcome a President who belonged to an established Christian sect. Eisenhower agreed with Graham and became re-baptized in the Presbyterian Church. During his early years in Abilene, Kansas, Eisenhower's family was deeply religious. His grandfather and father were Mennonites; his mother a Jehovah Witness. The Bible was read daily and became the family's guiding source of spiritual inspiration. Throughout his life, Dwight D. Eisenhower was devoted to the Bible and strongly held that a democracy and the future of Western civilization could not survive without the morality offered by Judeo/Christianity. He supported the Seven Divine Freedoms alluded in Psalm 23: Freedom from Want; Hunger; Thirst; Sin; Fear, Enemies and to live Abundantly. In addition to his feats in WW II and Korea in 1953, Eisenhower concluded his military accomplishments in the year 1956. Then, Israel,

France, and Britain planned to snatch the Aswan Dam on the Nile River from Egypt, a weakened power. Eisenhower said "no" by preparing amphibious troops to counter the plans of his once-allies. They backed down to Eisenhower..

CHAPTER 9

The Suppression of Freedom in Sino/Asia
The American Vietnam War

America did not lose the Vietnam War in the year 1975. It was the surrender and capitulation of the South Vietnamese Army that did not consider "freedom" worth the fight. In contrast to, the ferocity of the North Vietnamese troops and militia that won the Vietnam War hoping to preserve their tradition and long history of socio/political bondage to either their Sino/monarchies of yore and in the 20th century, to the slavery of Communism. At the bottom of it, America's military objective was to bring about God's gift of freedom to Southeast Asia as it did to South Korea a few years prior. However, this War was lost to the Communist North Vietnamese when the South Vietnam Army surrendered its arms to maintain their subconscious history of being governed by the despotism of modern-day Communism.

Throughout their history, Southeast Asians never have shown any inclination toward the ideas and ideals of democratic living. What happened two years prior to the defeat of South Vietnam, when America achieved "victory with honor" by way of a Treaty in Paris, President Nixon turned over all future combat to the South Vietnamese Army that became fully armed and supplied as early as the year 1973. Previously, the evils of Global subjugation and bondage by Russian and Chinese Marxism were contained by Eisenhower's threat of tactical nuclear involvement, abruptly ending the fighting of the Korean War. Then, God's offer of freedom shifted to Southeast Asia, where in this Global region all were of Chinese DNA origin. Vietnam, Cambodia, Burma, Thailand, Laos, Indonesia, Malaysia, Java, and Sumatra formed a potential Empire that spiritually yearned for a resolution to the socio/political freedoms of democratic living vs the tyranny of their repressive, age-old monarchies. Yet, trying to enter the Modern Era for them was not easy. As a interim alternative, these underdeveloped nations of Southeast Asia gravitated toward Communism or another monarchy in opposition to the past economic exploitations by the Western World. Specifically in Vietnam the French readily exploited the resources of this colony for years, but was defeated and expelled by a Communist Vietnamese militia in the year 1954. As expected, these Chinese hybrid nations of Southeast Asia leaned toward the ideological bondage of Communism rather than take the leap forward toward the freedoms offered by a democracy. Accordingly, by defending and protecting its hard-earned freedoms in both WW II and the Korean Conflict, America became misled and drawn into a long-shooting war in Southeast Asia that lasted over a decade,--from 1965 to 1975.

In tandem to this Southeast Asian War a social revolution already was taking place on the American Mainland. This incongruity impacted the military frame of mind of the American soldier who found himself rebellious, uncertain, hesitant, and placed him at greater risk during combat conditions. Tactically, American conquests in Southeast Asia often became ineffective, muddied, and confounded by the widening social revolution spreading across the USA. This rebellion among young adults introduced hard drugs, liberalism, free-for-all sexuality, and student protests opposing the war. Add to these disruptive social factors, the Vietnam War was conducted and micromanaged by Washington career-politicians and bureaucrats instead of knowledgeable Generals on the ground. The Secretary of Defense, who set both the strategies and tactics, along with the inept Officers chosen by them proved to be militarily bungling and incompetent.

Thinking ahead prior to the shooting war in Southeast Asia and during and after the Korean War American defense planners, commissioned funds for the building of a secret airbase in the frozen and freezing inhospitable surroundings of Thule, Greenland. Hundreds of cargo ships filled with construction materials arrived in Thule to build a huge facility to counteract the threat of a Russian invasion from the North Pole. On a regular basis, the weather in Greenland was clocked at 50 degrees below zero with sunlight during the winter months at seven minutes per day. So to, to protect its richly deserved Global freedoms, American strategists organized 40+ spy networks across the world, known as *Military Assistance Advisory Group* (MAAG) and *Army Security Agency* (ASA). These top-secret, spy programs, not unlike today's CIA, were expected to: (a) assist South Vietnam in their fight against the Communist Viet Cong that sadistically assassinated and beheaded village chiefs after the French defeat in 1954; (b) gather intelligence; (c) train soldiers; (d) escort refugees out of danger zones; (e) fly scouting missions; (f) encode and decode enemy messages; (g) protect the classified materials of the USA; and (h)) defend MAAG troops with force when threatened. Prior to the start of the official Vietnam War in 1965, there were 60,000 American spies assigned to MAAG across the Globe, who were supported and airlifted in and out of Clark Air force Base in the Philippines. Indeed, not unlike in WW II and the Korean Conflict, Southeast Asia became the next modern-day Empire opposed to political freedoms and universal human rights. God's gift of freedom to humanity was again challenged by another Global tyranny.

In response to these rapidly unfolding events, in 1965 America had no choice but to shift its role from defensive to offensive, from advisory via the MAAG and ASA spy programs to active combat. At this time, American bases were being attacked with mounting casualties. So, President Lyndon Johnson ordered a bombing campaign against North Vietnam, while American troop strength was being increased five-fold. Sent in, two battalions of marines and army units from the First Calvary defeated key Vietcong forces. By the end of 1965, as green, body bags carried dead soldiers back to the USA,

American college protests intensified. Politically America was becoming polarized. In the Spring of 1966, American forces scored decisive victories in the Mekong Delta in South Vietnam, while the 173rd Airborne defeated battalions of Vietcong and destroyed their "command and control" headquarters. Naively, to win the hearts and minds of the beleaguered Vietnamese, President Johnson offered to build medical and educational facilities for the North, hoping to lure them into accepting democratic living. However, surging waves of anti-war protests and the equal rights movement for Black America continued to sweep across the country. These civil Rights protests and riots disrupted the national peace. Hard drug usage swelled. Sport sexuality became immorally in-vogue. Liberals vs Conservatives competition flourished in academia, politics, churches, and the Media. Unexpectedly, the Southeast Asian war for freedom was attenuated by the social revolution in the American Homeland. Yet, as noted by Hanoi's Generals: (1) the various search&destroy missions; (2) the increase of American forces now numbering a half a million; (3) attempts at Vietnamese pacification; and (4) the heavy bombing campaigns launched, all failed as strategies to bring North Vietnam to its knees. Irrespective of the loss of 100,000's of military and civilians the defense of Vietnamese Communism proved to be a stronger obsession than to capitulate to the democratic West. The Communist Generals in Southeast Asia sensing the four-part, American strategic failures were willing to commit another million casualties to their cause to defeat both the Sino/monarchies of yore and the imperialism of the West. Hence, North Vietnam went on the offensive on January 31st, 1968. It was called the Tet Offensive, launched on their

Lunar New Year. With over 100,000 troops ready to die and with a brilliantly coordinated strategy, both the North Vietnam Army and the Vietcong militia attacked the American and South Vietnam forces across their principal cities, including Saigon and its American Embassy. These Communist victories exposed the incompetence and naïve predictability of the American commanders as well as the will and desire of the American soldier to fight and die. As their military MO, North Vietnam's make the most of civilian atrocities, not unlike the carnage committed by Communist Russia and Mao Marxists. It became recorded in war history as the evil crimes against humanity of the Southeast Asian Empire.

Outraged, with lethal fighter bombers America launched raids against the civilian Capital of North Vietnam from their nuclear powered aircraft carrier, the Enterprise. General Westmoreland, similar to the inept Generals of the Civil War who became promptly replaced by President Lincoln, asked for an additional 200,000 troops to cover his military failures. Rather than replace General Westmoreland, President LBJ, now with a 26% approval rating, announced that he would not seek the upcoming presidential election under any circumstances. Across the American cities, protests grew aggressively louder with Martin Luther King Jr. and Walter Cronkite's vocal oppositions to the Vietnam War. Civilian uprisings during the Democratic Convention in Chicago further embolded the spreading and growing, popular opposition to the Vietnam War across the USA. With political correctness, newly elected President Nixon began the withdrawal of American combat troops and turning-over the fighting over to the South Vietnamese. Surprisingly, the anti-war rallies worsen both on college campuses and major public streets. Secretly, Nixon who would not accept defeat sent an additional 40,00o troops to neighboring Cambodia and Laos, which only reinforced the steadfast resistance of the "Empire" of Southeast Asia to Western democracy.

Psycho/politically, it now seemed to American war-planners that all totalitarian and autocratic governments, including Chinese hybrid nations, favored social bondage, not freedom.

Accordingly in August, 1971, all combat operations were turned over to South Vietnamese forces, while American ships mined-shut all North Vietnamese seaports and aircraft heavily bombed Hanoi's civilian targets. Quickly, a call for a cease-fire accord was drafted with conditions that included: (a) release of all American prisoners; (b) the removal of all American forces from the South; (c) the end of fighting in Laos and Cambodia; and (d) the establishment of an international committee to monitor the conditions of the truce. The signing of the ceasefire agreement took place on January, 1973 that Nixon spun as "peace with honor." Only 2-years later on April 30th, 1975, North Vietnam, which had no official truce with the South, forced South Vietnam to surrender unconditionally to the Communist North. All American advisors were forcibly expelled from Vietnam-Proper. During the decade of active combat, the so-called American defeat was substantial; 50,000 dead and 300,000 wounded.

The historical questions raised by the results of the Vietnam War yet remain to be resolved. Why would the South Vietnamese military perform so timidly, passively, and submissively in their pursuit of democratic freedom? Conversely, why would the North Vietnamese be so willing to fight robustly and be willing to sacrifice a million casualties for the tyrannies of Communism or a Sino/monarchy that promised socio/political and individual bondage? So too, it might be said for the all nations of Southeast Asia. Even in the 21st century any derogatory remarks or suggestions against the monarchy in Thailand will assure extensive jail time. The riddle to these socio/political enigmas can only point to the original Chinese DNA and its bio/social effects on the Sino/hybrid nations of Southeast Asia. Not unlike capitalistic Singapore, the nations of Southeast Asia are Sino/ Hybrids; forming a composite Empire that genetically rejects, renounces, and fails to incorporate God's gift of freedom, universal human rights, and democratic institutions within their socio/expectations. In defense of freedom history will show that America choice to fight the Vietnam War and against the tyranny of Marxism was a noble venture. America was not defeated in the Vietnam War, instead, it was the Chinese, anti-freedom Genome that overwhelmed, impeded, and postponed the Asian evolutionary progress well into the 21st century.

In regard to the ideational and political evolution of Humankind, the "territorial expressions" of Mainland China and its subsidiary effects on Southea in defense of freedom st Asia have been: (a) more tangibly anchored than enduringly theoretical; (b) more practical than abstract; (c) more tribal than societal; (d) more preyed-upon that predator; and (e) more as ideo/emulators than ideo/contributors. For thousands of years, the key attributes of their irreal, intellectual discussions have centered about: (a) forcefields; (b) vortices; (c) wave propagation; (d) organic totality; and (e) organismic auto-regulation. These Sino/philosophical delusions about reality would place them at odds with the Western views of rational objectivity, freedom, universal human rights, and the merit of demoncratic institutions. Consistently to this day, the Sino age-old commitment to the political/economic Order has been non-democratic and hierarchically rigidified as: (a) authoritative; (b) autocratic; (c) traditional; (d) eco/centralized; (e) corrupt; (f) with grandiose, failed public projects; (g) anti-profit socio/values; (h) xenophobic; (i) overpopulated; (j) collectively over-disciplined; (k) educationally indoctrinare; and (l) bureaucratically spinnakers. As yin&yang, these mindsets have appeared over-and-over in Chinese history and in their hybrid nations in Southeast Asia. For 8-thousand years, these genetic patterns continue to dictate the life-and-love styles in today's, Peoples Republic of China and the nations of Southeast Asia. The outcome of the Vietnam War in the 20th century when freedom was rebuffed only can be understood genetically. For this reason, in order to comprehend the "democratic fitness and dynamics'" of the major and minor communities of the Sino/genome that includes the Chinese, Koreans, Vietnamese, and the full collection of nations of Southeast Asia, the appropriate starting point for any inquiring bio/anthropologist ought to be to first map-out the DNA-blueprints of the Asian citizenry; specifically to provide a base-point for the genomal profiles of the Mongol, Manchurian, Chinese, and nonChinese types, i.e. those who traditionally have been dotting the inland landscapes of the AsianContinent. As distinctive biobreeds, the histories of the mainland Sino have revealed that their archetypal genomes have dominated Asia Proper for millennia--as compared to the eugenic/mutational fluidity noted in the peripheral Asian-nations; that is, the Vietnamese, Burmese, Laotians, Indonesians, Malaysians, Javans, and Sumatrans. These are Asian hybrids, who have been the close relatives of the purer root of the "yellow race." Although Chinese history, arts, philosophy, architecture, and written language have been rich in style, their substantive contributions to a 20th-21st century ideo/world remains disputed and meager. For the Modern Age, the Sino, bio/cultural yesteryear suggests that they would be better "territorially conceived" as tangential, mercurial, and yin&yang, rather than cerebrally focused, prophetic, futuristic, and genetically fit for a democratic/capitalistic Age. When compared and contrasted to the Caucasian Genome, the more-elite of the modern-day Chinese communities still reflect traces of the conventional, bio/social behaviors and attitudes of their traditional ancestors. Thus, they have run-short of creative objectivity; as needed for the socio/politics of freedom, the pure sciences, innovative technologies, and higher mathematics. Simply stated, Chinese DNA/derivatives have functioned more as engineers than scientists. Furthermore even after many generations of interacting with the Western World, the socio/political patterns of the Orient don't lean toward a decentralized, democratic lifestyle; those which trust the political insights of the common man and the political will to permit individualized socio/expressions. By virtue of their options, the genome of the Asian tends to echo the political folklore of its forebearers. The political conclusion seems clear: the Vietnam War ended as a DNA/partiality for the bondage of Sino/monarchies and now the subgagation offered by Communism. In a 21st century, info/tech, Global context, the evolutionary impact of this yellow/skinned, racial branch of humanity must be considered non-democratic in their selection of the political lifeblood of their government, whether local, State or Federal. Their yan&yang history tried and repeatedly failed to introduce freedom, tried and failed to legislate human rights for all, tried and failed democratically, tried and failed intellectually, and tried and failed religiously. At best, the Chinese, North Koreans, and Southeast Asians should always be expected to function as unassimilated, unabsorbed "genetic visitors" in the Modern nest.

Is China really the next Superpower?

The suggestion by pundits that the ascendency of China will rise as a world leader by the year 2020 AD remains uncertain and most likely an extrapolative delusion. America and its commitment to freedom and universal human rights alone is the only, and perhaps last, hope for a dying Sino/world already in bondage. To achieve national grandeur, other than in a economic/military sense, the truly, great societies of the 21st century will be expected to adhere to four benchmarks as needed for any post-modern civilization. Within this Century, China and its DNA/derivative Southeast Asian nations, can't meet, or hope to acquire, these four standards. *First*, a democratic society fully committed to freedom and universal, human rights is basic. As in its political past, the Chinese Genome keeps relying more upon its socio/economics, than individual civil liberties. This misguidedDNA/policy is bound to cause most all Asian societies to fragment into regions governed by despots, monarchs, and warlords. There is little in the Chinese DNA, 8000-year history that suggests any inclination by its political leadership to trust the insights of the common man. Over time universal freedoms can never be subjugated to the availability of material goods&services. *Secondly*, the great societies of the future must be committed to the principles and practises of the free market. China-Proper, with its hard-core "stealth socialism" and its over-centralized planning, will never evolve into a Singapore, Taiwan, or Hong Kong. The Chinese civilization from its 2nd millennium B.C.; that is, its Neolithic Age to its Bronze Age of the Shang Dynasty to the Han, the Mongol, the Manchu, and Mao's Communism has always relied heavily upon over-centralized controls for its agri/economics and non/agri manufacturing and trade.

As an anecdotal sidebar of the proof of economic bondage, in today's alleged "Chinese capitalism" there are few "want ads" for employment opportunities published in their State-controlled Media. *Thirdly*, in a high-tech/info world, a truly free citizenry must possess and reflect a DNA/appropriate and Sino/adaptive "genomal pool." The political "genetic impulses" of the Sino peoples must be capable and preferring of individual self/reliance (not social dependency), expressive creativity (not a conforming technocracy), neighborly compassion (not a jaded acquiescence to overpopulation), and be politically proactive (not autocratically reactive). As their history has shown repeatedly, the demographics of China and its hybrid nations lack these DNA/urges. Hence, the failure of freedom in the Vietnam War can be best understood as genetic. *Finally*, the world leadership of the future must be pledged to the "Moral Evolution of Western Man." True democracy requires a bio/spiritual component. Communist China resists and impedes most all religious and Judeo/Christianity"s free expressions that are needed to sustain the souls of any citizenry. America has always been a religious nation founded by God's gift. Outherwise, the Hindu/derived religions of Southeast Asia don't meet the touchstones for God's gift of freedom. As the annals of civilization have taught us: any and all Empires will implode simply because "Man can't live by bread alone."

Language, acholars tell us: in Ancient China-Proper only those most-gifted with innate skills are able to take pleasure in and partake in their art of literacy--or being capable of developing a legacy of : (1) enduring ideas; (2) abstracted theorems of science; (3) symbolic laws of the Megaverse; and/or (4) high/mathematics. Instead what was conveyed was a beautiful, but clumsy, Chinese language, hampered with just 40,000+ characters taking the form of pictograms, ideograms, logograms, and singular symbols as scripted in the written word. By being moored to these non-alphabetized scripts which favor the immediacy, Asians have been able to produce the literati, poets, and artists who express only glimpses of *irreality*; while in parallel encumbered socio/politically with archaic layers of limited and perishable ways&means. As an axiom, when any national language is restricted by a insufficiency of an alphabet, whether caused by culture or genetics, both ideo/progress and freedom suffer. Language, ideals, sociology, politics, and religion are all intertwined. Ergo, individual liberty hinges upon the cerebral DNA/ attributes of a articulate "linguistic people."

As further evidence and as a sidebar to this thesis consider this analogy. During the Western Medieval centuries, a spiritually-tyranical, Roman Catholic Church kept its parishioners in a state of bondage and exploitation simply by restricting the personal readings of Biblical Scripture. In time, the Christian Reform movements by the German and English Churches were able to overturn this "reading despotism" simply by translating the Bible into everyday language. Similarly in China and its hybrid nations, common people didn't have access to a common language. Verily, traditional Asia has been unable to invoke for its masses a language that has a great deal to do with the politics and the economics of freedom. WithIn a bio/anthropological context, China's linguistic heritage couldn't have described for their populace, or led them to, the complexities of a range of great ideas as relished by modern-day mathematics, science, economic theory, technology, banking, and the political laws of freedom. The cerebral and political legacies of the Sino/ Continent have been mercurial, capricious, and yin&yang. For these reasons their future of bio/technology and theology must follow the identifiable, language DNA/markers attached to the Asian Genome. These genes have accounted for the Orient's reactionary, socio/politics that compromised their individualized, full-democratic living, as defined succinctly by their continual rebuffing of the universality of human-rights. If so, who would deny that during their Dynastic eras the "Asian person" has been chronically subjugated and victimized by the central authorities-at-large and military force and not the soul of Man. Throughout the 21st century for their children's sake, as a bio/spiritual statement this Eastern sector of the Globe must choose to pursue and emulate the West, and not all its failed "symbolic expressions" of human fulfillment, as been conceived by the DNA/tools of the Occidental mind.

If truth be told, the understanding of the results and dynamics of the Vietnam War can be tied to the genetics and political urges of the Chinese Genome and its effects on the nations of Southeast Asis. Simply stated, in lieu of freedoms, univercal human rights or democratic institutions, why would these countries prefer the bondage of a monarchy or the subgigation and repression of a Communist society? The answer must lie in both the workings of the genes plus the spiritual motivations of individuals and their societies. China's secularism and Southeast Asia's Buddhism would never be consistent with democratic ways&means. Surely, it would take a bio/spiritual explanation to fathom the socio/political preferences of Sino/.Asians. An examination of the orgins of democracy and God's gift of freedom via Judeo/Christianity, also known as the Moral Evolution of Western

Man, could also explain the sociatal limitatiojns of the Sino/ Asians and the dismal conclusions of the Vietnam War.

Mosaic Law and the Creation of Democracy

American Christianity and American Democracy run parallel. They both emanated in substance out of the Mosaic Law. At the near onset of human civilization, this covenant addressed the universal, socio/ political concerns of Mankind, which were then slighted by the tribal outlook and debauchery of those Ancient times. While the 10-Commandants set the stage as the core of moral living, the expanded Mosaic dictates dealt with false accusations, rights of the family and women, individual dignity, just economics, equal law, and rest on the Sabbath. From the Israelis to the message of Jesus to the development of the democratic order, this covenant accounted for the Moral Evolution of 21st century's Western Man.

By existential theme, there are three overriding, spiritual building-blocks featured within the 1200-plus pages of the Judeo/Christian Code, i.e. the Bible. *One*, is the command of *righteousness* that is a Divine, nonnegotiable condition that both the organic and inorganic realms within the Multiverse has been preestablished. Creation in itself is good, neither neutral, nor evil, nor in bondage to socio/political law, nor chaotic, and not devoid of inherent beauty. Indeed, goodness is beautiful. Righteousness or goodness or holiness is a primordial, metaphysical, dynamic attribute of all organic and inorganic creation. Why? Simply because the Nature of God is indubitably holy, good, free, and righteous. His creation must become this likeness of Divinity. *Secondly*, for living-and-loving on Planet Earth, *social justice* is another spiritually nonnegotiable reality, fundamental to all of human proceedings, including the freedom of socio/politics. Indeed, when a young man asked Jesus: what will it take to enter the Kingdom of Heaven, the answer was "…love your God (who is good) with your whole might" and "love thy neighbor as thyself." *Thirdly*, the aura of *love* is paramount to the understanding of creation. Love cherishes. Love serves. Love considers all creation as precious. Love can't exist without the freedom to love. In sum, although God's nature supersedes all of our capacities to fathom the totality of the Divine, four existential, conditions, i.e. love, justice, freedom, and righteousness, reflect the reason and justification of both our species and individual creation. God's gift of freedom encompasses all four of these Divine attributes.

In the 21st century, these four attributes became the Global forewarnings by Jesus, along with serving as socio/political beacons for democratic living. Straddling time from Abraham to the 21st century, personal holiness, love, freedom, and social fairness have been the religious presuppositions that have been avowed and affirmed throughout the history of the Moral Evolution of Western Man. The Mosaic Law, written over 3500-years ago, initiated and formalized these four spiritual themes for Western Mankind to abide by. No doubt, democracy is a Christian theme, not consistent with Asian socio/political inclinations. From a 21st century perspective, along with the results of the previous American wars cited, the role of the existential aura of "holiness, love, freedom, and justice" has been clear. The matter of socio/political manifestations of universal human rights, as building-blocks of the Creation Plan, hasn't yet been globally achieved. Surely as spiritual dynamics, personal holiness, love, freedom, and social justice can be best understood as partially overlapping bio/attributes (love and freedom) addressed individual relationships between Man and God, while one trait (social justice) tackled the spiritual mechanisms of community affairs. Holiness covers it all. Accordingly, in order to understand what "justice," as a spiritual entity entails, socio/political discourse on the transcendent evolution of government should cause us to see the glaring differences among evil, despotic dictatorships, autocratic oligarchies, benevolent monarchies, Communist ideologies --and the compassionate, Mosaic-based democracies.

As it stands today, historic logic should ordain that a 21st century American democracy ought to be considered the ideal consequence of Biblical expression. Unequivocally, the USA stands for universal human rights, civil liberties for all, social justice, and economic parity for those who dare apply. China and its hybrid offshoot nations don't adhere to these principles of social liberty. God's gift of freedom means little to most Asians. Biblical scholarship has revealed that freedom commitments have been originally implied and then codified by Mosaic Law, not Asian philosophies or their pseudo religions. Both structurally and operationally, the socio/political "justice devices" of America are the outcrop of Israel's tradition that has been spiritually crafted 3500-years ago. As related to survival and fulfillment of the Homo Sapien, throughout history Mankind has been victimized by "spiritually inept" political models, which summarily have failed to connect and recognize the evolutionary significance of "righteousness, love, freedom, and justice." The American democracy has been telling it otherwise. If so, adaptively and spiritually by virtue of its flourishing, 250-year tenure, America, has been the concluding socio/political paradigm, regarded as the last and only hope for a dying world.

Via God's Creation and Redemption Plans, both of which unequivocally featured freedom-of-choice for each soul, the Mosaic Decree became Divinely launched by way of a chosen people, the Israelis. In a theological capsule, this religious code formalized the rules, regulations, and spiritual laws for both individuals and the Hebrew, ruling bodies of government. Henceforth both in their leaderships and daily proceedings so as to survive and succeed as human, social institutions, all future regimes of nations, tribes, and communities must reorganize their socio/political ways&means so as to echo the preconditions of holiness, freedom, love, and social justice. So, what did the Mosaic Law allude about the spiritual attributes of democratic socio/politics?

<u>On Personal Worth</u>: *the right afforded every person to be respected; highlighting the non-exploitation of the powerless (rights of the poor, disabled, orphan, the sick, widows, and foreigners).* Moses told us....

...do not murder (Exodus 20:13)

...kidnappers must be killed...an assailant must pay...because of injury...if a slave is beaten and dies, the owner must be punished (Exodus 21:16-21)

...show your fear of God by treating the deaf with respect and by not taking advantage of the blind (Leviticus 19:14)

...cursed is anyone who steals another's property...or who leads a blind person astray...or who is unjust to foreigners, orphans and widows... or who kills in secret for pay...or has sexual relations with animals, or other family members (Deuteronomy 27:17-26).

<u>On Untrue Allegations:</u> *<u>(the right against perjury, slander, and libel.</u>*

...do not testify falsely against your neighbor (Exodus 20:16).

...do not pass along false reports...or tell lies on the witness stand...do not be swayed in your testimony by the opinion of the majority and against the poor (Exodus 23: 1-3).

...do not spread slanderous gossip among your people (Leviticus 19:16).

...never convict anyone of a crime on the testimony of just one witness (Deuteronomy 19: 15).

<u>Rights of Women</u>: the right of females to be protected from exploitation.
...if a slave owner's son marries a slave girl she becomes free and must be treated as a daughter (Exodus 21:9)
...on the Sabbath no one must work, including your daughters and female slaves (Exodus 20:10).
...if a man seduces a virgin, he must pay the customary dowry and accept her as his wife (Exodus 22:16)

...if you see a captive, foreign, beautiful women you may marry her, but not humiliate her or sell her or treat her as a slave (Deuteronomy 21: 10-14)
...do not accuse a virgin falsely or have intercourse with his father's wife (Deuteronomy 22: 13-30).
...a newly married man must not be drafted in the army but must be free to be at home to bring happiness to his new wife (Deuteronomy 24: 5).
...if a man dies and has no sons, give his inheritance to his daughters (Numbers 27:8)

Punishment: the right not to be punished cruelly and inhumanely.

...if a person is sentenced to be flogged, no more than 40 lashes may ever be given so as to avoid the public humiliation of the accused (Deuteronomy 25:1-3)

Social Dignity the right to be honored and safeguarded by society.

...if you buy a Hebrew slave, he is to serve for only six years. Set him free on the seventh year. (Exodus 21:2).

...if any of your relatives fall into poverty, support them and allow them to live with you. (Leviticus 25:35)

...the people of Israel must never be sold as slaves. (Leviticus 25:42)

...if any Israelite has not been redeemed by the time of the Year of the Jubilee, they and their children must be set free. (Leviticus 25:54)

...when you release a male servant, share with him some of your bounty. Don't send him away empty-handed. (Deuteronomy 15:13-14)

Family Solidity and Continuity the rights of inheritance.

...a "kinsman redeemer" assures the just sale of Israeli properties. (Leviticus 25)

…the Levitical pastureland may never be sold; it is their permanent, ancestral property (Leviticus 25:34).

…the Lord replied to Moses: the daughters of Zelophehad are right; you must give them an inheritance of land. (Numbers 27:5)

…none of the inherited land may be passed from tribe to tribe. (Numbers 36:7

Property rights:
.. you shall not steal (Deuteronomy 5:19

…if a thief is caught in the act of breaking into a house and is killed, the person who owns the house is not guilty (Exodus 22:2)

…do not use dishonest standards when measuring length, weight, or volume (Leviticus 19:35)

…if you see a neighbor's ox or sheep wandering away, take it back to its owner (Deuteronomy 22:1)

Rights of Workers
…always pay your hired workers promptly (Leviticus 19:13)

…never take advantage of a poor laborer (Deuteronomy 24:14)

On Sharing Food: rights of the hungry poor.
…let the poor among you harvest any crop that comes up …let the same apply for your vineyards and olive groves (Exodus 23:10-11)

...*leave the extra grain and grapes for the poor and the foreigners (Leviticus 19:9-10)*

...*your hired servants and foreigners may eat the produce that grows naturally during the Sabbath year (Leviticus 25:6-7)*

...*bring the tithes of your crops to the Levities who have no inheritance as well as to the foreigners, orphan, and widows in your towns (Deuteronomy 14:28-29)*

...*when beat the olives from your olive trees, don't go over the boughs twice; leave some for the foreigners, widows, and orphans (Deuteronomy 24: 20)*

<u>Honoring the Sabbath:</u> right for a seventh-day rest, gratitude, worship, and praise.

...*set apart the Sabbath as holy and as a day of rest (Exodus 20:8-11)*

....*the Sabbath day must be dedicated to the Lord your God (Deuteronomy 5:12-15)*

<u>Honoring Marriage:</u> society's right of inviolate, marital relationships.

...*do not commit adultery (Exodus 20:14)*

...*do not practice homosexuality, it is a detestable sin (Leviticus 18:22)*

Right to a fair trial: social justice is an ultimate, nonnegotiable entitlement.

...do not twist justice against people simply because they are poor (Exodus 23:6)

...take no bribes as it hurts the cause of the person who is in the right (Exodus 23:8)

...always judge your neighbor fairly, whether rich or poor (Leviticus 19:15)

...your Lord your God gives justice to orphans and widows (Deuteronomy 10:17-18)

...let justice prevail (Deuteronomy (!7:20)

...never convict anyone on the testimony of just one witness (Deuteronomy 19:15)

...a king must read a copy of the Law daily and obey all its terms (Deuteronomy 17:19)

Animal Rights:

...if you see an animal struggling under a load, stop and help it (Exodus 23:5)

...allow your livestock and wild animals to eat off the land's bounty (Leviticus 25:7)

...if you find a bird's nest on the ground with young ones, take the young. (Deuteronomy 21:6)

****

In support of the ideas of 21ˢᵗ century's democracy and by referencing and citing the five books of the Torah written by Moses millennia before the birth of Jesus, this is what was preached during the ministry of the Messiah concerning the socio/political rights of persons. All truly democratic societies are premised upon the Mosaic/Jesus ideas of social/political freedom.

- personal righteousness, love, and social justice are the ultimate, non-negotiable realities governing human life on Planet Earth; these are the overriding messages of the four Gospels of the NT.
- do not yield to evil temptations of injustice (See Matthew 4: 1-11)
- God blesses those nations which recognize their need for him (Matthew 5:3)
- Those who mourn will be comforted by God and community (See Matthew 5:4)
- God blesses the humble leaders of nations (See Matthew 5:5)
- Citizens who crave justice will be blessed by God (See Matthew 5:6)
- Societies which are merciful will receive mercy (See Matthew 5:7)
- The hearts of leaders must be pure (See Matthew 5:8)
- Striving for peace, forgiveness, and love of enemies ought to be the goal of just, legal proceedings (See Matthew 5:9; 43-48)
- Freedom from persecution must be assured by government (See Matthew 5:10)

- Democratic societies are the "salt and light" of the world (See Matthew 5:13-16)
- The Bill of Rights reflects, not rejects, the Mosaic Law (See Matthew 5: 17-20)
- Protection from murder, violence, and revenge is a primary task of free societies (See Matthew 5: 21-26; 38-42)
- Marriage and family are the building-blocks of free societies and must not be defiled by divorce and adultery (See Matthew 5:27-32)
- Democracies must be compassionate to the needy (See Matthew 6: 1-4)
- Public prayer by officials of free societies ought to be regularly scheduled (See Matthew 6: 5-13)
- Love of money is at the root of socio/political evils (See Matthew 6: 19-34)
- The Golden Rule, as Scripturally reflected in Court precedence, laws, rules, and regulations, ought to be the uppermost concern of democratic societies
- A democratic nation, which is premised upon the Mosaic/Christian ideal, will build, not on sand, but on the foundations of solid rock and deep roots (See Matthew 7: 24-27; Mark 4)

In succession and progression, from the Mosaic Law to the British Common Law to the Magna Charta to the Declaration of Independence to the US Constitution to the United Nations Charter, 21st century's "evolving7 Mankind" has etched within its socio/political consciousness the freedoms assured by the Bill of Rights, a Global commitment to universal human rights, the legal proceedings declaring civil rights for all, and an international marketplace includes freedom of the seas and skies, dedicated to economic parity, barring none who dare apply. The American model of socio/political freedom tells us that democratic societies, at first, evolved as compassionate communities followed by the operational and legal mechanisms of a free nation. In a variety of ways, and over 3500-years ago, the Mosaic Law was commissioned by God to bestow fundamental, socio/political rights upon the individual, human soul. Subsequently, about a thousand years later, the Hellenic Empire began to devise and formulate thoughts of democratic ways&means for the various nations of Greece. By way of the enlightened scholarship of Aristotle, Plato, and Socrates, the notion of the "good and just Man" was introduced as the basis for a "good and just nation," that might be both free and compassionate. Next, as many centuries passed by, democratic ideas and ideals continued to progress via the scholarship of the Renaissance (15th-16th centuries), the 18th century's Enlightenment, the Common Law and Magna Charter in England, along with the 18th century writers who fueled the French Revolution. However, the great experiment of a society bent on individual liberty eventually became crystallized in the New World. Implausibly, the Founding Fathers of America, led by the Christian character of George Washington, the classical persona of Thomas Jefferson, the legal/moral fiber of John Adams, the political charm of Benjamin Franklin, and the shrewd, sensible mind of Alexander Hamilton, put together a working model for a practical, democratic government. In a capsule, the US Constitution, scripted by God and James Madison became a revised, enriched, and expanded replica of the Judeo/Christian Code, which respected individual rights through a medium of theological compassion. Within five decades prior to the 21ˢᵗ century, this socio/political experiment began to cascade across the governments of the family of nations. Both in style and substance, the US Constitution became the archetype for the world communities to emulate. A government of individual freedoms, universal human rights, civil liberties bar none, and the opportunities for economic parity for those who dare of apply, became the inalienable touchstone for the Continents of the world. Although not trouble-free, in truth the "noble struggle" for human dignity endowed by God for all nations, which thusfar only knew of their political traditions of central control, entrenched caste-systems, and regal/military subjugation, is becoming brought to fruition across Planet Earth. Indeed, from the Mosaic Law as fulfilled by Jesus came the UN Charter of universal, human rights.

Alluding to the message of Sacred Scripture, our Founding Fathers understood:

> *...On the sacred rights of Mankind, these are written as a sunbeam in the whole volume of human nature, by the hand of Divinity itself; and can never be erased or obscured by mortal power. (Alexander Hamilton 1775 AD)*
> *...we hold these truths to be self-evident that all men are created equal and endowed by the Creator with certain unalienable*

rights. *(The Declaration of Independence (1776 AD)*

Such as:
- the right to free speech
- the right to worship freely
- the right to assemble
- the right of a free press
- the right to petition the government
- the right to bear arms
- the right for persons to be secure and equal
- the right to a fair trial
- the right to free and fair elections
- the right to life, liberty, and the pursuit of happiness.

In the 21st Century, we can expect to add Christian themes to the US Constitution with a Bill of Genetic Rights, a Bill of Patient Rights, along with a Bill of Victim Rights.

****

American Christianity move us up into the **fourth**, reform stage of the Moral Evolution of Western Man. Prior it was: (I) the Hebrews; (II) the Roman Church; and (III) the Reformation.

Its denominations are numerous, yet their primary Christian beliefs are few. **First**, American Christians believe in the inerrancy and inspiration provided by the Bible, a book that ought to be read and studied daily. For these New World

Christians, this Scriptural reading on a daily basis becomes an interactive conduit between the personal soul reaching upward to a personal God. *Secondly*, American Christianity understands that "it's all about Jesus," a living persona of the Divine, who protects, provides guides, loves unconditionally, and supplies the necessary grace/energy to make one's life meaningful. Spiritually, the forgiveness of individual sin, *salvation*, and a commitment to a life of love, righteousness, and social justice in thought, word, and action, are the basic building-blocks of *sanctification*—only then eternity with God is assured. *Thirdly*, American Christianity holds to the importance of honoring the Sabbath as an opportunity to praise and worship the One and only God, while offering gratitude for the many blessings of the past week. *Lastly*, the American Christian leadership must look to the Holy Spirit for guidance, and not trust the Old World, established authorities, i.e. the Papacy, the Patriarch, and/or the Church of England. All other theological issues, e.g. Baptism, Eucharist, etc, are worthy of spiritual speculation, but only secondary for the entering of the Kingdom of God. These four, primary, pillars of belief are the commitments of the numerous, New World denominations of America, i.e. the Evangelical people of the Gospel.

Consider this sequence of moral history that eventually led to the Vietnam War.

Since the 17th century, American Christianity experienced a number of "centennial steps" leading to the 21st century. Each hundred years or so, political freedom vs religion emerged and progressed in tandem, linked together and energized by competition, contention, controversy, and compromise. Freedom of religion and the paradox of separation of Church and State became the various denominations of the New World that challenged parishioners to seek and rise to a higher level of Divine intimacy by way of ideological and theological truths, as they might pertain to a free society. For sure, democracy as evangelically portrayed and as forged by the Founding Fathers and the Magna Charter of England, along with the principles of Christianity, together have socio/politically fashioned our a 21st century citizenry. As early as the 17th century, by escaping the religious and political intolerance of the Old Euro/World, Puritans, Quakers, Lutherans, Congregationalists, Baptists, and Pilgrims, sought to disestablish themselves from the autocracy, corruption, false doctrine, and the persecutions of the Churches of Rome, England, and Constantinople. These became the American pioneers who relied upon the guidance of the Holy Spirit, an inerrant Bible, living a personal, loving, righteous, and just, relationship with Jesus, and by honoring the Sabbath with praise, worship, and gratitude. In a capsule, American Christianity and its democracy became a noble struggle between rational Enlightenment and spiritual Evangelism. This ideational stressor accounted for the formation of democratic institutions and its subsequent free society called the USA.

Roger Williams, a Puritan, brought the first Baptists to America in the early 17th century. A few decades later, these Puritans formed the Massachusetts Bay Colony, along with the Pilgrims' Plymouth Plantation. Both sects joined forces when they realized and decided that they held in-common political, social, economic, and spiritual values. In chorus, they also resisted King Henry VIII's Presbyterians and Methodists, which together comprised Old Euro/World, Church of England derivatives. Pilgrims and Puritans called themselves Congregationalists. Subsequently, later in the 18th century, persecuted immigrants from Switzerland, Holland, Hungary, and other Euro/countries sailed to the New World to form the Synods of North America. Simultaneously during this period of time, the Quakers, who were persecuted in England, began to arrive in the New World. They were disillusioned with the demeanor of the English Church and its expanding ritualistic complexities, henceforth sought and opted for a simpler, more intimate, affiliation with God. Yet beleaguered, this religious movement, the Quakers, while blossoming in Boston, MA, continued to be persecuted, whipped, incarcerated, and socially rejected. Over the decades, their Christian values drew widespread, popular attention and became a focus of the American, political mindset. Quakers stood for peace, civil liberties, women's rights, the care of Native Americans, voting rights, the Underground Railroad, and in the 20th century assisted in the relocation of Jews. Indeed, Quakers became the model for the ideal, American democracy. Unquestionably, these persecuted, New World refugees were about to elevate the Christian Outlook to a new plane of political enlightenment.

Surely, the spiritual beliefs of the Founding Fathers of the USA typified the coming together of the American democracy with the New World version of Christianity. History has shown the American socio/spiritual concepts represented two sides of the same coin. Judeo/Christianity and a free society could neither be ideationally compromised nor politically disengaged. One without the other could neither attain nor gain nor acquire historical significance nor long-term, socio/political justification. Freedom to believe devoid of established, Church authorities became the rallying cry of the New World American. Liberty to worship propelled their patriotic efforts and personal sacrifices that were missing in the Vietnam War after the year 1973. Otherwise within an American political context, each Founding Father referred to Providential Divinity. God the Father, Jesus, God the Son, and the guidance and inspiration offered by the Holy Spirit were often mentioned in both their oratory and writings. The Founding Fathers were all professing Christians of some sort, either openly like George Washington, John Jay, Alexander Hamilton, and James Madison or tangentially as Deists or Unitarians, in concert with other colonial leaders, such as Thomas Jefferson, John Adams, and Benjamin Franklin. In their writings and political activities, the Founding Fathers sought to advance the notion of liberty by way of the Christian message by proselytizing both the Euro/loyalists and the Native American inhabitants. Not unlike Emperor Constantine of the 4th century AD, some of the Founding Fathers too had to conceal their true, Christian beliefs so as to avoid the possibilities of negative, political spinoffs. As a compelling analogy, Constantine was baptized on his deathbed, Alexander Hamilton died as a professing Anglican just prior to his demise. On occasion within the political realm, it would be difficult to reconcile openly one's, deeply-held, personal beliefs with the varying complexities of the political aura. Franklin, Jefferson, and Adams all agreed: *I think on morals and religion, as He left them to us, as the best the world has ever seen, or is likely to see.*

However, with freedom, whether spiritual or political, come the evils of immoderation and lawlessness. Political liberty brings about economic freedom or license, called capitalism or laissez faire. In the mega-churches we find that in the late 20th century the economic corruption of American Christianity has become endemic. Widespread, all to many super large churches of both liberal and conservative persuasions, Old World or New World convictions, are misusing funds, manipulating their accounting, exploiting their congregation, and for some, outright stealing of tithes. By way of their tax-free stewardship, which should demand a strict, Christian accountability of parishioner tithes and donations, the American "religious corruption" instead has become legally sticky. Jim Bakker, who misappropriated church funds, included the building of a carpeted, air conditioned doghouse. Jimmy Swaggart, who used church funds to solicit prostitutes on a regular basis. These were just a few examples of the systemic corruption of modern-day Christianity. As well, there are a growing number of cases-in-point of capitalistic/felonies being committed daily in other mega churches and tele/evangelistic ministries. Big-time Christianity has become big business perched upon the fulcrums of unethical illegality. Now in progress, the US Congress is conducting investigations of a number of the major, television, Sunday-services, which as a legal defense are alleging separation of Church and State for their financial lack of accountability,. In addition to their stealth, accounting practices, there are a number of ongoing, pseudo-respectable churches that consider their congregations to be a group of consumers, rather than souls to be spiritually saved and nurtured. Being perceived as serving customers, pastors become paid obscene, base, salaries plus outrageous, fringe benefits. A number of these "capitalistic churches" come out of the teaching traditions of Oral Roberts University.

However, the most egregious of all churches operating within the American Christian marketplace is the Roman Catholic Church. It functions as an administratively/financial, secretive organization, filtered through with sexual perversion, steeped in socio/hypocrisy, heretical, with its false doctrine and rituals that only can be described as idolatrous. Jesus and Sacred Scripture hold a low priority among its clergy, which instead promotes "Pope Worship" and praying to/thru Mary and the saints. In a theological context, nothing good can come about without Divine grace. Hence, any believer in the Holy Spirit as the prime source of spiritual enlightenment would conclude that God has pulled His approving grace out of the corrupted sinews of the Roman Catholic Church.

Furthermore, Catholics aren't encouraged to read the Bible daily, the only Divine system of communication between a soul and God. Regularly, these Romans pray, not directly to Jesus, a living, personal God, but to/thru saints and Mary as their prime source of idol worship. They are told that the daily Mass is a sacrifice for daily sin, ignoring the theological factoid that Jesus, as the ultimate sacrifice, already died for all human breaches of love, righteousness, and justice, in thoughts, words, and deeds. The Pope, who calls himself "His Holiness," is an affrontation to God, who is the one and only holy persona. Irrespective of the gains made by the Reformation, for Catholics the Pope is considered: (a) infallible under certain constraints: (b) one who claims to be able to forgive human sins via his priestly representatives; and (c) one who claims a legacy of continuity from Peter the apostle, These conjectures are spiritually unfounded and historical fabrications. In fact, the Papacy has been an administrative position, which was created on or about the 7th century AD and not in the 1st century AD so as to meet the needs of the growing number of Christian churches. Sound Biblical scholarship tells us that only Jesus can forgive sin. Only God is holy. Only the guidance of the Holy Spirit is infallible. The primary mission of the Roman Church is not the salvation of the individual soul, but rather the expansion and maintenance of their Global politics. Hence, their trumped-up theology is intended to control and exploit their Global constituency with fear, guilt, and institutional dependence. The false doctrines of purgatory, limbo, mortal/venial sin, the tenuous character of salvation, Eucharistic transubstantiation, Gnostic self-hate as demonstrated by the life of St. Francis of Assisi, covered up priestly sexual perversions, along with a range idol worship, all qualify the Roman Church as a Medieval cult that has become emptied of God's grace and approval.

In the Reformed Christian tradition, in spite of the prevailing, fiscal corruption operating in a number of American megachurches, which have become obscenely prosperous at the onset of the 21st century, there is a very influential, commanding, honest&holy, evangelical movement that has become a pulsating feature to both the American democracy and Christianity. These churches are large or small, coming from a number of varying Sepratist traditions, and as a composite represent the fastest growing, religious movement of the American spiritual and political life. They are the Evangelicals, the people of the Gospel, who believe and are dedicated to four, primary precepts. **One**, to read the inerrant and inspirational Bible daily. *Two*, to honor the Sabbath. *Three*, to seek their guidance from the Holy Spirit. And *four*, our brief life on Planet Earth is all about Jesus.

Some of these honest&holy churches come to us as tele/mega institutions directly out of the evangelical traditions of the mid-19th century. Both the Enlightenment and Great Awakenings of these times also produced and consolidated the Evangelical Movement that we find so robust in both the democratic politics and religious life of America of the 21st century. The supersized congregations of Billy Graham and his son Franklin, who have been the spiritual advisors of most of the Presidents of the 20th and 21st centuries; Robert Schuler, pastor of the Crystal Cathedral; Jerry Falwell, and his Moral Majority and Liberty University; Charles Stanley, an international tele-evangelist; John Hagee, and his political support for the Israeli link to the Judeo/Christian tradition; and Rick Warren, whose megachurch hosted the debates of presidential candidates, all have their Christian anchors set in the democratic processes. They carried forth the 19th Century's, Evangelical traditions of the Enlightenment and the Great Awakenings initiated by Francis Willard (1839-1898), Wayne Wheeler (1869-1927), and Billy Sunday (1863-1935). It's no wonder that Evangelical Christianity has become the largest and fastest expanding religion in America and on Planet Earth. Jesus' message is highly compatible with nations and communities which love the politics of individual liberty.

In India, a hardcore Hindu nation, there are 35-million Christians in its Southwest region, all part of the 1st century ministry of St. Thomas, one of Jesus' original apostles. Likewise, in Central and Southern Africa, Christian populations are exploding to new heights. South Korea too, since 1950 AD has megachurches with congregations as large as 100,000 or more. Similarly, once-Catholic, once-Orthodox European, which now professes to be part of a Post-Christian Era, i.e. secular humanist, are poised to redeem itself with a 21st century, spiritual revival. And, China, which has adopted Western capitalism, has a persecuted, underground Christian Church, numbering 60+ million believers. Indeed, Christianity and the politics of liberty have evolved to become two sides of the same coin.

As two macro-factors operating within the context of the ideational evolution of the mid-20th century, both the dynamics of: (I) the Chinese Genome; and (II) the absence of Judeo/Christianity, aka as the bio/spiritual factor, that were the principal determinates in the failed outcome of the freedom wars in Southeast Asia. America did not lose the Vietnam War in the year 1973, it was the "Bonding Genome" of the Chinese Hybrids living in Southeast Asia in the year 1975 that rejected and expelled God's gift of freedom from their socio/politics.

CHAPTER 10

The 21ˢᵗ Century War against Islamic Terrorism

Islamic Theology of Hate
Mohammad's Unholy Koran

Islam, the Koran, and Mohammad are evil. They refer to their god as Allah. Most all Muslims claiming to please Allah behave unjustly, hatefully, and wickedly. Otherwise, the God of the Judeo/Christian is fully just, bountifully righteous, and continually loving. In the Christian West, freedom is cherished and treasured, while Islamic bondage that typifies the socio/politics of the Imam is all-encompassing, merciless and unrelenting. Who would disclaim that *t*he socio/political proceedings engulfing the Globe of the 21ˢᵗ century point unswervingly toward Islam as a root cause of Malthusian evil that threatens God's gift of freedom along with the very survival of the human race?

It was only four years after the Vietnam War was over in the year 1975 that the next "evil Empire" emerged to challenge God's gift of freedom, universal human rights, and democratic institutions. As in the past, it was Islam again inflicting its gloom and darkness upon the human race. With its new found power in the oil market, which the modern world urgently needs to prosper and survive, that caused the Muslim nations to convince, subjugate, and militarily conquer the infidels by attempting to force them into submission. Indeed this Muslim plague that threatened famine, disease, and suicide bombers began on November 20th, 1979 when an Iranian militia seized the American Embassy in Tehran. A mob of hundreds of Iranian students raided the American Complex and took into captivity 90 marines and embassy workers. Then President Jimmy Carter invoked both military and diplomatic efforts to release the Americans, but his tactics proved to be ineffective and pointless. "Death to the Shah and America" were the celebrated, rallying cries that swept across Iran. This international incident marked the onset of the Islamic war with the Modern West and spiritually with God's gift of freedom. At the same time the invasion of Afghanistan by the Soviet Union, which hoped to exploit the oil reserves of this Muslim nation, further goaded the Islamic temperament. Diplomatically, President Carter's "phony Christianity" proved to be unfit in a belligerent world. His boycott of the Olympic Games in Moscow also did little to deter the USSR. Accordingly for the following decades Jimmy Carter became ranked as the worst President in Modern times, only to be replaced by Barak Obama in 2008-2016. These two encounters, i.e. Tehran and Afghanistan, with the Muslim

Oil Empire marked the onset of the next war against God's gift of freedom. On January 21st, 1981 under the leadership of a new President, Ronald Reagan and Iranian bribes, the maltreated, Embassy hostages were officially released by the Imam. Yet the depraved clashes with the Muslim World continued to escalate in Libya and Beirut, where the American Embassy was bombed in 1983., In Lebanon, justified as a Holy War dozens were killed and a 100+ wounded when a suicide bomber with 300 pounds of TNT demolished the American Embassy. Six months later also in Beirut, Lebanon, suicide bombers killed 200 American Marines and 47 French paratroopers. Suicide bombers targeting American and Israeli facilities along with the hijacking of commercial airlines, a 1985 TWA event became the MO of Muslim terror. In the late 1980s, America began to strike back with the bombing of Libya and Iranian Oil assets. All in all, for the past two decades of the 20th century along with two decades during the onset of the 21st century, the war between Western freedom values and the Muslim religious/politics has been raging with fury. Why is this happening?

Endorsed by Muslims-at-large, the revulsion of Islamic socio/politics, hypocritically embedded within the Koranic verses of religious justification, is being, and has been immorally occurring for centuries. To deny this demographic factoid with scholarly babble would be disingenuous. Even the moderate among them, who seem to act "Western friendly" when face to face, curse them as infidels behind their backs. Theologically and socio/politically, there can be neither reconciliation nor a cessation of hostilities between the heretical believers of the Koran and those of the Judeo/Christian Bible. Globally, dating back to the 8th century religious relationships have proven to be irreconcilable, simply because, Muslims, Hindi, and Judeo/Christians espouse incompatible imagery of God's nature, His intentions, and theological truths. Spiritually, Christianity is the only religion to spiritually understand the incarnate, indwelling, personal presence of Jesus. Otherwise, the Islamic tradition of indiscriminate, indoctrinated terror inflicted upon innocent non-believers comes directly out of a psycho/disturbed mind of Mohammad, the alleged the Last Prophet. As revealed by hallucinations and religious delusions, there are major differences between the US Constitution and the Sharia law of Islam. The Qu'ran calls upon God to justify religious murders via stoning, bombings, maiming, beheading. and the godless atrocities that have been executed by the godless leaderships of 20th century's Euro/Asia. Irrespective of their duplicitous, Friday-night, mosque prayers, the Muslim use of stealth, terror bombings by Shia vs Sunnis or vice versa, invalidates their claims of being spiritually justified and sanctified, Ever since the 8th century, the belligerent, spiritual disposition of Muslims only can be summarized as more political and military, than religious. By renouncing the message of God's love for all humans and peace among all communities, whether stated pseudo/religiously or politically, in itself confirms the hate-filled messages of the Koran. Above all its denial of the Divine incarnation of Jesus the "root factor" fueling a spiritual plague menacing the 21st century. Today's international security, national safety, and personal well-being must ooze directly out of Islam's bio/political Genome and its bio/spiritual Koran, both of which seek to cover-up its conspiracy to dominate the world with its cultural religious code of unsanctified beliefs. As been revealed by German researchers, the Muslim "unholy book" is a compiled document filled with pseudo-religious content embellished with a mixed bag of plagiarized, Judeo/Christian, biblical verses, set within a hate-filled context of a Holy War, known as the *jihad*. As narrated and authorized to scribes, the illiterate Prophet Mohammad sanctioned as spiritually defensible the conquest, terror, and mass-murders of innocent Westerners, Jews, tourists, Hindi, other infidels, and if need be, Muslims. Indeed, Mohammad has plagued the Globe with religious hate and violence since the 8th century.

Nonetheless, as many historical examples of military/philosophical contentions of yore have confirmed, the universal, insatiable thirst for citizen emancipation, ranged from the French and American Revolutions to today's Mideastern uprisings. What can't be indefinitely timetabled by the religious politics of tyranny is God's gift of freedom. Accordingly we can expect from any 21st century democracy that the spiritual principles of **Bio/Politics** will have to be discoursed, enacted, and embraced by most all nations; as intellectually viewed by the next higher plane of human, socio/religious enlightenment. From Iran to Tunisia, from West to East in the sprawling Muslim world, the violent protests emerging today substantiates the conclusion that the religion of Islam ranks as just another "grisly heresy." No doubt, the dissonance triggered by the easy accessibility of the social info/technologies, e.g. Facebook and Twitter, is bound to expose the charlatan, belief system of Islam and propel its hateful premises to the junkyards of religious ideas gone by.

Since its inception 14-centuries ago, the Koran, not unlike Marx's, 19th century, *Communist Manifesto,* Hitler's *Mein Kamp,* and Mao's *Little Red Book,* of the early 20th century has been enabling and justifying the Muslim objective of ever-escalating, worldwide domination through conquest via mindless terror. The continuation of the senseless conflicts between Muslims and the West, including Hindu India, can be attributed to the socio/political flaws in the Islamic "tribal Genome." Furthermore, in order to acquire and accrue a body of fanatic believers, as ISIS in the 21st century, the escalation of the evil-possessed revelations of Mohammad's hallucinations, along with, later on, as rubber-stamped by the subsequent interpretations by the Caliphs, and as compiled in the gratuitous script of the Koran's, traditional barbarism, Islam is, and has been throughout the many centuries a spiritual plague to God and all of Humankind. As an offer that can't be refused, everyday Muslims ought to consider adopting the "love thy neighbor" message of Jesus.

The Koran, aka Qur'an, was orally dictated to scribes by an illiterate soothsayer, Mohammad, whose early life and hallucinatory psyche became dysfunctional by the early deaths of both parents and later, by being cared for by foster parenting that was emotionally cold, unloving, and intimately distant. Jesus instead was securely raised by a stable, traditional Jewish family who educated him to read Scripture and become a highly literate Rabbi. Early family love and education are what separated the psychological lives of Jesus from Mohammad. Ultimately, the Koran became compiled and assembled two decades after Mohammad's death with 114 chapters and 6000 verses. The overall size of this Muslim tome is estimated to be the size of the Christian NT. While the Abrahamic heritage comes about from the direct line of Isaac, the Muslim link comes directly from his erratic brother, Ishmael. Much of the Koran was plagiarized from biblical and its theological accounts, with verses that were lifted-out and rescripted as Muslim revisions. Scattered throughout the Muslim Holy Book were amended verses taken from the Bible, confirming the assumption that Mohammad knew of Judeo/Christianity. As an example of "theological hate" of infidels found in the Qur'an (#4:95): "to suffer the jihad God has granted a higher grade to those who strive and fight." While otherwise, Jesus tells us to "strive and forgive."

As a military leader returning from battle, Mohammad often would cite the jihad as a holy "socio/political war" against those who reject the dictates of Islam. Over the centuries, most Muslims have interpreted the jihad to mean "violent detestation," justifiable murder, and warfare against the materialistic Western World. This commonly held Islamic ideal substantiates the premise that their common, tribal, self-image is DNA/flawed. The meaningless rivalry between Islam and the rest of the world has been continuing non-stop for over a dozen centuries, peaking with the vile acts at the World Trade Center bombing in NYC on September 1st, 2001, where 3000+ innocent people were trapped, fatally crushed, and/or burned alive. It would seem that one would imagine that any faithful, inerrant, and inspiring Sacred Scripture ought to be reflecting the true nature and intentions of the Divine; specifically those that feature His righteousness, His unfailing love, His gift of freedom, and His justice, as set within the operational context of universal human rights. Otherwise, in Muslim expressions of their concocted dogma, ala jihad, we find no *righteousness* resonating out of their endorsed murders, no *freedom* for political dissent, none for women's rights, lack of educational opportunities for girls, and/or no *justice* for other believers, including wrongly accused criminals. If God is *love*, then Islam joins the long array of heresies and false doctrines held by atheists, deists, gnostics, secular progressives, and the pagans of yore. If truth be told, the socio/politics of Muslims and their military terrorization of pagans, polytheists, Christians, Jews, Hindi, as well as all other non-believers, embody and qualify this pretense religion as pungent and a spiritual plague of the 21st century.

Clearly, the Koran, as narrated by Mohammad to scribes, must be considered a root cause of the spiritual curse threatening the Global well-being of the Post-Modern World.

Bio/spiritually, it would be reasonable to conclude that the Muslim plague against non-believers stems out of an inadequate, incompetent, tribal Genome that has been resisting progress and modernism for fourteen centuries. By the same token, bio/spiritually, Muslims must be considered quasi/aboriginals that covet the success of Westerners and the bounty gleaned from their "great ideas." Most extremist Muslims are evil-possessed. For centuries, they have been inoculated with envy and hate that feeds upon itself to justify their compulsive plots to subdue or kill infidels. Surely, future bio/technological research will confirm the "maladaptive inferiority" of the tribal, Islamic World. If so, only then will the Friday-night, mosque worshiper become religiously conscious enough to renounce the consent of terror and the sacrilegious delusions expecting the blessings of Allah. These Friday-night, prayer sessions never can be praiseworthy to a holy, just, and freedom loving One-God, but on the contrary always will be offensive, odious, and spiritually noxious to both Allah and the human, moral sensibility. Instead, Muslims ought to see themselves as common murderers destined to be marooned in the Outer Darkness surrounded by weeping and gnashing of teeth, forever. It remains a genomal enigma as to why Muslims don't feel mortified by their historic "guilt of hate" that continues to resist modernerity and spiritual decency.

Today, the *jihad* attacks by Muslim extremists, as fully condoned by Muslims-at-large, have mushroomed into a Global Terror network, their forming and fueling of a worldwide, spiritual plague. This immoral venom has been deeply imbedded within the Koranic, bio/social message. Especially noteworthy has been the Muslim raids by their marauders who inflicted terror upon vulnerable, small communities. As expected from the fatalistic message of Mohammad, the aboriginal, polytheistic tribes living in North Africa, who were conquered by Islamic incursions, hardly progressed out of their famine, beyond their myths, and above illiteracy.

So too in Moslem India, which still retains traces of its Hindu tradition, fatalistically postulates: "there is no reality." Likewise in culturally backward, Buddhist societies, which have adopted Islamic Thought, we see little modernism and woefully lacking progress offered by the Modern Era. Devoid of God's approval and grace all heresies and evil Empires of yore have been unsuccessful in fulfilling their delusionary goals for world conquest. Only Judeo/Christianity continues to spread, progress, and grow in ideational maturity, and advance true spiritually. Worth mentioning, in opposition to Islamic abhorrence of infidels was the 1998 novel *The Satanic Verses*, written by Salman Rushdie, who as a Muslim himself bravely launched a literary assault in defense of freedom of speech. Utilizing the power of fiction Rushdie tackled the flawed, spiritual premises of the jihad, as well as the full text of the Qur'an. Soon after publication of his *The Satanic Verses*, Rushdie was sentenced to death by the Ayatollah of Iran, via a worldwide, Muslim "murder contract." So too, fated to be killed for their criticism of Islamic violence were the famed Evangelical pastors-of-note, Jerry Falwell, Pat Robertson, and Franklin Graham. Yet without hesitation, the Koran easily can be compared to the unprovoked murders and repression of liberty connoted in Karl Marx's *Communist Manifesto*. Or, the same outrage scripted in Mao's, *Little Red Book*, along with, the genocidal atrocities preached in Hitler's, *Mein Kamp*. Looking back toward the 6th century AD, not unlike Rushdie's plight, during *Age of unChristian Heresies*, Bishop Augustine of North Africa challenged the false Catholic doctrines that defiled the message of Jesus. He too, lived under the threat of assassination. A thousand years later, Martin Luther confronted the corrupt Papacy and produced the Reformation of the 16th century. Like Rushdie, Luther lived his remarkable life under the Inquisition of the Roman Church. In common, Islam along with all of the Judeo/Christian heresies of yore can be typified and grouped as attempts to "proselyting through conquest," bent on world, religious domination. Only God's gift of freedom counters these historic evils.

For centuries, Muslims and the corrupt Papacy have pursued an invading "proselyting paradigm;" socio/political models initially proposed by Mohammad and the Popes of yore. As disseminated by the caliphs, scripted in the Koran, and now, embraced by the Muslims-at-large, time after time, the Islamic invasions have been and will continue to be defeated by true Christians, Hindus, and/or other Western armies. Surely in the 21st century, the Occident armed with the "great ideas" of the Western World and the ever-evolving, info/tech achievements of modernerity will defeat Muslim ignorance again. Not unlike the Battle of Tours in France in the year 732 AD led by Charles Martel and later by armies of five Crusades that led up to the 11th century. The Islamic armies repeatedly suffered defeat. Admittedly, by coming under the spell of Mohammad's theological delusions and deceptions, Damascus of Syria fell into the Muslim fold, along with Persia, Jerusalem, and Egypt. Also succumbing were North Africa, Spain, parts of India, China, Pakistan, along with most of the Mideastern nations. Nonetheless, the Muslim tacit rejection of the "great ideas," coupled with their tribal flaws, ignorance, and barbarous stagnation, incited the military expertise of the Western World to continue to trump and triumph over the Islamic Empire. This will again happen the 21st century. In the year 2015, history has been witnessing the unraveling of the Muslim world, first in Egypt, then Libya, Tunisia, and across the full range of the Mideastern, Muslim World. Their repulsive politics are rapidly disbanding and their dogma is fast approaching religious dissolution.

A thousand years ago in the 11th-12th centuries, the established Golden Age of Muslim Rule began to unravel and slowly decline. Iraq, Iran, and Palestine fell to the Turks, who then politically emasculated their all-knowing Caliph. In 1099 AD, Jerusalem was conquered by a series of Christian Crusades when their pilgrims were denied access to sites in the Holy Land. The Mongols, who sensed a tactical opening when Saladin, a Muslim, temporarily recaptured Jerusalem, advanced throughout Iraq and promptly executed the last of the Muslim "great Caliph." By the 14th century, Muslim military power provisionally returned. The Holy Cities of Medina and Mecca were returned to Islamic control, while Constantinople, now named Istanbul, also became Muslim occupied. Iran capitulated when they saw the Mongols converting and conquering parts of India.

Yet as a tribute to Islamic architecture, the famed Taj Mahal, in Agra, India, stands today as a singular work of Islamic beauty. Theologically, since God is the God of History, it becomes difficult to ascertain where or when Islamic bio/socio/politics or their fatalistic religion begins or ends. Today, the Global Terror Network of Islam, aroused by the hate-filled passages of the Koran, again seems to threaten the very survival of the Western World and the human race. This worldwide, Muslim conspiracy is well organized--ideologically, financially, tactically, and with no shortage of willing, suicidal/homocidal terrorists ready to be trained to kill infidels. Furthermore, "student terrorists" radiating out of the Mideast and across North Africa, including Egypt, Algeria, Saudi Arabia, Syria, Jordon, Yemen, and Libya, are actively forming "Muslim sleeper cells" in North America, Europe, and throughout the Orient. No doubt, out of its "core dynamic" the Koran, as the scripted motivator of the jihad, filled with religious and bio/sociological intolerance of infidels, fuels and maintains hate-filled prayer sessions during the Friday, mosque meetings, all happening under the watchful guidance of Imans. Again and again, robust, successful Western ideas and technologies have made little difference between winning and losing in the Muslim World. As analogy, the invention of the printing press in the 16th century, when viewed in "timeless tandem" with today's info/technologies, such as the Internet, worldwide TV, affordable and accessible commercial aviation, merged with the "great ideas" and the freedom progress of the Western World. During the 21st century, these Western achievements will again trump and triumph over Islamic fanaticism, its narrow-minded barbarism, its total reliance upon the economics of its Mideastern oil, and its terror war against the World-at-large.

In the light of current-day theology and bioscience, first and foremost all socio/political inclinations seem to be driven by both religious values and DNA/territorial preferences.

Throughout the Eras, as neuro/spiritually framed with words and symbols, these bio/spiritual expressions are becoming detectable in all segments of national life. It would be naive to assume that the art of international communications, i.e. diplomacy, is primarily resolved by way of the pressures of external, or enviromental stimuli. The internal pressures of the genetic realm seems to be a more scientifically plausible conclusion. Today, as the violent protests continue to fester in the Muslim world of the Mideast, what continues to be commanding are the values of democraatic politics, free market economics, and religious liberty. As deep-rooted in the human soul, only when politically mplemented by natural and enlightened leadership, do DNA/survival alternatives rule, by either elected officials or despotic nations. As many historical and current-day examples have established, the universal, insatiable thirst for citizen emancipation can't be indefinitely tabled by the politics of tyranny. This set-in-stone principle clearly is overlooked by the Islamic way of thinking. In due time, we can expect that within any 21st century democracy, the principles of **Bio/Politics** will be discoursed, enacted, and embraced by most all citizens; whether Oriental or Occidental, or whether Muslim or Judeo/Christian.

As viewed as the next higher plane of ideational enlightenment, in the immediate future, America, as a beacon of socio/political illumination, ought to consider making major modifications via DNA/Amendments to its US Constitution. With a *Bill of Genetic Rights*, primarily addressing educational, international, and enployment issues, a *Bill of Victim Rights*, addressing the DNA of law&order,

and a *Bill of Patient Rights*, addressing the specific diseases and their treatments arising out of an assortment of DNA-driven metabolics and immunities nestled within any bio/cultural diversity. Unquestionably, the gene-base that drives the caustic socio/politics of the tribal, Muslim World will attract a topmost tête-à-tête within the literate sector of civilized societies. Out of the wavering convictions of the 21st century, again came the clash of civilizations reignited by the Mideastern discovery of its vast, oil coffers. The effectiveness of tactical terrorism as originally devised by Osama bin Laden (OBL) came out of these oil fields. In the year 1979 AD, *two* momentous events aroused the Muslim passion, previously lying fallow since the 18th century, *One*, Osama, a Saudi multi-millionaire, was convinced, not unlike the leaders of the French Revolution, Marxism, Nazism, and Communism, that socio/political and religious change could never occur with peaceful resolutions, diplomacy, or any cooperative dialogue. Although inappropriate for the Western World, OBL professed that only the laws and ideals of the Muslim dogma ought to be the strategy for training extremists, as well as attract the support of the everyday mosque believers. Specifically for Muslim worshipers, OBL concluded that their religious beliefs must consist of: (1) pleasing Allah as the intention of life itself; (2) Mohammad and the laws of the Koran are to be their unwavering guide; (3) the jihad to become the tactical, socio/political mode of choice; (4) that dying for Allah and his edicts as the paramount hope to Paradise; and (5) the murder of infidels always can be justified as the preeminent road to heaven. *Secondly,* as evidence of God's approval has to be both the military successes by Muslim extremists in Iran leading to the expunging of their Western-leaning Shah, coupled with the Russian defeat in Afghanistan by village tribesmen. For the zealous Muslim, these two momentous events of the 20th century became the spark that flared-up into an Islamic wildfire for the next five decades. By scrupulously adhering to the injunction of Mohammad, who demanded that infidels religiously convert and politically submit to Islamic authorities, OBL and subsequent Muslim leaders began to plan a protracted war on the West to feature America and the Jews as satanic. Eventually, OBL expected that in Asia and across the Globe, all Hindu-derived nations and Christians to fall in lockstep to finally complete the Islamic ambition of the religious and political domination of all human life. To be sure in this historic context, Islam represents the spiritual plague of the 21st century. To this end, at the onset of the 3rd millennium, Islamic terrorists began to commit surprise acts of violence against t he soft targets of innocence; first across the Mideast, then Africa Proper, and Southeast Asia. In Africa, Kenya, Ethiopia, Tanzania, and Somalia, the military goals of Islam remained heightened and relentless. By always looking for symbolic targets, Islamic extremists, whether al Qaeda, Taliban or ISIS, became the international terror organizations of the 21st century. One of these groups launched coordinated, synchronized raids on a Jewish-owned, Kenyan vacation spot, the Paradise Hotel. Now as their MO, this attack included both suicide bombers with explosives hidden in a vehicle and the simultaneous launching of surface-to-air missiles aimed at an Israel, commercial plane. Internationally, yet-developing nations were of special targets to radical Muslims mainly due to the presence of 100s of millions of tribal people whose politics struggle as either fledging democracies or despotic monarchies. These yet-undeveloped countries are led by corrupt leaders, an ineffectual rule of law, and poorly trained police departments. Islam of the 21st century finds itself in a full mode of war operations by adding Russia, vacationing Australians and the British, the Philippines, Germans in Tunisia, French in Karachi, Somalian pirates on the high-seas, and a number of overseas American assets, including the bombing of New York's World Trade Center in 2001 AD where 3000 victims from all over the Globe were killed. Within a relative short period of time, these daily, terror bombings inspired by the hate-filled writings in the unholy Koran, many thousands of innocent men, women, and children have been slaughtered during these years of the "Big Oil Era." Now again, as in the past 14-centuries, Muslims, with a decade head-start, are seeking that Idyllic fix as a quick path to paradise by marching lockstep against the West and other infidels.

Is the Islamic plague primarily related to the bizarre delusions of Mohammad's revelations or are there other major factors operating as intervening bio/variables? Are the core problems within the Muslim society indications of a tribal, substandard Genome? As in the past 1400 years, ought Muslim belligerence to be attributed to pathological urges? Are the Genomes of all Islamic nations adaptively unfit and unsuitable for the ideational evolution of Mankind; so that they must seek to destroy the most successful societies, i.e. the Jewish and Western nations that ever graced the face of Planet Earth?, Via our territorial DNA/urges bio/anthrpologists know that our Ancient or Modern-day politics cover more than the possession of land rights. As in the past, our institutionalized, formal Codes, both Hammarabic and Mosaic, served and guided the built-in socio/spiritual needs of Western Mankind. However, Muslim tribalism, as scripted in the Koran, has not translated well into natural and transcendent DNA/prescripts.

Specifically, what has not succeeded in the 14-centuries of Muslim despotism and belligerence have been: (a) the delivery of economic freedom and affluence to their masses; (b) righteous governing power based on universal human rights; (c) the educational opportunities for all girls to explore; (d) just property rights; (e) fair inheritance; (f) the rule of Common Law; and (g) the military defense of their national borders. Because of the commonality found among and across all Muslim communities, ranging from the aboriginal clans to the larger yet-uncivilized, Islamic nation/States, most probably their territorial DNA operating within its "Genomal motherboard" must be fundamentally mal-imprinted or missing the full complement of normal genes.

Nonetheless to some degree, it is important to note that this same tribal DNA is only related to human, bonding urges. In part, the ***inter-species*** politics of Muslims is DNA/ poles apart from their ***intra-species*** "bonding." While the former is relatively impersonal and manifested as societal themes, the latter addresses the intimacy that adhere person-to-person. These factors determine when Muslims kill other Muslims on a regular basis with terrorist bombs, the bonding genes within the Islamic Genome that must be malfunctioning and counter-evolutionary. Humans and most all of the full range of life on Planet Earth seek to knit together, not kill each other aimlessly. Across a wide-range of living styles; courting, mating, sexuality, family modes, and nesting all are potentially identifiable as DNA/components of social bonding. Fourteen hundred years of inter and intra tribal belligerence embedded within the Islamic tradition must be signaling a flaw(s) in their Bonding Genome. Muslims neither bond naturally with themselves nor with the rest of humanity. For science with a genetic perspective, the bio/social studies of both the Muslim Political and Bonding Genomes ought to be researched as partially overlapping, but separate, DNA/subsystems. Concurrently as a broader, international picture, bio/political science ought to devote itself to the study of the macro-plagues of Humankind, to include: (a) perennial warfare; (b) unjust, ineffectual lawℴ (c) disease, health, and longevity propensities; along with, (d) recurrent famines and intractable poverty. With this deeper knowledge of the bio/spiritual and bio/political factors that must underlie the interactive manifestations of bio/bonding. the genetic science of cultural diversity might become clearer in explaining the never-ending cycle of Muslim, "extinction urges." Is it chance happenstance that at the onset of the 21st century the full-family of Mideastern nations are in a revolt-mode, craving the political successes of Western democracies and their free marketplaces? Does this political covertness include an orbit of ideas that underlie: (a) the structure of government; (b) the course of practical and just politics; (c) economic capitalism and central banking; (d) the reliance on science; (e) the use of higher mathematics and data processing; (e) the implementation of freedom and human rights; (f) the ongoing R&D of technology; all as modulated by (g) the roots of the Judeo/Christian Code, that serves as the "vagus nerve" of all "great ideas." Regrettably, while all can partake in these erudite, fundamental thoughts, not all human bio/breeds seem neuro/equipped with equal DNA/proficiency to live-out the ambitions and aspirations of this Western type of transcendent society. As an axiom: ***living successfully in a free society requires a fuller, comprehensive, transcendent, neuro/genetic development of its integrated brain.*** Tribal Islam seems to lack this socio/political potential.

Yet arguable for future bio/science, this theorem yet to be explored might hold true for individuals, the diverse bio/breeds of Mankind, and society-at-large. In potential and fit for 21st century governance, this assumed principle could become a plank in a political platform for any bio/cultural, democratic diversity. We now know beyond the shadow of doubt that the psyche level of the frrontal lobes and its ajacent tissues of the brain of the Homo Sapien delivers to democratic communities: (a) greater self-control; (b) better judgment; (c) socio/appropriate emotions; (d) organizational efficiency; and (e) the neuro/delay mechanisms needed to assure a more, adaptive self-reliance and decision-making. Indded, the fashioning of these required attributes of the Political Genome can only be realized in a democracy. The tribal, Islam nations lack these DNA/capacities for governing. Without eugenic intercession, not all the bio/breeds of the family of Mankind are fully capable of supplying these socio/political qualities for freedom living. Moreover as the floundering United Nations has verified, there remain few, useful solutions for the upgrading of the territorial plights of Humankind via Global politics. Since leaders continue to tread laterally in either a politically ultra-conservative or ultra-liberal direction, forms of spiritual plagues will be expected to continue to inflict war, terror, disease, bondage, and starvation upon the human condition.

Without the "genetic vision," the political denials and sidestepping of the UN are guiding the human race nowhere. So too without the "genetic vision," in the USA, especially in California where the diverse demographics might be Democrat, Republican, Independent, Left, Right, or Center, the spectrum and mechanisms of its political assortment have become stalemated and weighed down with inert, mounting debt, oversized, ceentral governing, with higher taxes, and the Liberal tyranny of political correctness. Similarly within the world context, national, diplomatic \relationships have become weary, dreary, confrontational, and idling by the reiterating babble of spinmasters of leaderships. Verily, no matter how hard they try with socio/political "slipping and sliding," the Western World remains stuck-in-the-mud, spewing bromides as regurgitated by the pundits of the international Media. This multi-factored circumstance has contributed significantly to the Western vulnerability to the barbarisms of Islamic onslaughts. All the while the insights needed for a more wholesome, less vitriolic internationalism remains genetically unattainable. Why so? Plainly, what is needed by the Global politics-of-the-day is the acceptance of a bold thrust of "vertical launches" of national courage and neo/ideas. At the bottom of it all, international, political discussions must be rotated and pointed "upward," away from the "lateral now" of politics-as-usual. Only by veering our "Global mindset" in this upturn mode will humanity be able to "find and fulfill" the designs and intents of the democratic "freedom hopes" for all. Surely with the lurking possibility of Malthusian extinction posed by the plague of Islam, now the world is ripe for a Global Renaissance. Verily as an historical simile, liken to the great, oceanic explorations of the 15th and 16th centuries, only the freeing-up of our "political ships of state" willing to sail assuredly in unchartered, neo/ideational waters can America and the free world discover the more useful answers to our 21st century's, socio/cultural challenges, dilemmas, and contentions. The genetic vision, when applied to the Muslim World promises a progressive thrust away from their antediluvian ideas and primordial values.

Here is how and why Islam is "failing and falling" precipitously. Unlike the spirritual "freedom messages" of the Bible, the Koran lacks the full density and intensity of righteousness, justice, freedom, and love, as Divinely set within the context of individual liberty. Instead, the Muslim World is possessed by hate, bondage, injustice, and evil. *For each of us, our thirst for freedom, love, justice, holiness, and intimacy with the Divine are the most-basic, operational, socio/spiritual compoenents of life on Planet Earth..* All of Creation is steeped in these Divine qualities. Politics too ought to be loving, not hateful, enacted as good, not immoral, freedom-loving, and just-for-all, bar none. This is the message of Jesus, not Mohammad. Love doesn't and can't exist without the freedom to love. Islam is not spiritually powered by these Divine qualities. It is just another major herasy. Accordingly, the yearnings for "political freedoms," as in democracies and capitalism, must be viewed as an irrepressible component of our very innate existence. The Islamic Code professes the opposite of life&love. As a matter of simple deduction, the genes must have been the carriers of our appetites for societal freedom vs bondage. Thus across a span of thousands of years, the "compassionate Bible" vs the "incompassionate Koran" both created societies that materialized out-of the governing experiments of Europe, Asia, and Africa. In the 21st century, we must think that which was once unthinkable. For example, demographically prowling at the American, political subconscious was the "communal gene" of the Northland People of Europe. They played a determinant role in the fashioning of our embryonic New World. In the 18th century AD a diverse confederation of Northland Europeans unified, gelled, and amplified as a migrating community in America. Driven by the DNA's "best and bravest" of Old World British, Irish, Skandia, Germans, Scots, Welcch, and French Huguenots, a New World bubblrd out of this Northern/European genomal cauldron. This bio/cultural merging of Viking ways were destined for the future populace of Americana. Iinitially animated by the territorial and militant vibrancy of the Viking DNA/stock, all the while in the Western Hemisphere the territorial ambitions of the Spanish, French, and Portuguese waned, ceded, subsided, and drifted apart and away from this momentous, American, eugenic miracle. Simultaneously, also seen in a DNA context, the Muslim World emerged and expanded out of the Genomes of aboriginal tribalism that fully accounts for their barbarism, ignorance, resistance to progress, and heretical theology.

Scientists of the future will be contending that it's the "territorial genes" of human bio/breeds which are producing either democracies or despotism, and/or affluence or poverty. Irrespective and independent of the axioms of universal human rights, civil liberties and the trade opportunities of the open marketplace are we willing to admit that our political/economic theories and obsessions with the cultural correctness of Secular Liberalism are running short-of-the-mark? If so, the philosophical acceptance of the "genetic vision" can only be sustained by the ongoing breakthroughs of the mega-technological feats of bio/science; especially as they might be conceived and substantiated by: (a) the output accretions of gigga-bite computers that are capable of extracting-out voluminous, yet-hidden DNA-patterns; (b) the fuller array of elements located within the genetic cosmos, as gauged by the highest form of bar-coding micro/technology; and (c) the amplification by scholars and mathematicians of bio/genetic theories. Moreover, socio/politically acting as a counterweight, delicately balanced upon a fulcrum, these DNA/equations can be: (a) offsetting the budgetary down falls of 20th-21st centuries failed and wasteful, governmental programs; (b) neutralizing the disillusionments of pan-victimization professed by the non-sequiturs of Liberal-driven, legal events; and (c) welcoming the differential, performance expectations in schools and the workplaces. Axiomatically trying to tip-over the fulcrum of progress with the promise of political spin-offs, true revolutions of thought always are beset with positive and negative valances. This repositioning of the human mind will be creating a new Philosophy of governing; mainly *The Age of Bio/ Politics,* while neutralizing the spiritual plagues, intellectual myths, and emotional superstitions-of-the-day. With a new scholarship, the search for the mathematical relationships of territorial genes and democratic politics will constitute the leading focus of national governance and international relations. Via bio/technology, the shifting among the DNA building-blocks, known as the A, T, C, G, along with the billions of combinations and permutations that they generate, ought to become the in-vogue, political science fit for a new millennium. Verily, the *Age of Bio/Behavior* is descending upon this scholarship. Moreover in support of the workings of the Political Genome, the principles of chemistry, biology, and physics will be called-upon to help solve the 21st century's enigmas generated by the falsehoods of the psychological, sociological, anthropological, and political establishments. All of which in common have been zealously committed to the efficacy of the micro-unit of *political experience*. With the creation and aid of future mega-computers, which already are capable of generating trillions of calculations per gigga/ second, the technological progress for new scientific efforts at first will be a trickle, slowly accelerating, then snowballing--so as to push Mankind's "envelope of bio/spiritual insights" up into a higher orbit; thereby cueing international leaders that a new era of scientific and philosophical enlightenment could be on-hand. With carefully worded hypotheses emanating out of the results of integrated, multi-science inquiries, scholars of both the hard and soft persuasions, will be able to better account for the puzzling array of complex, human behavior, especially our demoncratic politics of freedom vs the Islamic theology of bondage.

Other than Koranic, world-terrorism, who would deny that today's rate of bio/criminal behaviors has become an "unacceptable obscenity" to a free society. Especially, at an incidence-level that seems destined to encumber a free nation that is at the cutting edge of human evolution. As national policy committed to credible&just DNA/ blueprinting, criminals and terrorists who have relied upon the technological limitations of both military prowess and law enforcement, will quickly lose their sinister edge. The shroud of secrecy, which has been shielding the "dispassionate Muslim criminal," will be shredded and torn-away from their moorings of their traditional bio/social hate. When cleverly marketed by law-enforcement and counterterror specialists, the spiritual temptations of terror would cause potential perpetrators to realize that they run a high, personal risk of near-immediate identification, near-certain capture, along with, inevitable, long-term incarceration--or as some have suggested, more ideally, "public beheading." Ideally a political goal for the near future, might be that all heinous crime in a Jeffersonian democracy ought to be pegged down to a trickle. The national crime-rate and terror-threats combined, estimated between 1%-2% of the general population, should be pegged at least at par with the dubious, zero-tolerance of dictatorships. Freedom-based societies always have been undully victimized by the henious criminal. Then, and only then, will the dreams of our Founding Fathers approach their wishes for a transcending society laced with communities liberated from evil-possessed, heinous behaviors. Surely for society-at-large, genetically generated, asocial types, political extremists, and antisocial personalities, who accepted evil as a life-style, have accounted for most of the heinous, horrific, and flagrant crimes against vulnerable innocence, whether individual, against the community, or humanity at-large. With DNA research, it becomes possible to see that the dispositions toward bio/spiritual crime and despotic warfare. At first, these abberations can be identified, computer-cataloged, and then, within the code of human rights and liberties, eugenically backbred out of the evolutionary chain. All birthright citizens abiding in democratic societies deserve the political intervention of this line of tax-sponsored bio/research. Surely, this bio/spiritual advancement will become the renaissance of the future. How so?

Foremost, by the identification and integration of those genetic factors associated with innercity crime and Muslim terror management. Then, within a US Constitutional Amendment that formally recognizes the *rights of victims,* the knowledge gained from these DNA studies of lawbreakers and terrorists, might encourag ea number of creative, legislative bills to be proposed and enacted by lawmakers of all party and ideological affiliations. Concomitantly, urgently needed are preventive programs that are the building of DNA/ centers, which basic objectives ought to be to avert the escalation of the interbreeding of criminal/extremist genes. To boot, instead of the hideous practices of abortions in tax-suported clinics, a number of preventive "eugenic hubs" by family centers might be better enacted to advise childless couples, and those pre-wed and newlywed of their genetic composition and anti-social or asocial propensities. With time and legislative wisdom as partners, the DNA/control of bio/ criminal or terrorist behavior and their appalling outcomes of impersonal evildoing, are bound to wane. Especially, those sexual predators that victimize children or suicide bombers that spread terror by snuffing-out the beauty of innocence. With DNA-based enforcement, the rate of budgetary savings from incarcerations ought to tumble. In sum, with each passing day the bio/behavioral revelations of the socio/ spiritual DNA, conducted in tandem with the bio/tech labs and schools of theology; might define the workings of the internationally diverse *Political Genome* and offer hope to a frenzied Globe.

Egregiously offensive to God is the Muslim non-stop killing of thousands of innocence over the past 14-centuries with claims of Divine mandate. This horror ought to confirm for the Western World that a deep-rooted, dismal, evil reality is in play. An all-inclusive heresy, Islam has been an ongoing spiritual plague, and an existential wickedness that seeks to impede both the ideational and spiritual progress of Humankind. Indeed the reduction of the seemingly never-ending conflict between the Islamic and Judeo/Christian Worlds can prove spiritually essential to the well-being and growth of any society. Yet, irrespective of their commitment to either democratic freedom or Muslim slavery, all nations have the responsibility to protect well-founded, religious expressions. Nonetheless, to grasp the historic dynamics of this Global quarrel, first, what must be faced by both political and religious leaderships is that this irresolvable, socio/spiritual contention is hinged upon a single, core, philosophical factor. Liberty vs bondage, raging between the Muslim World and Judeo/Christianity, is the core issue at hand. Today, this obstinate conflict has resulted in a "war on terror" driven by the economics of oil. Thusfar, as in the past 1300-years, this socio/spiritual discord has neither subsided nor faded away. Yet history tells us that all socio/cultural oppositions or wars have been known to end in due time when the non-theological conditions of human life adapt to technological progress and become absorbed within the contending societies. So, why not so the Muslim/Christian disagreement?

Despite of what most historians would have us believe, for almost one and half millennia Islam has been jealously at war with the progress of the West due to the ongoing, basic differences that have proven to be more *theological,* than political, economic, militarily, or even ideological. Since the 7th century AD, by citing the dictates of their "unholy book," the Koran, Muslims vehemently have been opposing cultural and religious advancement, while confronting both the Judeo/Christian and Hindu beliefs that kept Planet Earth in a state of ideational and spiritual disarray. From its onset, Islam is, and has been an enduring, profane, hypocritical, Global sacrilege. Any religion that doesn't profess the Divine attributes of freedom, love, goodness, and justice is avowing a heretical doctrine. Unconditional love, goodness in lieu of evil and universal human rights are glaringly absent in the basic Code of Islam. This alone ought to confirm that the

Muslim world fails to meet the very benchmarks of liberty. Theologically, with our adamant search for true meaning, what eludes the hate-filled passages of the Koran is that the most ennobling drives of the human psyche are the longings for dependency to, and intimacy with God. In all religions professed, the creation of all heresies and schisms has thwarted this fundamental "psychology of the spirit." The denial or distortion of this most basic purpose of life, as misguidedly asserted in Islamic dogma, has accounted for the distorted holy *Message* of Jesus. What must be recognized by scholars is that there are different motivations for the formation of heresies and schisms that seek to challenge the fidelity of the freedom *Message of God* and the devotional *Media of religion*; both linked as two sides of the same coin leading to the spiritual journey of a Moral Evolution. As examples of justifiable, Christian **media**, Presbyterians, Episcopalians, Methodists and Anglicans, all attempt to put into practice truthful expressions of the Judeo/Christian Belief. They are neither wayward doctrine nor heretical schisms. As compared to, the idolatrous rituals of Hinduism and the false doctrines of Islam on the nature and intent of Divine life and its intent. Consequently, socio/political tolerance for denominational and liturgical variations seem wanting in the unChristian World. While the road to the Kingdom of Heaven is narrow. as historic fact Muslims have failed to grasp the Divine fiat of love for neighbor is nonnegotiable. As a divergence from Hinduism and Islam, Christian Scripture advises that the "highway to heaven" must be tapered, funneled, and paved with universal love, holiness, freedom, and justice. Hopefully, with the infusion of grace, the voyage of a soul, which is bound to stray, vacillate, or walk spiritually unsteadily, will lead upward to God with the indirect supervision of the Holy Spirit. That's why, neither Mohammad nor Shiva, only Jesus instructed us that it is never acceptable to judge or condemn the spiritual growth of any well-intention believer. That's why, moral ideas set in truth, which have a great deal to do with our spiritual expansion and escalation, deserve to be tested with meditation, spiritual reasoning, grace, and faith. Any particular stage of spiritual development of any individual soul doesn't deserve criticism and the finality of condemnation by anyone. In his ministry, Jesus condemned bogus and sinful ideas, but never sinners, or those honestly inquiring, seeking, or curious about, the road to the Kingdom of Heaven. All other non-Christian beliefs, especially the Muslim theology of terror, fall short of this spiritual principle. Always, vengeance or mercy remains God prerogative, who through Divine wisdom both approves or condemns human acts, words, and thoughts.

Prior to the, yet-puzzling conception and rise of the Muslim Faith by Muhammad in the 7th century AD, the evolution of "Christian Thought" during its first 400 years AD had believers meeting in homes, synagogues, or the Temple in Jerusalem as they tried to ascertain the veiled, multi-directional, spiritually complex, multi-factored, meanings of Jesus' nature, message, and ministry. Occasionally this early period of Christian history led to different perspectives and major heresies concerning the reasons to worship Jesus. However in the 6th century AD, some of these theological uncertainties drifted away from the truth to become formally established as major heresies and schisms. These errant doctrines became unveiled and disputed by a Bishop Augustine of Hippo, the foremost theologian of the 6th century, Christian Church, as ministered in North Africa. Over his lifetime, Bishop Augustine, with five million, carefully scripted words began to formulate and clarify the elemental doctrines of the Early Christian system of belief. No doubt, Augustine ought to be considered one-of-four of the superstars of Christian theology. The other three were Moses, Paul, and Luther. All other theological scholars ought to be considered having some substance, but as spin-offs of these four theologians. The formalization of Christianity, along with the guidance, administration, and activities of the later Church Fathers: St. Jerome, St. Benedict, St. Basil, and St Gregory added "hands-on flesh" to the yet-floundering, fragile skeletal Church of Early Christianity. Head-on Augustine challenged the heresies-of-the-day by addressing and defining the issues of baptism, the Trinity, resurrection of the body, the Divinity of Jesus, the Holy Spirit, Divine energy as grace, the Eucharist, the 2nd homecoming of Jesus, predestiny, faith vs. works, forgiveness of sins, the moral justifications for warfare, and the intercessional role of the Madonna. Later in the 8th century AD, while the Muslim heresy began to gel, pseudo/Christian expressions, which began to form as early as the 2nd century AD, included the Marconites. They developed an entrenched following of believers across Arabia, Italy, Armenia, and Egypt. This heresy challenged the "good God" view of Sacred Scripture. As well, and defiantly, by adopting the hardcore, dualistic, Platonic view of the human spirit and the Gnostics, not unlike Islam, denied the incarnation of Jesus.

By utilizing an array of magic and pagan myths, Arius in the 4ᵗʰ century AD, not unlike Islam, also denied the divinity of Christ and collected a sizeable following of heretics. Also defiling Jesus' ministry during the "Heretic Age" were the Valentinians, who as early as 136 AD, were led by a glib and slick Egyptian who abided in Rome. Persians too, added to the body of the Christian history of high-heresy. On and about the year 240AD, Mani proclaimed a new religion and claimed that he was the last of the great prophets, along with Abraham, Noah, Jesus, and Buddha. Four hundred years later Muhammad followed this array of pseudo/Christian cults by declaring to be the Last Prophet. By being part of this pattern of false, theological doctrines, 21ˢᵗ century's Islam, by virtue of the exploding high/tech revolution that info/intertwines the fabric of humanity on Planet Earth, must be considered the most egregious of all the high-heresies.. *Surely, Islam is the spiritual plague of the 21ˢᵗ century.* And so, in a capsule in one fashion or another the heresies and schisms of the past 2000-years have all centered about the misconceived, theological study of Christology. In the year 380 AD just three centuries after the Crucifixion, most-all of these early, theological oppositions to a newly and rapidly forming Christian Church, were counteracted and defused by the scripting of a "universal creed," known as the Nicene version that became the official, orthodox, mainstream doctrine of the Christian Empire.

The survival logic of the 21ˢᵗ century dictates that the homicidal extremists of Islam must be defeated, not appeased. Moderate Muslims seem to see eye to eye with the terrorists who kill more Muslims than infidels. Islam needs reformers who revere progress, not more moderates who resist the natural course of human ideo/evolution. For this reason, it becomes the responsibility of the Imans to seek a lasting, reform movement that brings about their archaic, 8th century perception of the world up to 21st century standards of democratic civilization. In the present day, as in the annals of yore, Islamic communities, culture, and religious allegiance have been anchored and chained to barbaric, tribal ways&means. Initially, the polytheistic and idolatrous tribes that were conquered by roving, Koranic gangs, fashioned a "tribal Muslim Empire." Universal freedom, justice for all, love of non-believers, and socio/political morality have been clearly absent from the core message of the Koran. Instead, Muslims accept as true the terror of wanton suicide/murder of neighbors, suppression of adult females, the lack of modern education for young girls, and their fanatical desire for the demolition of the Western World. Since the 8th century, Islam has been hate-filled, ademocratic and non-Christian. With paradox, the Islamic expansion of believers among bellicose, tribal people has resulted in a narrow-minded, fanatical "tribal deportment" unfit even for the few open-minded, Western-educated Muslim. Mainly due to this contending, socio/political dynamic, whereby a collection of small tribes eventually blossomed into a Global, Islamic, "tribal Empire." occurring in tandem with the ideological evolution of the Western World, might we begin to understand the temperament of the Muslim and Christian, 1200-year rivalry.

The turning point to this irreconcilable enmity came to pass when Pope Urban II in the 11th century decided that due to the belligerence and intolerant stance of the Muslim armies the very survival of the Judeo/Christian tradition has been placed in serious jeopardy. Pope Urban II was prophetic. Soon thereafter, his first of a series of Crusades was launched against these hard-line, Islamic incursions. Unlike the 11th century, today as a catalyst to Muslim/Western relations the economic contentions for the major, oil reserves of the world have been expressed through the Muslim terror-bombings of innocent bystanders. Whether denied or not, Embolded by the citations in the Koran, suicide murders of harmless people have become the acceptable media for the continuation of a1400-year strife between the progressive values of Christendom and those of the archaic, Muslim nations who ascribe to an antiquated, vintage, life&love modalities. Without "oil" as the tangible focus of economic and spiritual conflict, civilized Mankind would take little notice of the barbaric backwardness of the Islamic societies and would continue progressing beyond to the Space Age. Traditionally, the religion of Islam has been opposed to advancement, whether ideational or technological. However, at the bottom-line for those Muslim nations, which seek to move forward in the modern, geo/political arena, there is nowhere to go except to adopt the ideas, religion, socio/politics, and technologies of the Judeo/Christianized West. Otherwise as the Palestinian/Israeli conflict has shown, the bombings of innocence will continue to spread across the Globe, so as to eventually deplete, diminish, and impede any vibrancy left of Islamic barbarism. In due course, the Western World and its proven talents will not lose-out to an ignorant, backward-oriented, Islamic scheme. Out of the adaptive dynamics of Western evolution, a finalizing proposal to the Imams of the Muslim World might be: "reform thyself." This is a Malthusian offer that can't be refused.

Patently heretical, the worship of Islam has been the spiritual plague of the 21st century. Irrespective of whether it's of the original 8th century vintage or the archaic, modern-day versions of Sunnis vs Shiras, Islam remains as an immoral counterpoint to all other mainstream, religious practices on the Globe. *De facto*, most of humanity knows: God is love. And, as stated in Scriptural metaphor, good vines (i.e. good theology) don't produce bad fruit, such as the immutable, Islamic abhorrence of the murder of all infidels, as directed at the greater part of humanity. A jihadist teaching espoused by the Koran for both devotional rituals and scriptural mandates are immorally justified, aided and abetted by the modern-day, moderate, Muslim community-at-large. As religion, Islam is spiritually unsustainable, unpalatable to a healthy soul, and revolting to God. The sponsoring of indiscriminate "violence unto death" for the infidel never can be morally defensible within the current, World Order. Since the 8th century, there have been few "peaceful and loving thoughts" by the Muslim outlook toward their brothers and sisters, whether Hindu, Jew, or Christian. Packaged as a Jihad, i.e. a holy war, which comes directly out of the readings of Islamic Scripture, the socio/political style of the everyday Muslim has been unbendingly shaped out of the unswerving, overriding message of detestation toward the non-Muslim believer, i.e. the infidel. Hence, in toto, the verses of the

Islamic Koran must be considered as intellectually ignorant, liturgically immoral, valueless, socio/politically destructive, and a scripturally bankrupt pestilence of the 21 century.

A fuller appreciation of the message of Jesus in this high-tech culture of the 21 century must include both an "historical and theological" scrutiny of the Islamic allure. For the sake of the survival of Humankind, this biblical scholarship can neither be ignored nor tabled. The potential of today's info/military technology and nuclear weaponry can prove to be either a blessing or a curse to Christian/Muslim relations. For this reason, as stated in the Koran, the dogma originally put forth by the warped, deranged, illiterate psyche of Mohammad, demands a scholarly confrontation, not a conciliatory pretext of the Muslim World. In the context of today's ideas, religious insights, socio/politics, and high technologies, the dysfunctional life of the "Last Prophet," will supply insights into the nonstop disputation between Muslims and Christians. When compared and contrasted with the peaceful message of Jesus, the zeal of the Islamic expansion well over a thousand years, from the 8th thru the 18th centuries, reveals an evil obsession for socio/political aggression and world domination. The differences in truthful doctrine, concerning the nature, structure, intentions, and operations of the Godhead glaringly stands out. Granted over the centuries, both the traditional Roman Church and Muslim Mosque have stepped over the acceptable line of social decency, truthfulness, justice, freedom, and righteousness. Nonetheless, from a theological perspective, these disparities continue to become worthy of scholarly meditation and erudite analysis. Why so? Across the evolution of the religious/ spiritual journey of the Homo Sapien ranging from the mutant Adam of South/Central Africa leading directly to 21st century Man, there is an existential message that pits goodness vs evil, justice vs prejudice, freedom vs bondage, and love vs hate. Irrespective of Islamic claims, when viewed within the context of today's enlightenment and scholarship, the Muslim belief *isn't* an authenticate extension of the Judeo/Christian Code, but rather the practice of monotheistic high-heresy. The Muslim denial and dismissal of Jesus as the incarnate reflection of God fully confirm this postulate. At best, Islam has been a provisional "spiritual fix" for those bio/tribal souls of alienated, polytheistic, idolatrous Black&Brown&Yellow racial, sectors of Mankind. These successful incursions by Muslims across many centuries of history have been targeting the conversion of the vulnerable, polytheistic/idolatrous communities, consisting of the people of the Mid East, North Africa, parts of South Asia, and other, aboriginal areas of the Globe. To its credit, monotheism was a Judeo/Christian principle that became reintroduced by Islam for the sake of the spiritual enlightenment of the downtrodden, subjugated, ignorant, oppressed people. For the past two centuries, Islam has been on an ideational/theological decline due mainly to the illegitimacy of its hateful tenets. An honest assessment of their hopeless societies and their culturally barbaric ways&means should be enough to convince anyone that "good theology," not heretical doctrine, always will outperform and surpass those values which time has passed. Both ideationally and technologically, the Muslim, 8th century view of today's realities continues to clash with those of the Western World of the 21st century. Modernism has often been resisted by traditionally intolerant leadership. Numerically, any alleged swelling of its Islamic ranks can be attributed to spikes in family-size rather than to an expansion of converted believers. Prophetically by the end of this century, the branding of a "cult status" upon the hides of the societies of Islam, along with Hinduism and its religious derivatives, will continue to identify and highlight maladaptive dogmas. A steep decline in stature by Islam and pan-Hinduism will set apart and diminish their "religious carcasses" of yore. Only Judeo/Christianity has been and will continue to spike/trend upward and outwardly due primarily to its Divine substance.

Always bear in mind the psycho/history of Mohammad. Early in his emotional development, he was raised out of an unstable, dysfunctional, family. His father died before he was born. His mother died when he was 6-years of age. Throughout his formative years, Mohammad's upbringing was shuffled erratically from his grandparents to his uncles. Surely, the psyche of Mohammad was damaged--intellectually, emotionally, and spiritually. He never learned to read or write. Yet as an illiterate, uneducated, and uniformed nomad, his charisma, his natural intellectual brilliance, and military prowess appealed to those tribal societies consisting mostly of Black, Yellow, and Brown races. With the Islamic suppression of the notion of idolatrous polytheism unrestrained in the 8th century and by embracing monotheism, Mohammad was able to sate the souls of unsophisticated, uncivilized, tribal people of the Globe. As contrast, as an orthodox, educated Jew, Jesus came out of a tradition of Jewish scholarship. He was raised in a stable, healthy, loving family and for three years guided a ministry that appealed to both the non-Jew and Jew alike. Granted, both Jesus and Mohammad attracted great hordes of followers. Jesus did it with love, Mohammad with a spiritual/ military message of "religious elitism" that rationalized hatred, was financed with protection payments, ruled with spiritual bondage, and justified with the murder of the non-believer. Otherwise, about 800-hundred years prior at a tipping-point of no-return for the fall of the Roman Empire, well-prior to the scripting of the Koran, on Palm Sunday, Jesus entered the Holy City of Jerusalem on a "humble colt" in a background of cheering, adoring followers who knew of his miracles, healings, and unconditional teaching of love and salvation. Mohammad on the other hand entered into the Holy City in Saudi Arabia on a camel brandishing a sword, followed by a 1000-warriors. Hence as metaphor, we see in action social love vs. social belligerence vying for religious preeminence.

Eventually, these 1st and 8th century events led to the Crusades, a decisive, pivotal Medieval Epoch for both the followers of Jesus and those of Mohammad. Just prior to these 10th century wars of religion, Islam was spreading feverishly across the Mid East, North Africa, and Asia, sweeping across the homes and communities of mostly people with non-pink, skin tones. As bogus, the Koranic claim that Islam is for "all people" rang hollow for Westerners. De facto, Muslims abhor the Caucasian Christian, the Jew, and the Hindu, even though their Holy Book contains mostly plagiarized, fragments of Judeo/Christian references. In toto, the "Koran and Islam" is no more than a warped, heretical, fax-simile, and distortion of the Moral Evolution of Western Man. Its credo goes 180 degrees contrary to the set-in-stone, widespread, accepted beliefs of love, holiness, freedom, and justice. By their laws all females, women and girls alike, are kept mostly ignorant and browbeaten into submission without human rights. In Muslim societies, intolerance and revulsion of others are taught in their religious schools and mosques as standard curricula. In the context of the 21st century's illumination, who would deny that Islamic nations are primitive, archaic, barbaric, and unfit for the ideas, socio/politics, religion, and technologies of the Modern Age?

As if it pleased Allah, the kidnapping and slaughter of innocent bystanders via suicide bombers are the time-honored acts of hate by all strata of Muslim societies. At the genomal level of discourse, even their resistance to democratic ways&means, ideational progress, and the rule of law for both themselves and others suggest that irreversible "bio/tribal flaws" are operating within their DNA/profiles. Their psycho/social behaviors of tribal vs civilized people must be an ingrained, genetic statement. Primordial defects embedded with in the Muslim Genome that include: territorial preferences, family bonding, mating styles, socio/politics, Divine identification, and neighborly urges toward humanity-at-large suggest that a genetic factor is negatively operating within the Muslim DNA. Behaviorally, the Koran and its theocratic demands resonate a "genetic dynamic" that might be in play for those who are irretrievably, intolerantly disposed to hate. So too, reflected as a spin-off of Mohammad's psycho/pathology is the Islamic vision of the hereafter as an "erotic reward.'" In the Koran heaven is depicted as having unlimited sex with dozens of virgins, thereby makes dying as a homicidal bomber eternally worthwhile. This form of theology is bizarre and theologically incoherent.

For the most part, while the original appeal of Mohammad's dogma was a monotheistic, non-idolatrous, message--away from the polytheism and pagan worship by neo/aborigines of the 8th century, its spiritual value abruptly ends here. By seeking the direct genetic line to living Muslims, religious scholarship in the search for the core cause of the rise of the Muslim belief, points to Ishmael, the bastard son of Hagar and Abraham. That is, as compared to Isaac, the son of Abraham and Sarah, who was the direct genetic line to King David and Jesus. Beginning in Ancient times, at least biblically, it seems that the tribal attraction to a new, monotheistic religion must have been a genomal statement. Future bio/technological research can be expected to shed light on these conjectures. Granted, while the Arab intellectuals carried forth both the lost Classical and Ancient knowledge to the 15th century Renaissance, their historical contributions must be considered as no more than "carriers of knowledge" rather than as "ideo/creators" of human evolution. The proof is in the pudding. When one looks at primeval societies, which Muslims transformed before and during the Modern Age, what is bound to be concluded is that the Islamic World has been rejecting the progress of the "great ideas" of the West, including the soul-satisfying values of Jesus. Undeniably, it was the socio/spiritual factors of Judeo/Christianity that produced the free societies, the open marketplaces, universal human rights, care for the disenfranchised, tolerance toward all, along with, the full and open, cultural roles for women and girls in society. Even if radically reformed, the basic, religious tenets of the Koran will never sustain the Muslim World to ever be fit for any modern-day, socio/political reality. Ergo in the 11th century with a run of Moslem conquests, the Western World finally had enough of Islamic barbarism that plagued the known world from the 8th thru the 12th centuries. Thus in response and existentially threatened, the Western World replied in kind with their brand of counter-conquests. In reaction to the theological repression and military aggression of the Muslim Imans, a number of Christian Crusades were launched, ranging across a number of time periods. Consequently, the Euro/West reacted militarily and began to impede the "Islamic Pestilence." As of today and irrespective of the Global economics of oil, these terror-wars of religious ascendancy have marked the "beginning of the end" of the Muslim national cohesion and expansion. Today, most of the Islamic nations of the 21st century seem to be socio/politically geo/decomposing. Set into motion with an array of commercial/fiscal relationships between the East and West, sinking "oil banking" by the inflexible and barbaric nations of Allah are vying with the "flexible and creative" Christian West. Utilized as chips in the Global Marketplace, the oil reserves of the Moslem nations have become their fleeting, Global currency once-valued highly in international dealings are plummeting, new energy technology and sinking oil prices. These trends will give the Islamic cultures an offer they can't refuse: either to adopt the religion, ideas, socio/ politics, and high technologies of the Western World—or perish into an abyss of religious obscurity.

EPILOGUE

God's gift of freedom, which includes universal human rights and democratic institutions embedded within all socio/political communities, can best be cherished biblically.

In Exodus 6: 6-7 God tells us: ***I am the Lord and I will free you from your slavery. I will make you my own special people... who has rescued you.*** In Galatians 5: 13, Paul tells us: ***You have been called to freedom... not freedom to satisfy your sinful nature, but freedom to serve one another in love.*** In Exodus 21: 2 Hebrew slaves must be fully emancipated after six years. In Deuteronomy 15: 13-15 God tells us when male (and females) are freed; a farewell must include part of a bounty with which the Lord has blessed. He says: ***Remember that you were slaves once and God redeemed you.*** In Jeremiah 34: 17, God's wrath and fury were expressed toward those who withdraw freedom from others. Through the prophet Jeremiah, He declares: ***I will set you free to be destroyed by war, famine, and disease. You will be considered disgraced by all the nations of the Earth.*** Defending the Oppressed was of high priority to the

OT Prophet Nehemiah in his 5th Chapter. In Romans 6:17 *Thank God, once you were slaves of sin… now you have a new master, righteousness.* John 8: 32, Jesus tells us: *And you will know the truth and the truth will set you free.* And John 8: 36 *If I set you free you will indeed be free.* In Galatians 2:4 Paul says: *those who came to spy on us to see our freedom in Jesus Christ.* And in 5:1 Paul continues: *So Christ has really set us free, now make sure you stay free and don't get tied up again in slavery to the law.* In Romans 8: 15 *we are told not to be like cowering, fearful slaves… behave instead like God's very own children.*

In 2Corrintians 3:17 Paul tells us, *Now the Lord is the Spirit and wherever the Spirit of the Lord is, he gives freedom.* John 8:36 says: *If the Son sets you free, you indeed be free.* Romans 6: 7 tells us: *For when we died with Christ we were set free from the power of sin.* In James 1: 25 the bible instructs: *keep looking steadily at God's perfect law, the law that sets you free.* Romans 8: 21 of Scripture informs: *All creations anticipate the day when it will join God's children in glorious freedom.* Galatians 4: 3-4 gives us insight to His Redemption Plan: *God sent Jesus to us to buy freedom for us who were slaves to the law.* Colossians 2: 20 says: *you have died with Christ* and He has set you free from the evil powers of the world. Psalm 116:16: *Lord, you have freed me from my bonds.* 1Corintian 8:9: *But you must be careful with this freedom of yours.* 1Peter 2: 16-17: *You are not slaves, you are free. But your freedom is not an excuse to do evil. You are free to live as God's slaves. Fear God.*

Who is this God who demands freedom?

God is love, 1John 4: 8. God is holy, Leviticus 11: 44. God is eternal, Psalm 90: 2. God is infinite, 1Kings: 8: 27. God is immortal, 1Timothy: 1: 17. God is spirit, John: 1: 18. God is all-knowing, Psalm 147: 5. God is all-present, Psalm 139: 7-21. God is all-powerful, Isaiah 40: 6-7. God is unchanging, Malachi 3: 6. God is without equal, Isaiah 40: 18, 25. God is righteous, Psalm 145: 17. God is perfect, Mathew 5 48. God is beautiful, Exodus: 15: 11. God is gracious, Exodus: 34: 6. God is invisible, John 4: 24.

Consistent with Jesus, who shed His blood to free us from bondage and subjugation, who forgave us of our sins, and saved us from an eternity in the Outer Darkness, surrounded by weeping and gnashing of teeth, so too since the year 1776 AD, hundreds of thousands of soldiers, sailors, and aviators shed their blood in death and wounds to defend God's gift of freedom from the evil of Empires that sought Global slavery.

Revolutionary War: 1775-1783; 10,000 dead and wounded.
War of 1812: 1812-1815; 7000 dead and wounded.
War of Manifest Destiny: 1846-1848; 18,000 dead and wounded.
World War I: 1917-1918; 320,000 dead and wounded.
World War II: 1941-1945; 1. 1 million dead and wounded.
Korean War: 1950-1953; 150,000 dead and wounded.
War on Terror; 1982 to present; yet to be determined.

As of the early-21st century, there are thousands of American soldiers, sailors, and aviators buried in the cemeteries of 26 nations.

Edwards Brothers Malloy
Thorofare, NJ USA
March 21, 2016